A NOTE ON THE AUTHOR

SHRABANI BASU was born in Calcutta, graduated from St Stephen's College, Delhi, and earned her Master's at Delhi University. She has been the London correspondent of Ananda Bazar Patrika group since 1988, writing for *Sunday, Ananda Bazar Patrika* and *The Telegraph*. Basu founded the Noor Inayat Khan Memorial Trust in 2010 to campaign for a memorial for the WWII heroine. The memorial was unveiled by Princess Anne in November 2012. She is the author of *Curry: The Story of the Nation's Favourite Dish, Spy Princess: The Life of Noor Inayat Khan* and *Victoria & Abdul: The True Story of the Queen's Closest Confidant*.

FOR KING AND ANOTHER COUNTRY

Indian Soldiers on the Western Front, 1914–18

Shrabani Basu

B L O O M S B U R Y
NEW DELHI • LONDON • OXFORD • NEW YORK • SYDNEY

Bloomsbury Publishing India Pvt. Ltd.
Second Floor, Building No. 4
DDA Complex LSC, Pocket C – 6 & 7
Vasant Kunj, New Delhi 110070

First published in India 2015
This paperback edition first published in 2016

British Library Cataloguing-in-Publication Data
A catalogue record for this book is available from the British Library.

ISBN: 978 93 86250 92 6
2 4 6 8 10 9 7 5 3

Typeset by Manmohan Kumar
Printed and bound in India by Gopsons Papers Pvt. Ltd., Noida

To my parents

Lo! I have flung to the East and the West
Priceless treasures torn from my breast,
And yielded the sons of my stricken womb
To the drum-beats of the duty, the sabers of doom.
Gathered like pearls in their alien graves
Silent they sleep by the Persian waves,
Scattered like shells on Egyptian sands,
They lie with pale brows and brave, broken hands,
they are strewn like blossoms mown down by chance
On the blood-brown meadows of Flanders and France.

Sarojini Naidu
'The Gift of India', 1915

Author's Note

The term 'Indian soldiers' in the context of this book refers to soldiers from pre-partition India and comprises soldiers from India, Pakistan and Nepal.

In order to retain the authenticity of the period, I have used the old British names and spellings of the various Indian cities e.g. Calcutta for Kolkata, Madras for Chennai, Jullunder for Jalandhar etc.

Contents

	Map	xi
	Dramatis Personae	xiii
	Introduction	xv
1	Monsoon	1
2	Arrival	22
3	Comfort Kameti	39
4	First Blood	55
5	The Trenches	70
6	Winter	83
7	Bandobast Sahib	95
8	Neuve Chapelle	109
9	Clouds	122
10	Brighton	140
11	Funerals	156
12	The Maharaja and the War Cabinet	168
13	The Peace	176
	Epilogue	191
	Appendix	196
	Notes	197
	Bibliography	208
	Acknowledgements	212
	Index	215

Frontline, Western Front, 1914

Allied and German trenches
Main towns and villages in Belgium and France where Indian troops were in action

Dramatis Personae

THE INDIANS

The Soldiers:

Khudadad Khan – 129th Baluchis
Darwan Singh Negi – 39th Garhwalis
Gabar Singh Negi – 39th Garhwalis
Mir Dast – 57th Wilde's
Mir Mast – 58th Vaughan's Rifles
Manta Singh – 15th Sikhs

The Airmen:

Hardit Singh Malik – Royal Flying Corps
Indra Lal Roy – Royal Flying Corps

The Maharajas:

Sir Ganga Singh – Maharaja of Bikaner
Sir Pratap Singh – Regent of Jodhpur
Sir Bhupinder Singh – Maharaja of Patiala

The Official:

Lord Sinha – Representative at the Imperial War Cabinet

The Cleaner

Sukha

THE BRITISH

The Generals:

Lord Roberts – Former Commander-in-Chief of Indian Army
General John French – Commander-in-Chief of the British Expeditionary Force 1914–1915
General James Willcocks – Commander-in-Chief of the Indian Corps in France 1914–1916
General Douglas Haig – Commander-in-Chief of British Expeditionary Force 1915–1918

The Viceroys:

Lord Hardinge – 1911–1916
Lord Chelmsford – 1916–1921

The War Office:

Lord Kitchener – Secretary of State for War – 1914–1916
Sir Walter Lawrence – Commissioner for sick and wounded Indian soldiers in France and England 1914–16

Indian Soldier's Fund:

Lord Curzon – Former Viceroy of India, Executive Committee Member, Indian Soldier's Fund

The Cabinet:

Lord Crewe – Secretary of State for India – 1911–1915
Austen Chamberlain – Secretary of State for India – 1915–1917
Lord Montagu – Secretary of State for India – 1917–1922

Introduction

On a quiet country road surrounded by miles of flat farmland in Northern France stands a circular monument with 'INDIA – 1914–1918' inscribed on it. Flanked by two large willow trees, the memorial has a pillar with a tiger on either side. On it are the words 'God is One, He is the Victory' written in English, Urdu, Hindi and Gurmukhi. In the centre of the garden is an inscription: 'Their name liveth for evermore'.

Bathed in the spring sunshine, the memorial is a peaceful haven in the middle of the fields. Occasionally a car passes by, its owners largely unaware of the story that lies within the latticed walls. A café opposite advertises croissants and coffees, but it is shut. Few people visit the place, miles away from any tourist trail. It is hard to imagine that a hundred years ago, this tranquil spot near the village of Neuve Chapelle, was the scene of a pitched battle in the First World War, the sound of artillery fire drowning the songbirds and the cries of the injured shattering the silence of the countryside.

It was here between 10 and 13 March 1915 that Indian soldiers fought as a single unit and broke through the German defence for the first time. The casualties were heavy but they succeeded in capturing vital sections of the German line. Most of the bodies were never found. Carved on the circular wall of the Indian Memorial at Neuve Chapelle are the names of over 4,742 Indian soldiers and non-combatants who died on the Western Front in the First World War and have no known graves. Thousands of miles from their homeland, the names on the sandstone wall are all that is left to remember them by.

The memorial designed by Herbert Baker was inaugurated in October 1927, nine years after the end of the war. The opening ceremony was attended among others by the Maharaja of Kapurthala, Marshall Foch, the Earl of Birkenhead, Rudyard Kipling and several veterans. Over the years, the commemoration events slowed down. There was no one at the Memorial the day I visited. It felt almost surreal standing in a field in France surrounded by the names of Indians. A single poppy wreath lay near the plinth, laid by a British foreign office minister a month ago. It said: 'Our shared future is built on our shared past. We will remember them.'

The first Indian casualties of the First World War were not on the Western Front. Nor did they happen on the harsh deserts of Mesopotamia or Africa. They happened on Indian soil, before the troops had even reached the frontline.

It was an ordinary September morning, the third day of the Hindu festival of *Navratri*. The residents of Madras were going about their business. Moses and Company, the tailors on Mount Road, were advertising their woollen suits and woollen underwear for Europe-bound students. Madras Corporation was debating the closure of a road. The High Court was in session. It was less than two months into the war, but the guns seemed far away. All this would change in a few hours.[1]

On the night of 22 September 1914, the German warship *SMS Emden* silently entered the dark waters of the Bay of Bengal. The 3,600 tonne *Emden* was on a mission to sink commercial ships. There were no Allied ships guarding the port of Madras. It was almost as if the city was unaware of the war. The *Emden* boldly took its chance. Armed with 22 guns, the ship dropped anchor just 2,500 metres off the harbour, the starboard side facing the city.

The commandant of the ship, Karl Friedrich Max von Müller, asked his men to bathe, wear laundered uniforms and prepare for an attack. These precautions would reduce the risk of infection if there was any retaliation. The sea was calm and there was no activity on the coast. The lighthouse in the grounds of the Madras High Court was flashing as usual. The powerful beam clearly lit up three oil tankers positioned nearby. They were painted white with red stripes. It made the job easy for the gunners. The commandant had his target. At about twenty minutes past nine, he ordered his men to fire.

A volley of shots from the *Emden* struck the tankers of the Burma Oil Company. Within minutes, two tankers – packed with 5000 tonnes of kerosene oil – caught fire, the flames rising high into the night. The Germans let out a loud cheer. The *Emden* then indulged in some 'fancy shooting'. Though von Müller did not want to hit civilians, he wanted to cause panic in the city. Soon several buildings had been hit: the Madras High Court, the Port Trust, the Boat House of the Madras Sailing Club and the facade of the new National Bank of India. A merchant ship on the harbour was struck, five sailors died and 13 were injured. A giant crater opened up in the ground and unexploded shells lay around. The attack lasted 30 minutes. The *Emden* fired 130 shells.[2] By the time the field guns at Clive's Battery fired back, the *Emden* was leaving. None of the nine shells hit the German ship.

It would be the only time that the War would come directly to India's shore.

The bombing had its effect. Panic spread in the city and nearly 20,000 left every day. Crowds went out of control and the railways had to summon special police. Those who could not get the train took the road, leaving on carts and on foot. Prices of commodities shot up. *The Times* newspaper estimated that the *Emden*'s raid at the mouth of the Hooghly and down the Coromandel coast had left the province of Burma isolated for a fortnight, paralysed the trade of Calcutta, pushed up the cost of insurance on the seas and cost the country over a million pounds. [3] There were fears that the *Emden* would return.

A plaque on the Eastern wall of the Madras High Court building still today marks the spot hit by an *Emden* shell. So powerful was the effect of the bombing of Madras, that the word 'emden' entered the Tamil lexicon meaning a 'person who dares and works with precision'. The residents of Madras would not forget the day that German guns attacked their city.

The Indian connection in the First World War was not something I was ever aware of when growing up in the subcontinent. To me, it was a European war, in which I took an academic interest. In any case, it was the literature of the period that appealed more to me than the tales of battles lost and won. And therein lay a link.

When Wilfred Owen, the English war poet was killed in action in France on 4 November 1918, he was found with a notebook on him, inscribed with the words: 'When I go from hence, let this be my parting word, that what I have seen is unsurpassable.' Wilfred was only twenty-five when he died at Ors, just seven days before the guns fell silent in the First World War. The lines that he carried close to him were by the Indian poet and Nobel laureate Rabindranath Tagore from *Gitanjali (Song Offerings)*. Wilfred's notebook was returned to his mother, Susan Owen, who wrote to Tagore on 1 August 1920, nearly two years after her son's death. Reaching out to the Indian poet the grieving mother said: 'I have been trying to find courage to write to you ever since I heard that you were in London, but the desire to tell you something is finding its way into this letter today. The letter may never reach you, for I do not know how to address it, tho' I feel sure your name upon the envelope will be sufficient. It is nearly two years ago, that my dear eldest son went out to the War for the last time and the day he said goodbye to me ... we were looking together across the sun-glorified sea, looking towards France, with breaking hearts ... when he, my poet son, said those wonderful words of yours, beginning at "When I go from hence, let this be my parting word", and when his pocket book came back to me, I found these words written in his dear writing, with your name beneath. Would it be asking too much of you, to tell me what book I should find the whole poem in?'[4]

That the poetry of Tagore should have inspired the young English poet and given him courage in his last moments is something that has always moved me. It was the poetry of Wilfred Owen and Siegfried Sassoon that brought out the human tragedy of the war. It was many decades later that I realised that there were Indians too fighting in those same trenches, shoulder to shoulder with their 'Sahibs', with unquestioning loyalty. The soldiers were mostly illiterate and came from remote villages in India. They did not carry the poetry of Tagore with them, but they had their own poetry and composed their own songs. Today, few in India know about them.

Yet in the heart of New Delhi stands India Gate, a memorial designed by Sir Edward Lutyens on the lines of the Arc de Triomphe in Paris, and inaugurated in 1931 to commemorate the lives of the 90,000 Indian soldiers who died in World War One and the Anglo-Afghan War. The eternal flame that burns below – *Amar Jawan Jyoti* – is associated today with the twentieth century conflicts of post-Independence India. The memorial to the Unknown Soldier, the *jawan,* has been the site for all large-scale protests and demonstrations in the capital. However, few of the present-day protesters holding candles near India Gate would know the stories of the soldiers named on the memorial, who had crossed the forbidden sea – the *Kala Pani* or 'black waters' – for the first time in 1914 to die in foreign fields in a long-forgotten war.

The overriding image of World War One is always that of the Tommy. It is rarely that one associates the war with an Indian face. But in the numbing maze of white headstones that dot the flat land around Ypres in Belgium for miles, their names can be seen at the cemeteries at Lijssenthoek, Grootebeek and Bedford House alongside their colleagues from the Commonwealth. In the quiet calm of the Bedford House Cemetery, with its trees and surrounding moats, lie the first casualties of the war: Sepoy Mehr Khan, 57th Wilde's Rifles, killed on 28 October 1914 in the First Battle of Ypres, Sepoy Fazl Dad and Jemadar Muhammad Khan of the same regiment, killed a day later, all dead less than 48 hours of entering the trenches. The graves of the Indian soldiers lie in two rows close to the chhatri-style mausoleum in the cemetery. Far away from the land of their birth, they are looked after today by the gardeners of the Commonwealth War Graves Commission, who work quietly through the year keeping the cemetery in pristine condition.

Driving through the narrow roads that crisscross the area around Ypres, I come across a small memorial on the edge of a farmers' field in Hollebeke for the Indian soldiers who died in Belgium between 1914 and 1918. It marks the site where the Indians were first engaged in battle on 26 October 1914. The local farmer tells me that occasionally a busload of Sikh families arrives from London and lays a wreath. It was in Hollebeke on 31 October 1914 that 26-year-old Sepoy Khudadad Khan of the 129th

Duke of Connaught's Own Baluchis kept firing at the enemy till he was the last man left alive, for which act of gallantry he was awarded the Victoria Cross, making history as the first soldier from Asia to receive this award. At Grootebeek British Cemetery I walk past the graves of Indian soldiers who died in April 1915 within days of each other: Sepoy Sardar Khan, Sepoy Sharif Khan, Sepoy Elahi Muhammad. They would have died in the first gas attack.

In October 1915, a year into the war, a Muslim soldier wrote to his sister: 'This is a place where the earth and the sky need to be covered [because of the bloodshed], and I am taken in that calamity. Then you write saying, "Come here". My sister, I will come on that day when God shall bring me. Abandon all thoughts of my coming.'[5] Caught in the depths of a war that they could not understand, the soldiers despaired that they would never go back.

At the Menin Gate Memorial in Ypres the names of 414 Indian soldiers are inscribed on two giant columns to commemorate the hundreds of thousands of Commonwealth soldiers who fell in Flanders fields and have no known graves. The Memorial itself was constructed by the British, who carved it on the bombed out ruins of the fortified gates on the Eastern exit of the town. It was from this gate that the Allied troops took the main road to go to the frontline. Today, cars enter the town through the gates, driving past the 54,896 names inscribed on the walls, a chilling reminder of the countless lives lost in the war in the surrounding area alone. At exactly 7.45 p.m., the area falls silent and the traffic is stopped. At 8.00 p.m. a bugler plays *The Last Post* followed by a minute's silence and then the *Reveille*. The ceremony at Menin Gate has been carried on uninterrupted since 2 July 1928, except for a period during the Second World War when Ypres was occupied by the Germans.

In the continuous line of trenches that ran from Switzerland to the Channel, the Indian soldiers were at the heart of the action on the Western Front fighting some of the bloodiest battles in the first year of the war. They were needed to prevent the advancing Germans from capturing the vital ports of Boulogne in France and Nieuwpoort in Belgium, where the British supplies of food and ammunition arrived across the Channel. The memorial in Neuve Chapelle records the names of the areas in France and Flanders that the Indian soldiers fought alongside the Allied troops: La Basee (1914), Ypres (1914–1915), Givenchy (1914), Aubers, Bazentin, Morval, Messines (1914), Gheluvelt, Neuve Chapelle, Loos, Delville Wood, Armentiers, Festubert, St Julian, Somme (1916) and Cambrai (1917). I found myself wondering what the soldiers would have felt when they reached these places whose names they could barely pronounce. What would they have thought of the damp and cold so different from their homeland?

Less than four weeks after landing at Marseilles, the Indian troops were thrown into the First Battle of Ypres against the world's best-equipped army. They went into the trenches still in their cotton khakis, soon to face one of the harshest winters they had ever seen. Despite the freezing weather, and their unfamiliarity with trench warfare, they bore the shelling with undaunted bravery. They faced the first gas attacks totally unprepared and without any equipment. Yet they carried on. Within a month they had won their first Victoria Cross and ten more would follow over the next four years, as would several other gallantry awards. The soldiers could barely distinguish between the different European languages. Most thought it was a war between three Emperors. A soldier wrote home: 'It is not a war but a Mahabharat, the world is being destroyed'.[6] All they knew was that they had to defend the King Emperor at all costs. They fought with honour for their regiment and the '*jangi laat*', their commandant. Over eight thousand lost their lives on the Western front, blown apart by shell fire, buried alive in soggy collapsing trenches or choked by gas. Nearly five thousand were never found. The Indians arrived in the nick of time, when the British troops were exhausted in the first weeks of warfare. The armies from Canada, Australia and New Zealand were still on their way. It fell on the Indian Corps to hold the position. The Germans would have reached the ports, were it not for them.

By the end of the war, nearly one-and-a-half million Indians – including combatants and non-combatants – had gone to the frontline,[7] the largest volunteer army from any of the colonies and more than the combined armies from Scotland, Northern Ireland and Wales. The dead and missing were nearly 72,000[8] with many more wounded. Among the survivors were the shell shocked and disabled whose lives would never be the same again. They fought in all the theatres of war, from the Western Front,[9] where they helped hold the line in Ypres-Salient, to the deserts of Africa and the Middle East, in Palestine, Mesopotamia, Gallipoli and Egypt, where again they prevented the Turks and Germans from accessing the Suez Canal and let the British retain control of the oil fields of Basra.

The soldiers came from the length and breadth of undivided India, from the Punjab, Garhwal, the North West Frontier, Rajasthan and Nepal to Madras and Burma and represented different religious, ethnic and linguistic backgrounds. Most of the sepoys, flung into the greatest war of the century, were from peasant stock and hill tribes. A small village in the mountains of Punjab – Dulmial in Chakwal – sent 460 men to the First World War, the highest from a single village in South Asia. For four long years there were no young men left in Dulmial. They were all fighting at the front.

We have access to the thousands of letters written by the soldiers thanks to the records of the censor board, who translated and annotated them. The letters reflect at once the soldiers' despair, their anxiety and, at the same time, their undying loyalty to King and Empire. The photographs of the period tell their own story. There are images of turbaned soldiers outside a village in France, Sikh soldiers reading from the Guru Granth Sahib in Flanders, wounded soldiers playing cards in a hospital and French women giving flowers to the Indian troops as they arrive in Marseilles. Grainy film footage made clearly for propaganda, show soldiers doing a 'Cuttak dance' (Kathak dance) in the fields, others solemnly presenting their swords to their English commanding officers. Images of Indian soldiers playing football and tug of war and King George V visiting them in the frontline were sold as postcards in England and France. The Indians look embarrassed and self-conscious as they are filmed. Photographs of Indian soldiers held as prisoners of war in Germany and Turkey tell a different story: grim, frightened faces look straight into the camera, prisoners in an alien land. The photograph of a starving, emaciated Indian soldier in Kut captures the sheer horror of the siege that alone cost over 20,000 Indian lives. I felt the story of this silent – and forgotten – army had to be written.

One of the names carved on the walls of the Indian memorial at Neuve Chapelle is that of Gabar Singh Negi of the 39th Garhwal Rifles. Posthumously awarded the Victoria Cross for his bravery in the battle of Neuve Chapelle, he was one of the thousands whose body was never found. It was the personal stories of soldiers like Gabar Singh that fascinated me. I wanted to look at the background of Indian soldiers like him and trace their journey to the western front. I needed to go to where his story began, his village in the hills. My search took me to Lansdowne, a picturesque hill station 5,500 feet high in the Garhwal Himalayas, a place where time seems to have stood still since the days of the Raj. Displayed in the Officers' Mess alongside impressive portraits of Lords Kitchener, Roberts and Lansdowne, framed letters of Rudyard Kipling and Queen Mary, stuffed tigers and imperial stags, was a German flag with the words '*Gott Strafe England. Hoch Deutchland*' (God Punish England, Long Live Germany) captured by a Garhwali scout near Givenchy in 1916. Irritated with the flag that had been flying in different places each night in front of the trenches, the Garhwali crawled through the long grass one day, seized the flag, and brought it back in bright daylight.

The museum in Lansdowne – the Darwan Singh Negi Sangrahalay – is named after another Victoria Cross recipient from the regiment. Darwan Singh Negi was personally presented the medal by King George V for his bravery in Festubert in France. The Garhwalis and the Gurkhas shared four of the eleven VCs of the First World War between them.

Darwan Singh and Gabar Singh were not alone in their bravery. I could not write this book without telling the story of Sepoy Khudadad Khan, the first Indian from undivided India to win the Victoria Cross. His portrait enjoys pride of place in the Indian Memorial Room at the Royal Military Academy Sandhurst along with that of fellow Victoria Cross awardee, Mir Dast. Khudadad Khan was a machine gunner with the 129th Baluchis. In October 1914 his regiment faced the Germans as they attacked Hollebeke near Ypres. Despite his injuries, he continued firing till he was the last man left alive. His comrade Mir Dast of 57th Wilde's displayed outstanding courage in the face of the first gas attack in the spring of 1915.

There is also the inspiring story of Subedar Manta Singh, 15th Ludhiana Sikhs, who was fatally injured in Neuve Chapelle while rescuing his English officer, George Henderson. It was an act of sacrifice that led to three generations of friendship between the two families.

It was not just the soldiers who went to the frontline. Indian princes, who depended on the British for their livelihood, offered their troops, services and funding. They provided hospital ships, ambulance cars and generous donations. The Maharaja of Bikaner, the Regent of Jodhpur, the Maharaja of Patiala and the Maharaja of Cooch Behar were among the princes who left for the frontline. Two Indian students in London would join the elite Royal Flying Corps as officers, becoming the first Indian pilots in Britain. Indra Lal Roy and Harjit Singh Malik would make history in the skies. Even Mohandas Karamchand Gandhi, arriving in Britain from South Africa at the time, supported the war effort and wrote to the Secretary of State for India, offering to mobilise the services of Indians in Britain.

For the British, the logistics of taking the Indians to the battlefields of Europe was no mean task. The Indian Army regiments were largely organised along lines of caste and region. The Hindus could not eat food prepared by either the Europeans or the Muslims; some could not even drink water offered by a non-Hindu. The Muslims had their own dietary restrictions; they needed to eat halal meat. The Hindus would not eat beef and the Muslims would not eat pork. There was even a regiment of Brahmins who needed to have a bath before they sat down for their meals, not at all practical in the trenches. To cater to all these requirements, an army of followers had to be taken along with the troops. Cooks were brought in to cater to the different dietary needs. *Bhistis* or water carriers provided water separately to Hindus and Muslims.

This resulted in a grand march from every class of Indian society – from princes, soldiers and sailors to cooks, cleaners, drivers, and dhobis – a 'Band of Brothers' fighting their first Western war. At Neuve Chapelle Memorial, the names of the followers are carved on a separate section on the wall. Most are only a single name: Bhika, Chakara and Chhotu, the last for a young boy. Many, some as young as ten, managed to lie about their age and board the ships to Europe as kitchen hands and syces.

In a quiet corner of the Brookwood Military Cemetery in Surrey, England, are the graves of two cooks, Hansa and Babu. Hansa was from the Army Hospital Corps while Babu was from the Central Depot. Hansa died in September 1919. By then the war was over and the hospitals with the Indian soldiers had all been shut down.

There is also the moving story of a cleaner, Sukha, a low-caste 'untouchable' who died in a hospital in Brockenhurst in England and whose final resting place is a quiet church in New Forest, far from his home in India.

For Britain, taking the Indian Army to war sent out a powerful message to the world. To its allies, France and Russia, it demonstrated that Britain had the full support of its largest colony. To the Germans it sent the message that Britain, a powerful naval power, could call up the military might of its global Empire within weeks. Of all Britain's colonial armies, the Indian Army was the largest.[10] Moreover, it had actually fought in wars and could be mobilised at short notice. Lord Kitchener, who had been appointed war minister, was acutely aware that the 100,000 British troops who boarded the trains for the Western Front at the outbreak of the war, would not be enough. He called on India and the dominions to supply boots on the ground. The Viceroy of India, Lord Hardinge, proudly declared that the Indians were eager to fight for the Empire. He had received hundreds of messages of support from both the Princely states and Indian intellectuals. Indian political classes thought that their loyalty to the British Empire would earn them brownie points in any future negotiations for greater autonomy and eventual self-rule. At Britain's time of need, it made practical sense to set aside differences and help the motherland. India was not consulted, but the decision to send the soldiers to the front was unopposed, even welcomed.

To the soldiers it was a chance to go to *Vilayat* and fight shoulder to shoulder with English soldiers. The British were very clear that the Indian soldiers who had travelled thousands of miles to defend the Empire should be well looked after. The King and Queen visited the troops on several occasions, both in France and in hospitals in England. The Queen wrote personally to her 'sisters in India' in sympathy for those lost in battle. Injured Indian soldiers were treated in the opulent surroundings of the Brighton Pavilion, which was converted into a hospital for them. English women ran the Indian Soldiers' Fund, providing comforts to Indian soldiers and prisoners of war, sending parcels of treats.

Nevertheless, mail was strictly censored and Indian nationalist newspapers banned and confiscated from the hospitals. English nurses were not allowed to care for the Indian soldiers, their role was to remain supervisory. Strict rules for the Indians even led to a mini-revolt and a shootout at one of the hospitals. The large collection of letters from the Censors' office reveals the strong emotions the soldiers felt as they faced the endless shelling and mortar fire. A wounded Garhwali soldier wrote to his friend in India:

'As when the leaves fall off a tree and not a space is left bare on the ground, so the earth is covered with dead men and there is no place to put one's foot ... the whole world is being finished. We have been constantly fighting for six months, but we have not even seen the sun; day and night the rain has fallen; and the country is so cold that I cannot describe it.'[11]

As the war dragged on, the soldiers grew weary. They yearned for news from home and became anxious when they heard reports of plague and famine. They feared they would never return. However, despite the harsh conditions and the loss of their comrades, most remained firmly loyal to the King Emperor and were not afraid of death. 'It is the duty of young men to fight as lions in the field of battle,' wrote a young Pathan to his friend. 'It is of no consequence – to die is one's duty.' Another letter written by a wounded Dogra soldier from the hospital in Brighton echoed the sentiment: 'We must be true to our salt and he who is faithful will win paradise for his parents as well as for himself'.

For India, the first experience of Western warfare was to be a turning point as a nation. The country's educated elite began staking their claim for greater autonomy as a prize for the nation's contribution to the war. At the peace conference of 1919, two Indians were present – the Maharaja of Bikaner and Lord Sinha, the first Indian peer. The Maharaja signed the Treaty of Versailles along with the victors. The Indians had proved their worth and their loyalty, but unfortunately, there was to be no reward.

Barely five months after the guns were silenced, General Reginald Dyer opened fire on a gathering largely made up of Sikh men, women and children on 13 April 1919 at Jallianwala Bagh near the Golden Temple in Amritsar. Despite the loyalty of the Sikh troops, their contribution to the war and sacrifice, Dyer ordered his soldiers to continue till the last bullet was fired. It was an act that alienated the nation. The poet Rabindranath Tagore, who had so inspired Wilfred Owen, returned his knighthood in protest, and the Indian freedom struggle took on a new momentum.

But in June 1914, these issues were nowhere on the horizon. The main thing on the minds of most Indians that summer was when the rains would come.

1

Monsoon

Satoori was worried about the goats. She knew they were scared during thunderstorms. Their eyes would widen as they cowered under their flimsy wooden shelter as it was battered by the rain. The monsoons had come early this year, turning the hill paths into rivulets and the farmland into quagmires. She watched the lightning flash on the dark green mountain slopes followed by the deafening roar of thunder. She could hear the goats bleating in the dark, but there was little she could do. They would have to wait till morning.

She was also worried about her husband, who was on his way back from his regimental centre in Lansdowne. She hoped he hadn't got caught in the storm. The thirteen-year-old child bride was looking forward to his return. He could fix the roof on the goat shed. She had been married for just a year to 22-year-old Gabar Singh Negi, a rifleman in the Garhwal Regiment, but she rarely saw him as he had to stay in Lansdowne.

Named after the Viceroy of India, the picturesque hill station was built by the British in the Garhwal Himalayas. Unlike other hill stations like Simla and Mussoorie, with their malls and fancy British hotels, Lansdowne was built purely as a cantonment station for the Garhwal Rifles Regiment. It was in 1887, when the separate regiment was created for them, that the search for a centre began. The Deputy Commissioner of Garhwal, J.S. Campbell, suggested the area of Kalu Danda (Dark slopes), 5,500 feet high in the hills. With views of the magnificent ice-capped Himalayas and the hillsides below covered with oak, pine and rhododendron trees, the mountain station could be the perfect training ground for the officers and soldiers. The original village was painstakingly transformed. In the first few months, British officers lived in tents overseeing the construction of temporary huts. Soon the essentials of a cantonment, a parade ground and a post office were built. So tedious was it to build on the slopes that Earl Kitchener, on his first visit there in 1902 as Commander-in-Chief of the Indian Army, demanded to know 'who had planted troops on this pinnacle'? A cart road was laid down from the nearest railway station at Kotdwar in 1905, and water supply was pumped up in 1908. Electricity and telegraph lines would follow a decade later. In 1914 there was still no vehicular traffic on the road to Lansdowne. Goods were carried by mules, and soldiers and officers simply walked the twenty-four miles to and from Kotdwar.

The trek from Lansdowne to his remote village of Manjood in the district of Chamba took Gabar Singh nearly four days. He too was looking forward to the monsoon break and being reunited with his wife. He had been a soldier with Garhwal Rifles for nearly a year and wore the dark green uniform of his regiment with pride. The Army had not been a natural choice for him. His family owned a small plot of land and a few goats. Their house, nestling on the hillside provided a sweeping view of the valley below. Here Gabar Singh had spent his youth tending the goats and dreaming below the open skies. His idyllic world would soon collapse. In 1911, the village was struck by a plague of cholera. Gabar Singh's father, Badri Singh, died. Gabar Singh was only 18 at the time, the youngest of three brothers. He left home to search for work and took up a job with the Maharaja of Tehri. In 1913 he enlisted in the Garhwal Rifles Regiment.[1]

There were ten others from Manjood village who also joined the regiment. All of them were sent on furlough during the monsoon as it was impossible to carry on any work in the rains when the roads caved in and the drill field was flooded.

Also returning home during the monsoon of 1914 was Lance Naik Darwan Singh Negi. His village of Kefarteer in Chamoli in the Garhwal hills was even more remote. It would take him nearly a week to get back. 32-year-old Darwan Singh was a strong man and had walked this route many times since joining the regiment. With his possessions in a roll, he negotiated the slippery slopes and the narrow paths as he had done for years.

The Garhwalis were a simple, hardworking lot, who tended their mountain cattle and looked after small plots of land. They used the word '*bhulla*' (young brother), to refer to young Garhwali men. It was these rustic '*bhullas*' that the British were looking for. The potential recruits were typical Garhwali highlanders from the deepest interiors. They would be dressed in a homespun woollen blanket, draped over their shoulders like a kilt and fastened over the chest with two large pins (usually fashioned from large thorns or brass skewers). With bare limbs and long curly locks, the 'raw stock' as they were called, was usually illiterate but intelligent and quick learners. Often mistaken for the Gurkhas, with whom they shared certain physical characteristics, the British identified them as potential recruits as they not only had the physical requirements of 'strong arms and strong legs', but they were also known for their honesty and unquestioning loyalty. Years of walking on the mountains tending their herds had built their endurance. A Garhwali could walk fifteen to twenty miles at a stretch carrying a load, without feeling the strain. The Regiment preferred to catch them young – between the ages of 17 to 19 – where a good diet, regular exercise and military discipline would allow them to grow into tough soldiers.

The men from the mountains were preferred to those from the hot, low-lying valleys and plains, where fever was prevalent. The latter were never enlisted. Nor did the British recruit anyone who had previously done any menial jobs, as the caste hierarchy among Hindus would not favour a soldier from these ranks. The Garhwalis were intensely religious by nature. The Garhwal hills – famous for the temples of Kedarnath and Badrinath – were regarded as 'Dev Bhumi', the 'abode of the gods'. The regimental battle cry of the Garhwal Regiment – 'Jai Badri Vishal' – was with reference to the temple of Badrinath.

The Garhwal Regiment had been given a special place in the main parade at the Imperial Durbar of George V in the new capital of Delhi in 1911. Darwan Singh Negi had been part of the battalion and had seen the King and Queen – wearing their crowns and ermine furs – stand on the grand Royal podium in the Delhi winter. The King wore the famously heavy Imperial Crown of India, specially made for the Coronation Darbar, set with 6,170 diamonds. It was at this Durbar that the King announced that Indian soldiers would now be eligible for the Victoria Cross, the highest award for bravery. Three years later he would be personally presenting it to Darwan Singh Negi.

The Garhwalis and Gurkhas had a long shared history. Garhwal had come under Gurkha rule in 1803 after the latter invaded and subjugated the state. The Gurkhas were from the hills of Nepal, known for their bravery, loyalty and endurance. They too were staunch Hindus, who traced their roots to the 8th century Hindu warrior Guru Goraknath. In the First Nepalese War of 1814–15, they had fought the British under their commander Amar Singh Thapa. Though they were defeated, their bravery had left its mark. The British recognised them as a martial race and soon grew to depend on them. The Garhwalis and Gurkhas who had surrendered in 1815 were absorbed in the British Indian Army and until 1887 fought together in the ranks of the first five Gurkha regiments.

It was General Lord Roberts, the Commander-in-Chief of the Indian Army and the hero of the siege of Kandahar, who in 1886 raised the proposition that the Garhwalis should have their own regiment. 'The men would be of an excellent fighting class,' said the General, famed for his love of India and Indian soldiers. Over the next few years the cantonment was built, and on 21 September 1890, it was decided to rename it after the then Viceroy, Lord Lansdowne.

It was to Lansdowne that both Gabar Singh Negi and Darwan Singh Negi went after their recruitment to be trained as soldiers in the British Indian Army. As they returned to their homes in June 1914, they did not realise that the world was about to change.

Thousands of miles away in Germany, Kaiser Wilhelm II was enjoying watching the ships on the Kiel Kanal. The German Emperor was attending the Kiel Festival, an annual regatta of music and sailing, held in the last week of June. Passionate about the German Navy, he loved nothing more than seeing the display of ships at the Elbe Regatta and even sailed his own racing yacht, *Meteor V*.

As the grandson of Queen Victoria, he had a unique position: he was both Emperor of Germany and a British Admiral of the Fleet. Even as a boy visiting his grandmother, the young Wilhelm had always been fascinated by English ships and dreamt of building his own when he grew up. As the Kaiser he wanted to possess a fine navy that would rival the English. He knew that the global spread of the British Empire was based on its maritime supremacy and it was the powerful Royal Navy that made the island nation a player in European politics. To the Kaiser who craved 'world power', building the German Navy would be a priority and he passed five Naval Laws to enhance the Imperial German Navy. 'Our future is on the seas' he famously declared in 1900. Britain had always feared German naval ambitions and in early summer of 1914, the British government was not happy with the news that Germany intended to widen the Kiel Canal as this would allow German ships to move swiftly through the Baltic Sea to the North Sea. Yet there was nothing that outwardly reflected any tension between the two countries. On 26 June, the Kaiser proudly wore his Admirals' uniform and went on board the English battleship *King George V*. The only diplomatic incident that day was the Kaiser commenting on the sartorial choice of the Counsellor of the British Embassy in Berlin, Sir Horace Rumbold. The diplomat had arrived in a morning coat and top hat, prompting the Kaiser to explode: 'If I see that again, I will smash it. One doesn't wear tall hats on board ships.'[2]

He was much calmer next day when he attended a reception hosted by the commander of the British squadron, who noted the great camaraderie between the German and English sailors.

On 28 June the crowds in Kiel converged on the Bay to watch the yacht race. The Kaiser was competing too, on board his *Meteor V*. As he was leaning over the rails, a launch drew up by his yacht and the sailor threw a cigarette case across to him. In it was a telegram: The Archduke Franz Ferdinand, heir to the Austrian throne, and his wife, had been assassinated in the Bosnian capital of Sarajevo.

The Archduke had been a close friend of the Kaiser's. He had been Ferdinand's guest on a shooting holiday in Konopischt near Prague just a fortnight ago. The Kaiser called off the race and hurried back to his Palace in Potsdam. Kiel Week was brought to an end. It would stand cancelled for the next four years.

It was a warm summer day when Franz Ferdinand and his wife, Sophie, arrived at Sarajevo station on 28 June 1914. The 51-year-old heir to the Austrian throne had scheduled an inspection of the Austro-Hungarian troops. They were met at the station by Gen Oskar Potiorek, the Governor General, and Lt Col Count Franz von Harrach who would be the Archduke's bodyguard for the day. Soon the royal entourage was sweeping away in six cars. The Archduke and Duchess sat in an open top six-seater convertible, so the crowds could see them clearly. The party were to drive to the City Hall, have lunch with the Mayor and then head for the inspection. Amongst the crowds that lined the streets to watch the royal visitors, was a nineteen-year-old high-school student Gavrilo Princip, a Bosnian Serb. The night before, he and five other Serbian nationalists – part of a group called the Black Hand – had been given guns and bombs. All six had been asked to line the route of the Royal visit. Months had gone into planning the assassination.

It was all timed to perfection. At 10.00 a.m. the motorcade was to leave for the town hall by way of the Appel Quay. Muhamed Mehmedbašić, was placed at the first post armed with a bomb. But the crowds were too thick and he could not throw it. Next to him was Vaso Cubrilovic, who had been armed with a pistol and a bomb. But he too failed to strike. The third assassin, Nedel Cabrinovic, was positioned near the Miljacka River. He hurled his bomb at the car at 10.10 a.m. But it bounced off the back and exploded under the car that was coming up behind, injuring Ferdinand's Aide-de-Camp and 20 other people. In the confusion of the blast, Cabrinovic swallowed his cyanide pill and jumped into the river, but the poison was not strong enough and he was pulled out and beaten up by the crowds. Meanwhile the Archducal car sped towards the City Hall. The car was now moving so fast that the other three assassins *en route* could not shoot.

The shaken and angry Archduke reached the town hall and shouted at the Mayor, 'What is the good of your speeches? I come to Sarajevo on a visit, and I get bombs thrown at me. It is outrageous.'[3] Calmed down by his wife, he later read out his bloodstained speech, which had been retrieved from the blown-up car.

At the end of the fraught City Hall reception, the Archduke decided to change his plans and go to the hospital to visit those of his party who had been wounded. At 10.45 a.m. the Royal couple ill-advisedly got back in the open-top car. A member of the Archduke's staff suggested this might be dangerous, but General Potiorek replied 'Do you think Sarajevo is full of assassins? I will take responsibility'. Nevertheless, the Governor decided that the royal car should travel on an alternative route straight along the Appel Quay to the Sarajevo hospital. But he forgot to tell the driver of the change of plans. The driver took a wrong turn and entered Franz Joseph Street. Realising his mistake, he tried to reverse putting his foot on the brake. The gears locked and the engine stalled.

At this moment, emerging from a *delicatessen* was Gavrilo Princip. Disappointed at the failed assassination attempt in the morning, he had gone into a café. As fate would have it, the Archducal car with its royal passengers was directly in front of him as he walked out. He reacted quickly, pulling out his Browning pistol and fired three shots. One bullet hit the Archduke on his neck rupturing the jugular vein, the second hit him in the leg and the third hit the Duchess in the abdomen. As the Duchess slumped forward, the Archduke cried out to his wife: 'Sophie, live for our children.'[4]

For the second time that day, the driver, Leopold Lojka, drove through the streets at high speed, while the Archduke and Duchess lay dying in the car. By the time they reached the Governor's House, the Duchess was dead. Franz Ferdinand died ten minutes later. Within hours anti-Serb riots broke out in Sarajevo. The news of the assassination spread quickly around the world.

The events in far off Sarajevo had passed Sukha by. He was enjoying the rains. The small brick-and-mud hut he called his home in Gangapur in the town of Bareilly in the United Provinces had not provided much relief from the dusty summer. The monsoon clouds were a welcome sight to everybody in the hot plains. The urchins in his neighbourhood were dancing delightedly in the rain, splashing in the muddy water. The buffaloes looked content as they settled heavily in pools of water and enjoyed a mud bath.

Sukha lit his beedi and inhaled thoughtfully. He had seen his sahib reading the English papers that day with keen interest. There was talk of unrest and even war. He had only heard snatches of conversation as he swept their veranda and cleared the leaves from the drive. As a low-caste sweeper, he was known as an 'untouchable' and had very little to do with others outside his caste. Brahmins would cross the road if he approached and some would be forced to have a bath even if his shadow fell on them. His sahib was indifferent and barely noticed him as he went about his work. The heat was usually too much for the memsahib who remained indoors most of the time. Sukha was happier back in his shack with his own people, who carried the night soil, emptied the garbage and kept the town clean. He stroked his black beard and thought to himself: he must pay attention to the sahib's conversation tomorrow. If there was trouble ahead, he should be fully prepared.

His hometown of Bareilly had borne the brunt of the Mutiny in 1857 long before he was born. It lay in the heart of the plains of the United Provinces, surrounded by cities where the soldiers had risen up against the Sahibs. In Lucknow, the rebels under the protection of the Nawab's wife, Begum Hazrat Mahal, had pounded the Residency with mortar shells. In Meerut, the sepoys had mutinied. And in Cawnpore, the memsahibs had been trapped in the Bibigarh and killed. All that was history now. The Mutiny had been strongly suppressed and the administration reorganized directly under the Crown. It was well known that the Sahibs did not recruit any soldiers from the plains. They now preferred to work with India's martial races, the Pathans, the Sikhs, the Dogras, the Garhwalis and the Gurkhas. Sukha looked around him thoughtfully. He needed to know what was worrying his sahib and learn who was going to war and where.

At Queen Victoria's funeral in January 1901, her grandchildren, George, the Prince of Wales, and Kaiser Wilhelm II, had knelt together beside her coffin and paid their respects. Thirteen years later the family was torn apart. Victoria had arranged the marriages of her children and grandchildren with European Royalty. Her family was spread across the continent like a giant spider web linked by birth and matrimony to the kings and queens of Europe; family feuds and filial alliances were to create the complicated backdrop for the Great War. The Kaiser was the son of the Queen's eldest daughter, Victoria, who was married to Kaiser Wilhelm I. Tsar Nicholas II was married to Victoria's granddaughter, Alix of Hesse. Yet the relationship between the cousins had always been fraught with tension. The Kaiser did not care much for his English cousin with whom he clashed directly as he pursued his dream of becoming a naval superpower. It did not help that the Queen Mother, Queen Alexandra, was a Danish princess, as Germany had fought two wars with Denmark over the Schleswig-Holstein question in the nineteenth century. As long as Queen Victoria had ruled, she had kept the extended family together, but after her death, the Kaiser – known for his erratic behaviour – would often be excluded from family get-togethers and was isolated.

Despite the differences, in August 1914 the three cousins were still in contact trying to avert a crisis. On 1 August, King George V wrote to the Tsar: 'I cannot help thinking that some misunderstanding has produced this deadlock. I am most anxious not to miss any possibility of avoiding the terrible calamity which at present threatens the whole world.' A day earlier two telegrams had crossed each other between Berlin and St Petersburg. 'To try and avoid such a calamity as a European war, I beg you in the name of our old friendship to do what you can to stop your allies from going too far,' the Tsar wrote to the Kaiser. The German emperor too had sent a telegram the same day, 'I am exerting my utmost influence to induce the Austrians to deal straightly to arrive at a satisfactory understanding with you.' Both telegrams were sent in English, the language of their British cousin George V. The two Emperors had signed the telegrams 'Nicky' and 'Willie'.

In the month after the Royal assassination, Europe and Russia had been thrown into turmoil. As a wave of anti-Serbian feeling swept through Austria, the Kaiser declared that the Serbs had to be disposed of. The Austrian Emperor, Franz Josef, had already ordered partial mobilisation. On the afternoon of July 25, the Serbian army began to assemble as it feared an imminent attack. Trains began criss-crossing Europe carrying troops to their destination as war seemed inevitable. On 28 July, exactly a month after the assassination of Archduke Franz Ferdinand in Sarajevo, Austria declared war against Serbia. The next day the German Fleet began to gather and the British Fleet took up positions in the North Sea. By the afternoon of 30 July, the Russians ordered full mobilisation. France followed, the crowds reacting with jubilant cheers. One by one the great empires of Europe were coming under a domino effect preparing for a war that would consume them for years.

On the afternoon of 1 August the Kaiser ordered the mobilisation of all German forces. By that evening, the German ambassador to Russia went to the Russian Foreign Ministry in St Petersburg and formally handed over the German declaration of war. That day a public meeting was held in the Odeonplatz in Munich. Amongst the cheering crowds, baying for war against Russia and France, was a failed Austrian-born water colour artist, Adolf Hitler.

At 7 p.m. on 2 August, Germany sent an ultimatum to Belgium asking for free passage for its troops. Belgium refused. On 3 August Germany declared war against France and moved its troops into Belgium. Britain, now, had to act. She was a signatory to the Treaty of London of 1839 which guaranteed Belgian neutrality. Britain sent an ultimatum to Germany that there must be no attack on Belgium, and gave them 24 hours to respond. Germany chose to ignore it.

At eleven o'clock on the night of 4 August, Britain declared war against Germany. The Kaiser said that he had been proud of being a British Field Marshal and Admiral of the Fleet, but now he would 'divest himself of these honours'. Queen Victoria's grandchildren – three cousins and Emperors – were now at war and the world would change for ever.

In his desert palace in Bikaner in Rajasthan, Maharaja Ganga Singh was going through a flurry of emotions as he heard the news from Europe. On the morning of 4 August he put pen to paper and sent a telegram to his friend, King George V. Britain had not yet entered the war, but the Maharaja was anxious.

'Having just heard of the outbreak of hostilities between Russia, France and Germany, I beg leave most dutifully, should Great Britain also have resort to arms, to place my own sword and services at Your Imperial Majesty's command, either as member of Your Imperial Majesty's staff or at the head of my troops and Rajputs, all of whom are equally eager to fight for Your Imperial Majesty in Europe, India, or elsewhere for the safety, honour and welfare of your Imperial Majesty and your dominions.'

The flamboyant six-foot tall Maharaja, known for his sartorial elegance and carefully-chosen turbans, had been an Aide-de-Camp to King George V longer than any other Indian chief. Being perfectly fluent in French and English, he was on first name terms with the great and good in Paris and London.

The Maharaja declared that the personal military service was the 'highest ambition of a Rathore Rajput Chief' and that he was prepared to go anywhere and in any capacity to serve the King. He even informed him that he had made all the necessary arrangements for the administration of his state in his absence and was 'ready to sail immediately'. It was signed simply 'Ganga Singh'.[5]

The 33-year-old Maharaja's telegram was at once beseeching and proud, begging the King Emperor to use his services, and at the same time reminding him of the glory of the Rajputs. The Maharaja was no stranger to warfare. In 1900 he had become the first Indian prince to go abroad to fight for the British. He and his Camel Corps, the Ganga Risala, had gone to China to quell the Boxer rebellion. Though the Maharaja had arrived at the tail end of the war, he participated bravely and was 'mentioned in dispatches' and impressed the Viceroy, Lord Curzon, who awarded him the China Medal on his return.

The Maharaja also wrote to the Viceroy, Lord Hardinge. Soon the Viceroy received a flood of telegrams – from several native princes – all offering their services and financial help. *The Times of India* dramatically reported in August 1914: 'The swords of the martial Princes leapt from their scabbards...' The Viceroy had to choose which Maharajas would go to the frontline as there was quite a scramble. He shortlisted a few and had to personally write to the disappointed ones. The Viceroy's list included Sir Pratap Singh, Regent of Jodhpur, who had been well acquainted with Queen Victoria, had attended both her Jubilees and her funeral, and was eager to fight despite being in his seventies. Travelling with him would be the 16-year-old Maharaja of Jodhpur, Sumer Singh. Also included were the Maharajas of Patiala, Ratlam, Kishengarh, the Nawabs of Jaora, Sachin and Bhopal. The Maharaja of Nepal placed his formidable Gurkha troops at the disposal of the British. The Maharaja of Mysore was one of the first to offer financial help. He put Rupee 50 lakhs at the disposal of the Viceroy, who immediately said he would use it to pay for the transport of troops. The Maharaja of Gwalior sent a fleet of 40 motor ambulances, which was photographed making its way to Buckingham Palace. The Maharaja also gave 4,000 horses, thousands of pounds in donations and a contribution along with the Begum of Bhopal for a hospital ship.

Among the Maharajas in the frontline was a cricketer, famous in England as the Test player Ranjit Singhji who scored 154 not out against Australia in his debut test for England in 1896. Widely regarded as one of the greatest batsmen of all time, the legendary Ranjit Singhji, the Jam Sahib of Nawanagar, immediately offered his support when war broke out. He let his house in Staines to be used as a hospital and left for the frontline in November 1914.

On 4 August 1914, the Secretary of State for India sent a telegram to the Viceroy: 'Clear the line. Army at home is mobilising. Is it proposed by you to call out any reservists of the British Army in India?'[6]

On the morning of 5 August a second telegram followed, more urgent than the first. 'War with Gemany has started. Preface defence scheme to be seen.'[7]

On 8 August 1914, four days after Britain declared war on Germany, the British War Office ordered that two divisions of the Indian Army should be mobilised. The Viceroy had suggested that the Indian Army should fight shoulder to shoulder with their British colleagues in defence of King and country. The British Indian Army had fought in campaigns in Afghanistan and the Far East, but they had never travelled to the Western Front. The King approved, Parliament assented and the secretary of state for India was cheered loudly as he read out the Viceroy's telegram about how Indian princes had rallied to the war effort offering troops and money. India, he said, with its large standing army, was giving its full support. The Secretary of State for War, Lord Kitchener, was an old India hand. He had been Commander-in-Chief of the Indian Army between 1902 and 1909 and knew the soldiers well. His predecessor, Lord Roberts, declared that Indian troops could fight on any terrain and under any circumstances. Had he not seen their bravery in the Afghan wars and the storming of Kandahar?

The declaration of war was met with wild enthusiasm in Britain. 'For more than four hours the singing and cheering of the crowd was maintained without a break,' *The Times* reported on 5 August 1914, the day after the declaration. Kitchener's call for 100,000 troops for the front led to such a crush that mounted police had to be called in to control the crowds in London. The mood in India was euphoric too. Many felt it was an honour to be invited to fight along with the British Expeditionary Force. Hindus, Muslims and Parsees offered prayers for the success of British arms and there were demonstrations of loyalty throughout India.

Newspapers of the country carried wildly patriotic articles. *The Bengalee* newspaper edited by Congress leader Surendranath Banerjee, declared: 'Behind the series ranks of one of the finest armies in the world, there stand the multitudinous people of India, ready to co-operate with the government in the defence of Empire, which for them means, in its ultimate evolution, the complete recognition of their rights as citizens of the freest state in the world. We may have our differences with the government – and what people have not? But in the presence of the common enemy, be it Germany or any other power, we sink our differences…'[8]

Indian leaders addressed meetings all over the country expressing their support for the King Emperor. Bhupendra Nath Bose, President of the Indian National Congress, said: 'Whatever intrigues Germany may stir up in Turkey, Muslim and Hindu in India are alike united in their unswerving devotion and loyalty to the Empire in this crisis.'

In a large public rally held in Bombay, attended by the city's wealthy merchants, a unanimous resolution was passed expressing unswerving devotion and loyalty to the British Crown. In the town hall at Calcutta, the mood was equally upbeat. Prominent Bengali Hindus, Bengali Muslims and Parsees addressed a public meeting and called for the show of loyalty 'to the Empire and the Motherland'. Most Indian nationalist leaders at this stage were satisfied with British rule, but wanted greater autonomy or dominion status as enjoyed by Australia, Canada and New Zealand. Consequently, the rhetoric was always about 'putting aside the differences' at this time of crisis and giving their full loyalty to the King Emperor.

The most resounding voice of support came from Dadabhai Naoroji, the first Indian to win a seat in the House of Commons. The eighty-nine-year old, a strong critic of the British government's impact on the Indian economy, who had only the previous year described India's unequal export ratio with Britain as 'all loss, loss, loss', rallied to Britain's cause. In an open letter to the Indian public on 10 August 1914, Naoroji said that Britain had declared war on Germany not out of the desire to extend its dominions, but to keep her word of honour and discharge her obligation to peace: 'The War in Europe. What is our – India's – place in it… We are above all British citizens of the Great British Empire… Fighting as the British people are, at present, in a righteous cause, to the good and glory of human dignity and civilisation, and moreover, being the beneficent instrument of our own progress and civilisation, our duty is clear – to do everyone our best to support the British fight with our life and property.'[9]

The letter published in *The Times of India* drew an immediate response. The Governor of Bombay, Lord Willingdon, wrote to the elder statesman: 'Truly, India by her loyalty and devotion to the King Emperor, which shall be proved during the war, will gain her rightful place in the future in the 'sun' of the British Empire.'[10]

Indians in Britain too added their voice to the display of support for the King. At a meeting of prominent Indians in London, a resolution was passed for submission to the King Emperor. The signatories included among others Sir Mancherjee Bhownagree, who had served as a Member of Parliament between 1895 and1906, industrialist and philanthropist Sir Ratan Tata, Congress politicians like Lala Lajpat Rai and Mohammad Ali Jinnah. Pledging their loyalty to the British Empire against an 'aggressive foreign power', they declared: 'we, the subjects of His Majesty's Indian Empire, who are now residing in the metropolis, feel it our duty and privilege to express what we believe is the prevailing feeling throughout India – namely, a sincere desire for the success of British arms in the struggle.'[11]

Writing in *The Times* newspaper from the Hotel Majestic in Harrogate, Abdur Rahim, Member of the Royal Commission on the Public Services in India, explained why educated Indians backed the British in the war. This, he said, was because the British government in India had a 'higher purpose' to serve than merely the maintenance of peace and order. 'That purpose is to enlist by means of western education the sympathy and cooperation of the people in the ideals of Western civilisation, so that they may ultimately be fitted to administer the affairs of their own country as an integral part of the British Empire,' wrote Rahim, and added: 'From the Germans we can have no similar guarantees.'[12] Rahim believed like many other Indian intellectuals that the ultimate goal of a sovereign India would be gained by showing loyalty to the British at their time of need.

Even Gandhi who arrived in London by ship from South Africa on 4 August – the day Britain declared war on Germany – was quick not just to lend his voice of support, but to organise signatures from Indian residents in London as well. Gandhi's ship had been held up in the English Channel as mines were being laid there to prevent the incursion of German warships. However, within days of landing, the 44-year-old, who had already become famous in South Africa, wrote to the undersecretary at the India Office on 14 August 1914 from his residence at Talbot Road, Bayswater:

'It was thought desirable by many of us that during the crisis that has overtaken the empire and whilst many Englishmen, leaving the ordinary vocation of life are responding to the Imperial call, those Indians who are residing in the United Kingdom and who can at all do so, should place themselves unconditionally at the disposal of the Authorities,' wrote Gandhi. This, he said, was out of a desire 'to share the responsibilities of membership of this great Empire, if we could share its privileges.'

There were a total of 53 signatures including that of his wife Kasturba Gandhi, the poet and nationalist Sarojini Naidu, physician and surgeon Jivraj N Mehta and law student Sorabji Shapurji.

However, Holderness replied on behalf of Lord Crewe that the government did not think it advisable for Indian students to volunteer for military duties as they would probably not be able to leave it for three years. Lord Crewe advised instead that the Indians helped in rendering aid to the sick and wounded. He suggested that Gandhi set up a Voluntary Aid Contingent committee.

On 3 August 1914, Hardit Singh Malik, a second-year student at Balliol College, Oxford, was batting for Sussex against Kent on the opening day of the county cricket match in Canterbury. By evening next day, Britain had declared war. The match was abandoned, and with it Malik's dreams of playing county cricket in the summer holidays. However the mood was generally upbeat. He watched as the troops marched through the town cheered along by the crowds. Some even shouted, 'Bring us back some German sausage, lads!'[13] When Malik returned to Oxford in October he found that nearly all his fellow students had volunteered for the war effort. He felt that he should go too, even though Indians in England, were in an anomalous position. 'We were told that this was a war for freedom… But as Indians, we ourselves were under foreign rule, so how were we supposed to join in this war for 'freedom'? In spite of this I had a strong urge to join up,'[14] he said.

In Britain, however, Indian students were looked at with some suspicion as they often had nationalistic feelings and were not encouraged to join. Malik was told he could be an orderly in a hospital for Indian soldiers in Brighton. But that was not his idea of war service. The young Sikh wanted to see action in the front.[15]

Born in Rawalpindi and brought up in wealth and privilege – 'a lavish house, good food, horses and carriages, servants galore and money'[16] – Malik's family were devout Sikhs and his family had strict principles and convictions. At the age of fourteen, after being schooled in India by private tutors, he left for London, where after a short stint in a Notting Hill finishing school, he joined Eastbourne College, a 'good public school'. Malik faced an incident of bullying on his very first night. A group of boys surrounded him after supper and asked him to take off his turban as they wanted to see what was underneath. Malik told them that he was a Sikh and would not. When they advanced towards him saying they would take it off for him, Malik faced his assaulters calmly. He told them that he was outnumbered and would not be able to stop them now, but the first one who touched his turban he would kill, 'sometime, somehow'. The boys backed off and Malik was never teased again. He thought that word had gone around that Sikhs carried a kirpan on them, as any student who accidentlly collided with him during football or hockey and knocked off his turban, looked terrified and would apologise profusely.

Malik's academic and sporting talent – he was an all-rounder in cricket – made him the perfect candidate for Oxford and he joined Balliol College in 1912. Even as a teenager in London, he had kept up with the political struggle in India and the activities of the Indian students in the city. The assassination in London in 1909 of Sir Curzon Wyllie, Aide-de-Camp to the Secretary of State for India, by the young Madan Lal Dhingra had aroused a wave of patriotic fervour among the Indian students in Britain. Malik was thrilled when he heard that another Indian student, Veer Savarkar, who had been arrested for acclaiming Dhingra as a hero, had escaped from his ship at Marseilles. He remembered being furious when he heard that the French had captured Savarkar and handed him over to the British.

Yet, despite the dilemma he faced about British rule in India, Malik was determined to join the war effort and was not prepared to accept a refusal from the authorities. The adventurous young Sikh wanted to become a pilot. However, there was no chance of that, as the British were not prepared to accept Indians as officers. Malik knew that he would have to find a way in.

In their home in Kensington in London, the Roy family heard the news of the outbreak of the war with mixed feelings. The street was full of cheering men and women. Many of them had gathered outside the gates of Buckingham Palace and were returning home after seeing the King, Queen and the Prince of Wales wave to them from the balcony. It felt like a street party. But Lolita Roy was worried. The 49-year-old mother of six did not know what uncertainties the war would bring. She was the wife of Piera Lal Roy, eminent barrister and director of public prosecutions in Calcutta.The family had moved to London in 1901 so the children could gain a proper English education. Piera Lal Roy, born into a wealthy land-owning family from Barisal (now part of Bangladesh) believed that since Indians had to live under British rule, they should learn their ways. In Calcutta, he would often take his eldest son, Poresh, with him to the High Court, father and son riding out in their carriage on Calcutta's broad tree-lined streets. He would also take him for a walk every day. Piera, or 'Parry' as he was known, believed in physical fitness and taught his boys cycling and horse riding. A governess was engaged to school the children in English manners and etiquette. When the family moved to London, the boys were sent to St Paul's School for Boys in Hammersmith and the girls to St Paul's Girls' School.

Poresh found his calling in boxing and soon started training in school, where unfortunately, he faced an incident of racism. In 1912 when he entered his name for an inter-school boxing tournament there was a crisis. 'How can an Indian native compete with English boys?' roared their Physical Education teacher. 'Even though we considered ourselves English, he clearly did not think so,' said Poresh. 'I may have been fair-skinned, but there was clearly a difference.'[17] However, Poresh went to the tournament and defeated his opponent John Burns from the Irish School. When the victorious Poresh lifted the cup, the same P.E. teacher had the grace to tell him that he was the 'pride of the school'. He also told him he would make a name in boxing in the future.

While elder brother Poresh was becoming the school's boxing champion, Indra Lal 'Laddie' Roy was playing rugby and captaining the swimming team. The boys had to swim a mile every day. The refined Bengali family lived in a large house in Glazbury Road. Music could often be heard wafting out from the living room as the family – daughters, Lilavati (25, married), Miravati (24), Hiravati (18), and sons, Poresh (20), Indra (15) and Lolit (13) – listened to the songs of Tagore as well as to Western classical music. While Piera Lal continued to work in Calcutta, it was the sari-clad Lolita who was in charge in London. The house buzzed with the comings and goings of the boisterous family who – though very westernised – were still very attached to their Indian and Bengali roots. The news of the war provoked an immediate and animated family discussion.

Fifteen-year-old Indra knew at once what he wanted to do: join the Army. So did elder brother Poresh who had just graduated in Economics from Emmanuele College, Cambridge, where he had continued his winning spree in amateur boxing and gained a Cambridge blue. 'We were keen to prove that the non-martial Bengali could fight as well as any other soldier,' said Poresh."[18] As with Hardit Singh Malik, the fact that the King's Commission was not open to Indians, barred the gate for him. However he swallowed his pride 'and being a bit of a seeker of adventure and wanting to prove myself to myself' enlisted in the elite Honourable Artillery Company (HAC) on his twenty-first birthday, becoming the first Indian to do so. The HAC was the oldest regiment in the British Army, and Poresh began his training within weeks. He was soon sent to France. Indra signed up for the school cadet force at St Paul's. The teenager was determined to live his dream. If the war was to go on, he knew he wanted to play his part in it. Lolita was proud of her sons. They had grown up to be true Englishmen, dedicated to King and country.

As the Indians rallied to support Britain and the Empire, King George V sent them a message from Buckingham Palace. The King had a special bond with India. He had visited the country twice, once as the Duke of York and once as King. He had written to his grandmother, Queen Victoria, about the wonders of seeing the Taj Mahal and experienced the thrill of hunting in India and the opulence and hospitality of the Indian Maharajas.[19] He now felt that he needed to make a special appeal to his Indian subjects:

'During the past few weeks the peoples of my whole Empire at home and overseas have moved with one mind and purpose to confront and overthrow an unparalleled assault upon the continuity, civilisation and peace of mankind… In this hour of trial, the destinies of Great Britain and India are indissolubly linked.'[20]

The poet Rabindranath Tagore was visiting Ramgarh, a beautiful spot in the Himalayan foothills, but he could not sleep. A deep sense of foreboding was enveloping him. As the monsoon rain lashed against his window pane, Tagore felt that the world he loved was facing a catastrophe that would affect humankind for years. He wrote to his friend, Charles F Andrews: 'God knows it is the death pang that is tearing open my heart…' The poem he wrote that night captured his agony[21]:

Look, there comes the all destroying.
The flood of agony spreads out in a sea of pain,
The thunder roars in the dark and the lightning flashes amid the blood-shot clouds –
A lunatic shaking with laughter in his sport of death.[22]

Meanwhile, mobilisation orders were going out from the regimental centres in India. At 6.00 a.m. on 8 August Major Harry Hill of the Jullunder Brigade received a telegram at the station in Dalhousie ordering the mobilisation of the 3rd Lahore Divisional Headquarters.[23] By 8.45 a.m. he had issued the order to his units. By 9.00 a.m. 15th Sikhs were directed to proceed to Karachi. With seasoned military discipline, troops from the different regimental centres began to fall in. The soldiers would be asked to cross the *Kala Pani* for the first time. Crossing the seas was forbidden to orthodox Hindus as they could lose their caste. Any Hindu who crossed the seas would have to undergo an elaborate purification ceremony on their return. The commandants were apprehensive that many of the Hindu soldiers may be hesitant or superstitious. Yet the main job was tracing the soldiers who were mostly on leave and bringing them back to the regimental centres.

In Jalandher cantonment, Subedar Manta Singh of the 15th Sikhs got his call. Born in the village of Selampur Masanda in the district of Jalandhar in Punjab, Manta was the eldest of five brothers. After finishing his education in 1906, he signed up for the army. The recruiting centre was close to the village and many of the youngsters saw the army as a way out from the poverty of the area. Manta Singh's father, Khem Singh, was an influential landowner and knew many of the recruiting officers. It was his decision that led Manta Singh to choose the Army.[24] Soon he was promoted to the rank of Subedar (the equivalent of Captain). He said goodbye to his parents, his wife and young son, Assa, and left with the Jullunder Brigade attached to the Lahore Division. With him was his young English officer, George Henderson.

The Gurkhas had left on furlough for their houses in Nepal and the surrounding Himalayan regions. It would take nearly two to three weeks to reach them. Men were sent off to the remote mountain areas to track them down. Afridis left for the North West Frontier areas, where there were no post offices, to search out the soldiers and reservists and bring them back to station. From the deserts of Rajasthan, cavalry soldiers mounted camels and started returning to their cantonments. Where there were post offices, mobilisation letters were sent out by mail. In remote areas, the postmen would have to walk the last few miles to deliver them. The news of the war spread quickly in the villages. Many soldiers started heading back to their posts before they even received their letter. In regimental centres around the country, from the remote North West Frontier to the Central Provinces, the Indian troops were gathering, ready to make a journey into the unknown. The Gurkhas, Dogras, the Baluchis, the Garhwalis, the Sikhs and the Frontier Forces assembled at their centres for kits and final orders. India's martial races were ready to join the British Expeditionary Force.

Darwan Singh Negi was in his village in Kefarteer when the messenger arrived asking him to report for duty. The veteran soldier readied himself. He would have to make his way over the mountains and across the precarious rope bridge on the gushing river to reach his regiment in Lansdowne. A practised soldier, he said goodbye to his wife and began his journey back.

In Manjood village, Gabar Singh Negi had barely spent a few days with his young bride when it was time to return. Satoori did a puja for her husband, marked his forehead with red vermilion and prayed for his safety. The young man climbed up the steep path behind the house with a roll of bedding on his back, his hat tipped to protect himself from the rain.

Satoori would never see him again.

2

Arrival

The ports of Bombay and Karachi were hubs of frantic activity in the second week of August as the Indian contingent prepared to leave for France. Troops, camp followers, weapons, supplies, and animals had to be loaded on the ships which were not built for such unusual cargo. Curious observers at the port watched as hundreds of magnificent horses were tied up in slings and lowered on to the ship deck. The notoriously stubborn mules were practically dragged on board, not an easy task, but effectively carried out by the followers. Two hundred artisans and carpenters worked on the ships, building stalls for the animals, bunks for the soldiers, and shelves to store guns and artillery. Coolies, cooks and bhistis all waited at the embarkation ports, carrying their luggage in small bundles. They were going to *Vilayat*, the land of the English (the word *vilayati* would soon evolve into the word 'blighty'). Young Gurkha boys from remote villages, eager for an adventure and hoping to make some money, managed to enlist as followers by increasing their age. Waiting alongside them, in complete contrast, were middle-aged soldiers with greying beards. They were the reservists, who had also been asked to report for duty. Many of the reservists had not seen action for nearly fifteen years, and they looked scared and apprehensive about the long journey ahead.

Everything was done with military precision. Once the ships were prepared, embarkation began. The heavy kit and machine guns were loaded first by a working party of fifty men. They were followed by the animals – the machine gun mules and horses. Coolies carried the supplies:

rice, atta, dal and vegetables. Last on board were the troops, carrying their kit. As the ships waited at port, followers could be seen feeding the mules and walking them on deck to keep them exercised. Soon thirty ships were ready for the journey.

On 17 August, as the monsoon rains lashed the Apollo Bunder pier, the smartly dressed regiment of the 1/34th Sikh Pioneers arrived from their station in Ambala, Punjab, and were the first to board at the port of Bombay. The battalion consisted of nine British officers, nineteen Indian officers, 806 rank and file, fifty-seven followers and the mules and officers' chargers.

At 9.00 a.m. on 11 August, the Manchester Regiment, the British regiment which was part of the Jullunder Brigade, left Dalhousie by road for Pathankot and boarded the train to Jullunder. They were to embark at Karachi.[1] The troops from the 47th Sikhs, also part of the Jullunder Brigade, were all at their stations by 4.00 a.m. on 18 August, kitted out and ready to leave for Karachi by train. They were, however, in for a surprise. While their train was passing through Lahore, a wagon containing divisional supply personnel had been attached to their train. At Samsatta two of the followers in the wagon developed cholera. The train was immediately halted, the wagon cut off and on 20 August the 47th Sikhs were sent off on quarantine at Pilgrim Camp, four miles from the cantonment station at Karachi.[2] Luckily the troops were not infected and the battalion were cleared for travel. On 21 August, the 15th Sikhs, with Manta Singh and Captain Henderson in its ranks, arrived in Karachi at 6.30 a.m. and proceeded to their camp. Dressed in their long cotton kurtas and loose trousers, with the symbol of their Sikh faith on their turbans, the 15th Sikhs looked every bit the martial race they represented. Meanwhile, the 47th Sikhs, relieved at being released from quarantine, boarded the *SS Akbar* at Karachi on 29 August, only to find to their dismay that it was crowded, uncomfortable and short of rations.

More troops were to arrive from the Punjab. However, the *Indus* was in full spate, had flooded its banks and the troops from 57th Wilde's Rifles had to delay their departure. Eventually, after a tumultuous journey, they crossed the river and caught the train for Karachi. Arriving in the port city the next day they were congratulated for their 'keen and smart appearance'.[3] They boarded the *Teesta,* owned by the British India Steam Navigation Company. Despite the problems, all were ready to embark, and on 24 August, the Lahore Division with the Secunderabad Cavalry Brigade were set to sail.

Among the troops were two men who would go on to win the highest gallantry awards: Jemadar Mir Dast who would win the Victoria Cross and Havildar Gagna Singh who would receive the Indian Order of Merit. Travelling separately as part of 58th Vaughan Rifles (Meerut Division) was Mir Dast's brother, Mir Mast. Both brothers would win bravery medals before their paths took them on radically different directions. Mir Dast would have his medal of honour presented to him by the King. Mir Mast would have his honour withdrawn. But in the August of 1914, the brothers were not to know what lay ahead.

Also on the ship was 25-year-old Khudadad Khan of the 129th Duke of Connaught's Own Baluchis. Within less than two months he would be making history. Born in the village of Dab in the Chakwal district of Punjab, Khan was the only son of three siblings. His parents had died when he was still a teenager and he had studied only up to the fourth grade.[4] A close relative had helped Khan to join the Army. The mountainous area of Chakwal had no irrigation system and the land was not fertile. Enlisting in the army was the only way out for most men as it brought regular pay and earned the respect of the villagers. Life in the army was all that Khan had known. Travelling with him were the men from his neighbouring village of Dulmial, which had sent the highest number of troops to the war.

On 29 August, the 15th Sikhs and 59th Scindia Rifles embarked on the *RMS Takada*. Soon seven transport ships were lined up at the port of Karachi. Escorted by *RIMS Northbrook*, the 'ships sailed from the harbour for port unknown to any on board'.[5]

The Indian Expeditionary Force consisted of three infantry and one cavalry divisions. The first to be mobilised was the 6th Poona Division which was sent to the Persian Gulf. The next two – 3rd Lahore Division and 7th Meerut – would form the core of the Indian Army along with the Secunderabad Cavalry Brigade and head for Europe. Each division had four brigades which in turn consisted of different regiments. Each brigade would have one British regiment attached to it.

It would be the first time that Indian regiments would set out for battle alongside British troops.

Many British soldiers and officers had gone home to England for their summer holidays. They would all be recalled and join the Indian troops in France or Egypt. The Garhwal Brigade was part of the Meerut Division. It comprised the 1st and 2nd Battalion of the Garhwal Rifles and included in its ranks Gabar Singh Negi and Darwan Singh Negi. The Ferozepur Brigade was part of the Lahore Division. Its ranks included Khudadad Khan of 129th Baluchis and Mir Dast of 57th Wilde's Rifles. The Jullunder Brigade consisted of the 1st Battalion of The Manchester Regiment, the 15th Ludhiana Sikhs, the 47th Sikhs and the 59th Scinde Rifles (Frontier Force). Manta Singh and Captain Henderson were part of the ranks.

The Meerut Division was to leave nearly a month later. They were delayed as the German warship, the *Emden*, was in the waters of the Bay of Bengal dangerously close to Madras and likely to head towards Calcutta. There was a possibility that it could surface on India's Western shore as well, near the ports of Bombay and Karachi. The $2/2^{nd}$ Gurkhas and half of the $1/9^{th}$ Gurkhas embarked on the *SS Angora* in Bombay while the other half of the $1/9^{th}$ boarded the *SS Arancola*. The Gurkhas, coming as they did from the mountains of Nepal, had never seen the sea. They swam in the salty water and watched in wonder as the waves of the Arabian Sea crashed against the embankment near the Gateway of India. This was the famed *Kala Pani* that their religion forbade them to cross. They marvelled at the sea stretching endlessly to the horizon and wondered what it would be like to sail on it. The smartly dressed Gurkhas in their slouch hats caused quite a stir in Bombay when they went on their route marches. The people of Bombay had never seen soldiers from the Eastern Himalayas. Most mistook them for the Japanese. Like the *SS Akbar* in Karachi, the *Arancola* too proved to be far from comfortable. Originally meant for 500 men, it was now groaning under the weight of 1200 men and 100 animals. The convoy boarded the ship on 13 September but had to wait for a week at the docks before getting the clearance to leave. Many were seasick even before setting sail. On board were Kulbir Thapa and Karan Bahadur Rana both of the 3rd Queen Alexandra's Own Gurkhas. In less than a year Thapa would be awarded the Victoria Cross for his bravery in saving an officer and other comrades in Fauquissart in France and Rana would be awarded the Victoria Cross for action in El Kefr in Egypt in 1918.

The 39th Garhwal Rifles regiment was quick to mobilise despite having to recall many of their soldiers from remote hill areas. The 1st Battalion marched out of the regimental centre at Lansdowne on 20 August, and the 2nd Battalion on the 21st. They made their way to Dugadda and then to Kotdwar. But the rains made it difficult. At Dugadda, the camp site was flooded and the Garhwalis were finally able to settle for the night after borrowing tents from the 8th Gurkha Rifles. Darwan Singh Negi and Gabar Singh Negi were among the troops. The next day they marched 12 miles in the rain and reached Kotdwar, only to find that the next train would be available after nine days. Setting up camp in Kotdwar was not easy. Monsoon and malaria combined to make an unpleasant start to the journey. Soon most of the men were down with fever. On 31 August the troops finally caught the train for Karachi arriving at the port on 2 September. Many were still under the weather and would remain in poor form on the sea voyage ahead. The 2nd Battalion of the 39th Garhwal Rifles were specially commended for their discipline. They arrived at the dock in Karachi on 16 September at exactly 11.15 a.m. to board the *SS Coconada* and by noon had boarded all their kit and their men. By the time the Meerut Division set sail on 21 September, nearly a month after the Lahore Division, the troops were straining to go. As the ships gradually pulled out of the ports, crowds of people lined the docks to wave the soldiers goodbye.

A day later the *Emden* attacked Madras. The war had reached India.

As the Indian soldiers prepared to travel to Europe, the search began in London for the person who would command them. He would have to be familiar with India, understand the soldiers well and be able to gain their respect. The choice fell on Lieutenant General Sir James Willcocks, stationed at Murree, a picturesque hill station in the Punjab now Pakistan. Just a few months short of finishing his four-year tenure in the area, the general was delighted to receive his new appointment as Commander-in-Chief of the Indian Corps in France. He set out immediately for the port of Karachi and the sea journey to Marseille.

Born in India in Baraut, thirty-three miles from Meerut, in 1857, James Willcocks was just three weeks old, when Indian soldiers in Meerut had risen up in revolt against the East India Company leading to what came to be known variously as the Sepoy Mutiny and the First War of Indian Independence. The rumblings of protest against the policies of the East India Company had been growing for a few months before. The aggressive annexationist policies of the Company had led to political discontent, particularly when Oudh, the kingdom of Nawab Wajid Ali Shah was seized on grounds of mal-administration. Meanwhile, the soldiers too were feeling aggrieved. The Enlistment Act of July 1856, introduced by the Company's administration meant that Indian sepoys could be deployed anywhere, even overseas, which meant crossing the forbidden *Kala Pani* (The soldiers of the Bengal Army had previously been deployed only to areas where they could go by land.) However, the flashpoint was the introduction of the British Enfield Rifle. There were rumours that the bullets had been greased with beef and pork tallow, forbidden to Hindus and Muslims respectively. The soldiers had to bite open the paper-wrapped cartridges before ramming it down the barrel of the gun. On 24 April when Col Edward Carmichael Smythe of the 3rd Bengal Light Cavalry ordered a parade of eighty-five soldiers to load their rifles, the soldiers stood still, refusing to obey the order. They were immediately arrested, court martialled and sentenced to ten years rigorous imprisonment. It was not to end there. On 9 May the convicted soldiers were brought to the parade grounds, stripped, shackled and surrounded by the 60th Rifles and the 6th Dragoon Guards, who had their sabres drawn in order to intimidate and humiliate them. The heavy-handed action sparked off an immediate response.

The following day was a Sunday. As the European officers prepared to go to Church or spend the day at the club or at home, the Indian troops broke into revolt. By evening around fifty Europeans, including civilians, were killed in Meerut, and the eighty-five soldiers freed from the jail along with some other detainees.

The flame lit in Meerut spread across the plains of Bengal and United Provinces like a bushfire. On 11 May several European men, women and children were massacred in Delhi. As the Company's administration came under attack, James Willcocks' father, Captain William Willcocks, left for Delhi. Young James had to be guarded by two sowars at home, such was the danger to the Company's soldiers. James was just over a month old when his father fought under the command of Major General George Pollock who descended on Delhi from the Ridge with 5000 men and reclaimed the city. The Mutiny was crushed on 20 June 1858. The East India Company was dissolved and power transferred directly to the Crown. Captain William Willcocks retired from the army and took up civilian service. Young James was sent to England to complete his studies and graduated from Sandhurst in 1878. In 1879, he returned to India, took part in the Second Afghan War as a transport officer and in 1900 became Colonel Commandant of the Frontier Force. After a stint in the Boer War, he returned once again to India as Brigadier General. In 1910 he was appointed the commandant of the Northern Army.

A flamboyant man, given to writing poetry, he had a great love for the land of his birth, and admired the Indian soldiers. The General was a keen polo player and proficient in pig-sticking and tent-pegging. He also enjoyed hunting big game along with duck and snipe shooting. Willcocks spoke Hindustani and a number of other Indian languages and was well known to the Indian soldiers and officers. With his clipped moustache, deep blue eyes, and a chest-full of medals, he looked every bit the British General. It would fall on him to lead the Indian soldiers in what would be the most difficult war that they had ever fought. After the war he would write *With the Indians in France,* a memoir of his time on the Western Front, poetic in its praise of the Indians.

The Indian Army at this time owed its structure largely to the post-Mutiny changes carried out by Lord Roberts in the nineteenth century. Roberts had declared that it was the 'Mutiny which compelled us to reorganize our Indian Army and make it the admirable fighting machine it now is'.[6] Following the 1857 uprising, it was decided that the proportion of British to Indian troops should never fall below one to three and the field artillery should be completely in British hands.

Born in Kanpur in India in 1832, Roberts was educated in Eton and Sandhurst and returned to the land of his birth as a second lieutenant in the East India Company. He earned his spurs in the relief of Lucknow during the Mutiny and was awarded the Victoria Cross in 1858 for action at Khudaganj. It was the famous siege of Kandahar during the Second Afghan War in 1878 that led to him being praised in Parliament and knighted the following year. In 1885 he became Commander-in-Chief of the Indian Army. The Baronetcy followed in 1892 and he became known as Lord Roberts of Kandahar. He ended his forty-one year career in the Indian Army in 1893, to be replaced by Lord Kitchener.

Lord Roberts had a clear policy: he preferred to recruit from the martial races of India and also from those classes that had been loyal to the British during the Mutiny. According to Roberts: 'No comparison can be made between the martial value of a regiment recruited amongst the Gurkhas of Nepal or the warlike races of Northern India, and of one recruited from the effeminate peoples of the South.'[7] He favoured the Pathans from the North West Frontier, the Baluchis, the Punjabi Muslims, the Rajputs and the Dogras. The old Bengal Army, which had mutinied in 1857, was disbanded and Roberts had little time for the new recruits. Nor did he have a place in his ranks for the 'so-called fighting Marathas of Bombay'.[8]

The Sikhs were well known as a martial race. Their tenth leader, Guru Gobind Singh had founded the military order of the Khalsa that established the Sikhs as warriors. Sikhs made up a large number of the Indian Army, comprising mainly Jat farmers from Punjab. The Punjabi Muslims from an agricultural background, spoke the Punjabi language along with the Sikhs. The Rajputs from the deserts of Rajasthan had a thousand-year history of military warfare and were staunch Hindus. The agricultural Jats were closely allied to them and comprised Hindus and Sikhs from the region of Sindh, Haryana, Rajasthan, Jammu, and Western United Provinces, while the Dogras, orthodox Hindus considered solid and dependable, were descended from the Rajputs. The Pathans were staunch Muslims prone sometimes to unpredictable behaviour. There were instances of Pathans murdering a British officer for (unknowingly) sleeping with his feet towards Mecca. There was only one all-Pathan regiment in the Indian Army – the 40th Pathans –

and it was often referred to as 'The Forty Thieves'. However, those who were subjected to the discipline made very good soldiers and the first Victoria Cross from undivided India was awarded to Khudadad Khan, a Pathan.

The Gurkhas were the elite fighters of the Indian Army, the ultimate martial race, known for their endurance, bravery and loyalty. They were descendants of the Rajputs with a strong mix of Mongolian blood. Their favoured weapon – the *khukri* – a rounded dagger that could decapitate at one fell swoop, was much feared by the Germans, as was their war cry, '*Ayo Gurkhali* [The Gurkhas are coming]'.

Roberts never recruited from India's intellectual classes, leading to the criticism that the British chose soldiers from the less literate regions, to ensure they would follow commands without question. When war broke out, it was the intellectual classes, however, who came out strongly in support of the war effort. Roberts loved his Indian soldiers but he also believed that they lacked leadership skills and did not make good officers. According to him, no matter how well-educated or how brave, the native soldier needed to be led by a British officer. It would not do to have an English soldier placed under an Indian officer. Consequently, Indians were not allowed to go to Sandhurst and graduate as the King's Commissioned Officers. However, they were allowed rank as Viceroy's Commissioned Officers (VCOs) or junior officers of the regiment. Even here, there was a discrepancy, as the most senior Indian VCO would still be considered junior to the junior-most English officer.

There were strict rules for the English officers chosen for the Indian Army. They had to learn Hindustani and familiarise themselves with Indian history and culture. All officers were given a handbook on India before they left to take up their posts. Most English officers were popular with their regiments and those not getting on with the Indians were quickly transferred. The officers often went to the soldiers' villages and met their families. The Indian soldiers called them 'Sahib', and the officers too returned the courtesy. It was a carefully established order that spelt out clearly who was in command. The British knew that for the Indian soldier, the King – living as he did thousands of miles away – was a distant figure to proclaim loyalty to. They focussed on the regiment, which was very much like a family. The soldiers of the Indian Army swore allegiance first to the King, and second to their regiment. Usually from the same region and often from the same village, they spoke the same language and worshipped together, giving them a strong sense of community. The traditions of the regiment were taught to them at the temple, the mosque, the gurdwara and at church parades. A young soldier knew that if he did well in battle, he would be the hero of his village. Both Gabar Singh Negi and Darwan Singh Negi were the pride of Garhwal and their villages. New recruits were shown the regimental trophies on mess nights and saw the honour that came with the decorations and valour. The concept of 'being loyal to the salt' or loyal to the one who had provided for them ran deep. In letters home from the frontline, even during the worst days of the war, the soldiers always pledged loyalty to the hand that fed them.

The Indian Corps had begun its journey. Soon, they were streaming across the Indian Ocean on a moderate sea. The ships leaving from Karachi coordinated with those from Bombay and the convoy travelled towards the Suez Canal escorted by ships from the Royal Navy and the Royal India Marine. Later they were joined by the ships of the French Navy. Lt Col Merewether and Sir Frederick Smith, official historians of the Indian Corps, described the voyage as 'uneventful' and the weather 'perfect'. Considerable excitement was caused when a shark swam around the *S.S Edavana* on 1 September.[9] Apart from many soldiers on the *Edavana* falling ill and the Commander of the *Castalia*, Captain Mitchell, dying suddenly in his cabin (probably of heatstroke) the journey was smooth.[10] The soldiers were given regular exercise and there were lectures on board. The Sikhs were pleased that there were two *Darbar Sahibs* (the Sikh holy book) on board. 'We pray and sing hymns continually,' a soldier wrote.[11] 'There are ships without number passing hither and thither and there is no fear of any kind. The Sikhs, Dogras and Musalmans all subscribed towards scarfs to cover the *Darbar Sahibs*; we collected 2*l*, 19*s* and two franks. The *Darbar* is exhibited even on board ship. We are very fortunate.' Muslims were allowed to go up to the promenade deck of the ship and pray in the direction of Mecca.[12]

On board the ship en route to Calais was Sir Pratap Singh, the Maharaja of Idar and Regent of Jodhpur, accompanied by the Maharaja of Jodhpur, the sixteen-year-old Sumer Singh. Sir Pratap was leading his cavalry troops, the Jodhpur Lancers. Known to the officers as 'Sir P', the sprightly Maharaja addressed the two squadrons of cavalrymen on the ship. During a halt at Port Suez he told the soldiers about the supreme value of being prepared to sacrifice their all, including their lives, in upholding the traditions of loyalty and devotion to duty. By virtue of his age and status, 'Sir P' was regarded by the Rathores, who made up most of the cavalry, as the head of their clan. They listened to him in earnest and prepared to fight for their regimental honour.

The troops knew they were travelling westward, but had no idea of their destination. Speculation was rife that they would be sent to guard the Suez Canal. Given the experience of the Boer war – where the Indian troops were not taken to the frontline – they felt they would never be sent to Europe. The wireless message on 30 August that announced Lord Kitchener's statement in the House of Lords – that the British Expeditionary Force in France was to be reinforced by two Divisions from India, one of which had started out on its route – was greeted with cheers on the ships. 'This is the first information we have received giving us a clue to our ultimate destination,' wrote Hill.[13] The troops were delighted that they were going to be on the frontline in Europe, fighting with the British against a European enemy. The war cries of the different Indian battalions could be heard echoing from the ships: *Jo Bole So Nihal, Sat Sri Akal, Ayo Gurkhali*, and *Jai Badri Vishal*, as the regiments geared up for the fight ahead. Despite the cramped conditions, sea-sickness and poor rations, the spirits were high. They were going to *Vilayat* with their '*Janral Sahib*'.

On 12 September the soldiers received a wireless message from the Reuters news agency. On 9 and 10 September, the Germans had retreated in France on their right and the British Expeditionary Force had advanced in a Northerly direction across the River Marne for thirty-seven and a half miles.[14] Amidst cheers the British troops told the Indians soldiers that the war would probably be over before Christmas.

The Lahore Division reached Suez on 15 September. From here, two regiments – the Ferozepur and Jullunder Divisions – travelled by train to Cairo and then onwards to Alexandria and Port Said. Route marches were held in Egypt to show the population that there were a large number of Muslims in the Indian Army including the Pathans and the Punjabi Muslims. This was to emphasise that Muslims were ready to fight against Turkey, an ally of Germany, if the need arose. The troops boarded their ships on 18 September and sailed on the 19th. It was at this point that their destination was finally disclosed to them. They were to go to Marseilles. On 23 September they learned that the *Emden* had attacked the Bay of Bengal, dampening their enthusiasm briefly.[15]

King George V sent a message to the Indian troops on their arrival: 'You are the descendants of men who have been great rulers and great warriors. You will recall the glories of your race, you will have the honour of showing in Europe that the sons of India have lost none of their ancient martial instincts... History will record the doings of India's sons and your children will proudly tell of the deeds of their fathers.' It was greeted with a cheer by the troops who were elated that the King himself was reaching out to them. Each soldier now strained to prove himself. Hopes of gallantry medals and fame filled their hearts.

Lt Col Merewether captured the mood:

> No one who saw it will ever forget the landing from the great transports which began to swing into the harbour of Marseilles in the autumn of 1914, or the laughing sunburnt, careless faces of the young British officers who leaned over the bulwarks and called aloud to learn whether they were coming too late. In six months nearly all were dead.[16]

At 7.00 a.m. on 26 September the Indian ships arrived at Marseilles. The first to drop anchor was the *SS Taiyebeh*, carrying the twenty Company Sappers and Miners of the Lahore Division. The ship was seriously leaking by then. By 9.00 a.m. the entire flotilla of the Lahore Division had lined up at the port.[17] The Indians crammed the deck to look at their final destination. Excited voices asked if they could see the firing. Others marvelled that they were finally in *Vilayat* as they looked in wonder at the scene that greeted them – the port of Marseilles was a sea of regimental colours: the blue jackets and red trousers of the French infantry, the khakis of the Tommies and the red fez and baggy pantaloons of the troops of the French colonials. Officers carried swords and wore crested helmets. The soldiers called out to each other and officers gave directions. Dogs, horses and mules were led around and porters were busy unloading the artillery and supplies.

As the Indians disembarked they were greeted with loud cheers from the French. It was a glorious autumn day as the soldiers marched five miles to the camp site on the racecourse, watched by crowds of local residents, who packed every road, window and roof-top in the town, straining to get a vantage view. As ship after ship from India brought in the troops, the citizens of Marseilles showered them with flowers. Sikh soldiers were embarrassed to find French ladies eagerly embracing and kissing them as they marched through the town. Cries of '*Vive les Hindoues*' and '*Les Hindoues*' filled the air. The Indians replied with the one cheer they had learnt from their English officers: 'Hip, hip Hurrah.'

To the French crowds in Marseilles, the Indians looked like kings. The reporter from the *Manchester Guardian* wrote: 'The Indian Lancers sat proudly in their saddles, with their heads upright under the Oriental crowns; then came a regiment of Sikhs, walking at a brisk pace, all big and strong men, with curled beards and the wide '*pagri*' round the ears; the Pathans followed, carrying on their heads that queer pointed bonnet, the '*kullah*', which reminds one of the warriors seen on old Persian tapestries – a more slender type of men, but equally determined, and with faces at the same time smiling and resolute.'[18]

The Indians marched to their camp outside Marseilles at St Marcel, La Barrasse and Borley. They were followed in the dusk by the cheering and curious crowds who then watched them prepare their evening meal and eat chapatti and dal by the light of the campfire. At Marseille a minor crisis with regard to the food supplied to the Indians had been averted. While the Indians were still on board the ships, they were sent tins of canned mutton. However the labels on these tins showed a 'well-natured ox'.[19] The label, immediately noticed by the Indians, was brought to the attention of the British officers. It was pointed out that the meat could not be eaten by Hindus. The label was actually the manufactuer's logo, and not indicative of the contents of the tin, but the Hindus could not be persuaded. The tinned meat was abandoned.

On 30 September the Lahore Division left for Orleans. The journey was long, with regular stops to collect firewood and make provisions for the men to cook. Once again crowds gathered at the railway stations on both sides of the platform and watched the troops. 'Along the whole route, fruit of all kinds, coffee, biscuits and flags and flowers was given to the troops by the French people. Nothing could possibly have exceeded the kindness and hospitality with which the French civilians and soldiers received all ranks,' recorded Harry Hill.[20] Following the tinned meat disaster, the British decided that livestock would be supplied directly to the soldiers. Separate slaughtering facilities were set up for the Hindus and Muslims in the camps. To the French, the Indians seemed to be from another world. They often commented that the Indians were strong because they ate trees in the morning (the Indian soldiers cleaned their teeth with neem sticks). They watched in wonder as the Indians went about their ways.

Among the Indian followers was Sukha, the untouchable sweeper from Bareilly who had enlisted for war service. The pay was better than what he received in India and it was an adventure he did not mind. He had not enjoyed the sea journey or cleaning out the ships and the animal waste, but had felt better since they had landed at Marseilles. He enjoyed walking with the troops through the green countryside and marvelled at the cheers they got. No one had ever cheered for him before. Sukha was filled with pride. The followers were divided into groups: the cooks, grooms and bheestis. Cleaners like him were at the bottom of the pile, but Sukha did not mind. He was beginning to enjoy his time in France.

The train journey to Orleans was an adventure for the soldiers. The British officers travelled first class and the Indian sepoys, followers and Tommies were crammed into third. It felt very much like the crowded trains back home. The air was full of smoke from the *beedis* and cigarettes. Huddled next to each other the Indian soldiers sang, smoked, chatted and watched the French countryside roll by. As the train hurtled through the night, there was a minor disaster. One of the sepoys, Zaman Khan from 57th Wilde's Rifles, had covered his face with a handkerchief and propped himself against the door of the railway carriage to take a quick nap. He did not notice that the door was gradually coming loose. Khan was in deep sleep when a train coming from the opposite direction made the carriage rattle even louder. The door flew open and Khan fell out. The sepoys were in a state of complete confusion. They had no idea how to stop the train which was speeding on. Finally after much screaming they managed to reach the engine and get the driver to pull on the brakes. A search ensued, and Zaman Khan was finally found several miles away. He had escaped with a few cuts and bruises.[21] The rescue operation over, they continued through the night to reach Orleans on 2 October.

The Indians were surprised that the French spoke a different language from the English and that even most of the English could not understand them. 'No one has any clue to the language of this place,' a Sikh soldier wrote to his uncle in Jullunder. 'Even the British soldiers do not understand it. They call milk DOOLEE and water DOOLO…' He was referring to the French words *du lait* and *de l'eau*.[22]

The weather had turned by 13 October when the Meerut Division landed in Marseilles. There was a biting wind and sleet as the battalions marched to Camp La Valentine which was further away than the camp used by the Lahore Division. The field was muddy and tents were pitched in a quagmire. Both battalions of the 39th Garhwal Rifles, including in their ranks Gabar Singh and Darwan Singh Negi, were among those marching in the cold and rain, their clothes inappropriate for the weather. From the camp they left for Orleans where they arrived on 21 October along with the 3rd Gurkhas. At the camps, the troops were re-armed.

They marched through Orleans and were particularly taken by the statue of Joan of Arc in the centre of the large town square. Enthralled by the story of her bravery, they assembled in small groups around the statue and some companies which were marching came to attention and turned their faces towards it. A soldier who tried to buy postcards of Joan of Arc wrote to his family in India 'I could not find any more pictures of that woman who stands clad in armour with her glance turned up towards heaven. I am looking for them and searched many shops. Four hundred years ago that woman gained some notable victories in war against the English. However she was caught and the English burnt her alive. I think that is why the sale of the pictures has stopped, lest it should affect adversely the present friendship between the French and the English.'[23] Some Indian soldiers compared her to the Rani of Jhansi who had famously donned armour and fought against the British during the Mutiny.

It was in Orleans that the Indians saw their first aeroplane. They watched in wonder as the mass of steel and propellers flew over their heads, the pilot inside clearly visible. The Indians were just beginning to see the wonders of *Vilayat*.

Back in camp they had pressing problems to deal with. The Indian Army had been supplied with Lee Enfield Rifles Mark II, but the British Army had Mark III models. The soldiers were now given the new model, but they had little time to train as they were needed in the trenches. They would end up learning to use the new Rifles in the frontline. Though the winter was setting in, the Indians still did not have adequate clothing. They remained in their thin cotton khaki drill and jumpers which provided no protection in the wind, sleet and rain of the dark October and November months.

There was some attempt to supply warm clothing to the soldiers when they arrived, but it descended into comic farce. The batch of pullovers, long johns and British warm coats were made to fit the larger-built British soldier. The slightly-built Gurkhas found to their concern and embarrassment that the long johns simply fell around their knees when they they tried to pull them up. The men were sent off to the local market to purchase 3,000 safety pins.[24] Their underwear pinned up like diapers wasn't the best way for the men from the mountains to face the Germans. There weren't enough blankets either. Each soldier was supposed to be issued with an extra blanket on arrival but the Lahore Division found that there were not enough to go around. It was not unusual to see the tall bearded Pathans of Wilde's Rifles wandering around the campsite, desperately cold, wrapped in anything that they could find to keep themselves warm: from eiderdowns and table cloths to cast-off curtains. One of the sepoys wrapped in a thin blanket was Sepoy Khudadad Khan, unaware of the gruelling battle that he would soon be facing.

When the Indian Army had been ordered to mobilise in August, there had been no clear plan for them. Initially it was thought they may be used as reserve or garrison troops, but Lord Hardinge had suggested that this would be a waste of time for trained soldiers and not good for their morale. It was decided that the Indians would be used as a unified Corps under the command of General Willcocks. On 30 September, the General disembarked at Marseilles ready to join his troops.

One of the other major problems facing the Indian Corps was the shortage of artillery, which would cost them heavily. In addition, they were short of soldiers. In the confusion of the early weeks of the war, cavalrymen would be made to disembark and fight as infantry and battalions would be split up and used to plug gaps in the British lines, often under officers they did not know and who did not speak their language. Used to working as a team, the units were confused and demoralised. Despite this, the loyalty of the troops remained unfailing.

The official history of the war records a famous conversation between General Willcocks and an Indian officer. When the General visited the battle site of Neuve Chapelle in 1915, he was overcome with the huge loss of lives around him and told the Indian officer, 'There are very few of you left, *Subedar Saheb*.' To which the heavily wounded officer replied: 'There are twice as many as there were before the General Saheb visited us.'

Willlcocks describes the contribution of the Indian soldiers in his memoir praising their unfailing loyalty. In a poem 'Hurnam Singh' he relates what the soldier Hurnam Singh would be telling the villagers back home about the adventures they had after crossing the *Kala Pani*: 'The village yokels round him flocked to hearken to his tales… For India's sons had sealed their oath, according to their laws/Sealed it with blood across the sea… And died in England's cause.'[25]

The cold weather was setting in, freezing the bones of the Indian soldiers. But there was little time to worry about that. It was time to get closer to the action. Barely a few weeks since landing at Marseilles, the troops set out again. On the night of October 14, the train carrying over seven hundred troops from the 57th Wilde's Rifles left Orleans for the North. The Lahore Division was on the move. Sitting in the train was Khudadad Khan. By 26 October the 39th Garhwal Rifles left Orleans. For Gabar Singh Negi and Darwan Singh Negi, the journey so far had been fraught with difficulties. They had survived the bouts of fever and malaria, the overcrowded leaky ship and the sparse provisions, but the most trying times lay ahead.

3

Comfort Kameti

As the ships containing the Meerut and Lahore divisions were arriving in Marseilles, a high-power meeting was being held on 1 October 1914 at St John's Gate in Clerkenwell, London. An impressive line of dignitaries could be seen entering the sixteenth-century building of the Museum of St John. It was a clear autumn night with a slight nip in the air, as they made their way to the Chapter Hall, a room with beautiful stained-glass ceilings, medieval coats of arms and imposing portraits of British monarchs. Seated below the ornate chandelier from the Farnese Palace in Rome, the delegates discussed an important question: how to look after the Indian soldiers during the war?

Chaired by Sir John Hewett, an old India hand, the members tackled the problem of providing comforts and provisions to the soldiers who had travelled thousands of miles and were in an alien environment. It was unanimously decided to set up the Indian Soldiers' Fund.[1] The solid, heavy-jowled, Hewett, with his love for hunting, had served as the lieutenant governor of the United Provinces and proved himself to be an efficient administrator. It was Hewett who organised the labyrinthine twenty-five-mile tent city, housing 250,000 people in Delhi for the coronation durbar of George V and Queen Mary in 1911, which earned him a knighthood. Every bit the colonial administrator, he was joined on the committee by his sometime adversary, the former Viceroy of India, Lord Curzon, who had once described Hewett as an 'able, plausible, self-seeking, not too loyal individual, who plays for his own hand.'[2] These differences were however put aside as Hewett focussed on the present issues.

Present at the first meeting was also Lord Roberts, whose love for his Indian soldiers was legendary. The former Commander-in-Chief of the Indian Army was planning to visit them in France in the next few days and raise their morale as he had often done in the past. Only a few hours before he started on his journey on 9 October, he made a passionate appeal for funds hoping to get at least 1500 donors on his list. Members of the committee included the good and great of British society, many with strong India connections: Adeline, Duchess of Bedford, the Marchioness of Lansdowne (wife of the former Viceroy of India), the Countess of Scarborough, the Countess of Minto (wife of the former Viceroy of India), the Maharani of Bharatpur, Lady Ampthill, Lady Sydenham, Lord Hamilton, His Highness the Aga Khan, Sir Mortimer Durand, Sir Richard Havelock Charles, Sir Ratan J Tata and Mr C.C. McLeod. Lord Curzon kicked off the proceedings by generously announcing that he would provide office space at 1 Carlton House Terrace, a short walk from Trafalgar Square.

The objective of the fund was to establish and maintain a hospital for Indian soldiers and followers, to provide comforts and clothing for them in the hospitals and the front and to repair 'promptly and efficaciously the immense wastage of war.'[3]

On 23 October, by the time the Indian soldiers were in action in Belgium, the Indian Soldiers' Fund put out a second appeal under Lord Roberts. It was decided to build two hospitals for Indian soldiers in Brockenhurst in Hampshire, a short distance from Southampton, where the hospital ships from France would arrive. A site was obtained in Brockenhurst Park, and by November, the firm of Sir John Jackson & Company started work. The Order of St John of Jerusalem granted £10,000 towards the equipment for the Lady Hardinge Hospital. The Viceroy of India donated Rupees 100,000 from the Imperial Indian Relief Fund.

Soon a well-organised plan was in place. Having learnt the lessons from the Mutiny, the British administrators wanted to ensure that the Indian soldiers were well looked after and would not have any complaints. A clothing, comfort and warehousing sub-committee was formed and two depots set up in London – one at 29 Somerset Street and the other at 21 Park Lane – in houses lent by Lady Scarborough, so that the public could donate gifts in kind.

Run by the efficient Hewett, everything worked with military precision. Hewett contacted Willcocks in the field to establish what exactly the troops required. Soon the requests came flooding back, from the mundane to the unusal. Items like socks, shirts, cardigans, dressing gowns, overcoats and slippers were standard requirements. More specialised were items like waterproof *pagri* covers, *pagri* cloth, khaki muslin and *kulas* (a conical cap around which the *pagri* was folded). In the incessant rain in the Western Front the waterproof *pagri* covers were imperative. A special design was drawn up by Lt Col O'Connor and a large order placed in London.

The Indians needed comfort items to help them cope with the harsh life in the trenches. Food from back home was always welcome. Spices, boiled sweets, chutney, curry, pickles, papad, *gur*, puffed wheat and rice, semolina, tea, coffee and fruits, made their way to the frontline. Recreation too was all-important. Boxes of board games like chess, halma and *pachisi* were packed for the soldiers as were gramophones and outdoor games.

Convoys of lorries marked with the logo of the Indian Soldiers' Fund could be seen on the roads in France and Belgium, travelling from the depot at Boulogne to the base hospitals and frontlines. Even Indian Maharajas were involved in the elaborate chain. The Jam Sahib of Nawanagar was given charge of receiving and distributing goods to the cavalry, usually large consignments of cigarettes and tobacco.

The soldiers knew of the existence of what they called the *Kameti* (Committee) and they thought the gifts were sent by the *Sarkar* (government). The Committee proposed that the cigarette boxes should have a card enclosed saying that it was a gift from the Indian Soldiers' Fund. The Committee sent thousands of towels, handkerchiefs and soaps to the soldiers who welcomed these after they returned from fighting in the muddy trenches. There were large demands for these items from depots at Marseilles, Rouen and elsewhere. To the soldiers in the frontline, the supplies provided by the Comfort *Kameti* were a lifeline and kept them going. For those recovering in the hospitals, it was a sign that the English cared for them.

The Indian soldiers, especially the farmers from Punjab, quickly developed a taste for condensed milk; 50,067 tins were supplied in the first six months alone. Also popular was Horlicks Malted Milk (15,278 tins were sent by March 1915). The Indians consumed cigarettes in enormous quantities and many in the front and in the hospitals took to smoking the briar pipes used by the Europeans. For those who needed Indian tobacco, this too was taken care of. A considerable amount was supplied by donors from India. Hookahs and *chillums*, which could not be easily procured in Europe, were sent from India, though many broke *en route*. The dedicated volunteers of the Comfort Committee found that *lotas* (small brass pots used for drinking water) were required at the front. These were immediately ordered from a firm in Lyndhurst, Hampshire, and the design was much appreciated by the Indians.

For soldiers recovering in hospitals there was a constant demand for notepaper and envelopes as well as playing cards. London clubs donated a large number of the latter. Illustrated papers were popular among the soldiers – most of whom were illiterate – and the London clubs provided these in large numbers. The soldiers liked to read copies of *The Times History of the War*, both the British Army and the Indian Army editions. Photographs of the King's visit to Brockenhurst hospital were also popular, as the soldiers would keep these as souvenirs or post them to their families in India.

The Sikhs needed coconut oil for their hair, and efforts were made to source it from India. The Chesebrough Manufacturing Company of London, famous for Vaseline supplied in glass bottle jars, generously donated 50,000 small tins of petroleum jelly and camphor ice that was forwarded to the front as an emollient for chapped skin during the frosty weather.

There was nothing quite like music to lift the spirits of wounded soldiers. However, Indian music was difficult to locate in England and arrangements were made for 200 records to be shipped from India. The arrival of the gramophone players in the hospitals caused much excitement. As the music floated over the wards, the soldiers momentarily forgot their pain. There was also devotional music which the soldiers eagerly listened to. In a year's time the supply of gramophones increased for both hospitals and the front. 300 Indian records were supplied by the Gramophone Company, Hayes, Middlesex, and 500 were purchased from India.

The patients needed some outdoor exercise while they were recovering, and the Committee set aside funds for a shooting gallery, sets of quoits, croquet and other games. Footballs, cricket bats and hockey sticks were also supplied. Footballs were so popular at the front as well as in the depots, that their price had gone up nearly 50 per cent since the beginning of the war.

Writing to his friend in India from the Meerut Stationary Hospital in Boulogne, an Indian soldier, B. Dass, said: 'Here we have all sorts of games, football, cricket and tennis. I have become quite mad on ping pong. You must wonder at our playing games in the midst of this terrible fighting with the shells falling around us...there is no doubt that there are heaps of shells around us, but we don't mind in the slightest. One needs real bravery here, not the sort of bravery shown by dacoits in India.'

As they faced the relentless shell-fire in an alien land, the Indians, more than ever, felt the need to pray and there was a strong demand for religious books. Two hundred copies of the Quran were purchased from London and sent to the front, while the Begum of Bhopal sent a 'very large, almost embarrassing supply of copies.'[4] A further 1000 volumes were distributed by the secretary of the All India Muslim League, with the help of the *maulavi* from the Woking mosque. The Committee also received further gifts of 500 Qurans and 100 amulets from Mirza Hairat, editor of the *Curzon Gazette*, Delhi.

The Sikhs needed copies of the Guru Granth Sahib and these were arranged to be supplied from India by Sir Charles Pardey Lukis, the Director General of the Indian Medical Service. The distribution was organised through the Sikh Dharamsala at 79 Sinclair Road, West Kensington. When a consignment containing the Sikh holy book, reached the Secunderabad Indian General Hospital in the coastal town of Hardelot near Boulogne in France, the Sikh soldiers were so delighted that they threw a party.

'The Granth Sahib was received with great enthusiasm,' Col Jenney, head of the hospital, wrote to the Fund. 'The Sikhs insisted on meeting the expense of the installation out of their own pockets and are entertaining Hardelot to celebrate the occasion. There was a tremendous run on the Bhagwad Gita and the rosaries. The Granth Sahib has to be kept like the Church Bible of old, enthroned and guarded.'[5] A tent Gurdwara was installed for the Sikhs at the hospital.

Every care was made to see that the soldiers could practise their religion even on the frontline. A marquee erected in a field in Flanders was used as a mosque, another would serve as a gurdwara, and another tent, a temple. The sound of the Gurbani could be heard from tents and farm houses. The sight of Sikh soldiers carrying the Guru Granth Sahib on their heads as they walked through the flat French farmland, always invited curious locals. The only request from General Willcocks was that the Granth and Quran not be sent to the trenches, as there were elaborate procedures of moving them and it was not always possible to do so when a trench was being evacuated under shellfire.

The committee ordered Sikh religious objects – like the *kara* (bracelet), *kachcha* (short drawers), *kirpan* (dagger), *kangha* (comb) – mainly from Sheffield. While the *kachcha* was not difficult to replace (or likely to be lost), the *kara* was often lost or given away as souvenirs to friends in France. The *kirpan* was reproduced in miniature but the *kangha* was difficult to procure in Europe. The saws to make the fine teeth in the little wooden combs were only available in Germany and hence could not be ordered during the war. A large supply of combs was ordered instead from India. The governor of Punjab saw to it that nearly 4,000 combs were shipped to the soldiers in the first consignment.

The Maharani of Bhownagar gifted 1,500 *janeos* (Brahmanical threads). These were sent to the hospitals and convalescent depots and officers concerned were asked to observe the 'precaution of giving the threads only to members of the "twice born" castes.'

An item that was popular among the Muslim soldiers was a miniature Quran enclosed in a small metal case to form a locket. The print was so small that the locket had a small magnifying glass attached to the side. The small pendants, which the soldiers called 'Pansuras', were procured in England and sent out to the front in large quantities. The Muslim soldiers regarded them as talismans.

The ladies of the Committee were quite used to unusual requests. The Sikh community in London wrote to them that, while their countrymen found European sweets palatable, and they were grateful for the large amount supplied, the sweets did not possess the same nourishing properties as Indian sweetmeats prepared with flour, ghee, nuts etc. The Committee, not to be daunted, placed a small order for *pinnis*, to be manufactured in India and sent to the base depot in Marseilles. If they arrived in a good condition and were commended by the men at the front, the arrangement would be continued permanently.

One thousand great coats were purchased by the clothing committee and many were donated by supporters of the Fund. They could be used by the injured soldiers on the hospital ships as they crossed the channel, since the soldiers were usually placed on the boats in the same clothes and condition in which they had left the trenches. A large supply of rubber boots were also sent out for use in the flooded trenches. The St John Ambulance Association in India shipped a large consignment of 6,000 little pillows, which the patients in the hospitals found most comforting. For the soldiers who had lost their headgear in the frontline, blue and gold *pagri*s were specially sent out. From Mrs Leopold de Rothschild came a present of forty-eight handsome blue hospital uniforms with slippers to match. The King and Queen presented an ambulance for the use of the Indian troops at the front. When it was noticed that some of the Indian officers had not been able to dye their beards, as they could not get henna in France, hair dye was ordered.

To tackle the problem of vermin in the trenches, the soldiers were sent two large sterilisers and casks of formaldehyde. Oil stoves were supplied in order to cope with the severe climate in Northern France. For relief from the rheumatic conditions caused by the cold and damp, they were sent packets of thermogene. Electric torches, fly flaps to deal with the swarms of flies in the front, and even 2,400 yards of logline (a strong cord to tie the Indian *bistara* or bedding rolled up as a carpet) were some of the items that the Committee sent across to France. Another useful gift was a Hindustani-French phrasebook – of which 39,000 copies were sent. The Indians were quick learners and soon picked up French words and phrases enabling them to converse not only in French but also with the British soldiers who could not speak Hindustani. The committee also provided for benches and garden seats for the patients in the large hospitals in Boulogne, and raised funds for small tombstones for the Muslim soldiers who had died in French hospitals.

Donations poured in from Britain and India. The British American Tobacco Company supplied one million cigarettes in the first six months while the Maharaja of Gwalior sent two and a quarter million. The India Tea Association sent 106 chests of tea, the Maharaja of Rewa sent a large supply of condensed milk and The Ceylon and Eastern Agency sent two tons of peppermint. Individuals also sent gifts. The meticulously kept list of donors includes a Mr C.M. Seal who sent 863 spice bags and 'friends in Bombay' who sent a ton of chocolates. Mrs Sutro sent two tons of sugar candy. Mrs Beasley opened a canteen for the Indians near the cavalry lines in France and the fund supplied her with large 60 gallon tea boilers, invaluable to the soldiers. The members of the Order of St John of Jerusalem were prepared to meet all the demands from the Indians and show them they cared.

While the boiled sweets and jumpers for the troops were being packed in England, back in France, the Indian troops were getting closer to the action. The train from Orleans had brought the troops from the Lahore Division to the North. On 21 October, the Ferozepur Brigade of the Lahore Division had marched to the area around Wallon Cappel and Lynde in Northern France and billeted with the civilians staying in farms or private houses. The Indians from peasant stock were comfortable living on the farms and impressed by the hard-working French women who worked the land as their husbands were away at the front. They remarked how the French ladies looked after them, making their beds and cleaning their rooms, not distinguishing between caste or class. As the sepoys were generally well behaved, and even helped out when they could with the farm work, they were popular tenants. It was short-lived billeting, a brief chance to see the French countryside, even taste some wine, before they were asked to march again.

On the morning of 22 October, the troops stared with disbelief at the transport that was to take them to the frontline in Belgium. They had expected transporter vans or trucks. Instead, standing in front of them were 36 red London double-decker buses still with the advertisements painted on them for 'Glaxo, 'The Food That Builds Bonnie Babies' and

Carter's Little Liver Pills 'for biliousness, torpid liver and constipation.' There was much amusement among the British troops too, particularly the 1st Battalion, The Connaught Rangers, the British battalion in the Ferozepur Brigade. They were the first to board the buses at 8.30 a.m. and begin the journey further North. The rest of the brigade, including the 57th Rifles and 129th Baluchis, began to march to their destination. More than a thousand London buses were sent to serve in France and Belgium during the war. The volunteer drivers found themselves in armed units overnight and within a week were out in France.[6] Drivers would stay on the road for eighteen hours a day, going back and forth collecting the troops.

Khudadad Khan boarded the bus for the last few miles, looking out as the driver negotiated his way through the narrow roads. The dark October days were setting in and the Indian troops knew that they were only miles from the action. They would strain their ears and look out for the sights and sounds of the firing. Soon Khan would see the bullets whizzing past and the darkened skies ahead.

Mir Dast and Zaman Khan were part of the first Indian battalion to enter the trenches. Each soldier carried 200 rounds of ammunition, a day's cooked ration and an emergency ration of biscuits and raisins for a second day. They joined the 1st Battalion, the Connaught Rangers, who had arrived by the London buses earlier. The 129th Baluchis, with Khudadad Khan in its ranks, were the next to enter the trenches. The Indians were occupying the area around Ypres in a single line stretching eleven miles from the Mont des Cats in the West to Wytschaete in the East. The land was flat all around except for the ridge, which rose at times to several hundred feet, with a breadth of two miles. It was vital at all costs to prevent the Germans from gaining a foothold on the ridge as it would mean the evacuation of the British from Ypres and Poperinghe. The Cavalry Corps took up their positions between Zandvoorde and Wytschaete near a sparse wood nearly two miles long. The ground was mainly bog and the slightest rain made the road impassable. In October 1914, much to the despair of the Indians, the rain seemed never-ending. Unlike the monsoon rain in India, which provided a welcome relief from the heat of summer, the rain in Europe chilled them to the bone. The winter coats being readied by the Comfort Committee were yet to reach them.

Landing at the British headquarters at St Omer, General Willcocks felt that 'Asia had dropped into Europe...the descendants of Timour, of Guru Govind, of the ancient Hindus, had come to fight the Huns on the historic plains of Flanders.'[7] However, he rued the fact that compared with the British Army Corps, the Indian Corps was 5,400 bayonets short. Did the commanders realise, he asked, that 'our reinforcements were precarious, and had to come thousands of miles across the seas'.[8]

With the Indian soldiers arriving in the frontline, the British authorities faced two troublesome issues: the censorship of letters written by the soldiers and the fear of seditious activities in the field and the hospitals. In the early months of the war the authorities were not yet certain about whether the letters should be censored but were clear about withholding seditious material from the troops. The minutes of a meeting held in India Office Whitehall stated that 'It is not considered necessary on military or political grounds to institute a strict censorship of postal correspondence to and from the Indian troops in hospitals or depots in this country. However, instructions [to be given] to officers in charge, (to be kept under lock and key), the circular regarding certain seditious newspaper and possible undesirable visitors.'[9]

On 30 November, barely a month since the Indian troops had entered the trenches, Lt Gen A.J. Murray, Commander-in-Chief British Forces wrote to the Secretary at the War Office: 'I am directed to inform you that the only specific instances are the discovery of copies of "Ghadr" in the house of [Sardar Singh] Rana. The report [is] that Madam Cama was at Marseilles, distributing seditious literature among the Indian troops, and the distribution of leaflets, printed in Hindustani, by German aircrafts.'[10]

Bhikaji Rustom Cama, known popularly as Madam Cama, was an Indian nationalist leader based in Paris. She was the first to hoist the Indian flag on foreign land at the International Socialist Conference in Stuttgart in Germany on 22 August 1907. Inspired by Christabel Pankhurst and the Suffragette Movement, she was a strong campaigner for women's rights. Together with another Paris-based Indian nationalist, Sardar Singh Rewabhai Rana, she formed the Paris Indian Society which campaigned for a free India. In 1906 they started the *Bande Mataram* newspaper in Paris, the name inspired by the eponymous revolutionary poem that featured in the nineteenth century novel *Anandamath* by Bankim Chandra Chattopadhyay, which had been banned by the British. Later Rana and Cama went on to publish the *Talvar* (Sword) from Berlin. Both newspapers carried nationalist articles including a cover on Madan Lal Dhingra who was hanged in Pentonville prison on 17 August 1909 for the assassination of Curzon Wyllie, aide to the Secretary of State for India. Repeated attempts by the British government to seek extradition of Madam Cama had failed, and she had carried on her campaign. However with the outbreak of the First World War in 1914, the dynamics changed when France and Britain became allies, and Cama was advised to go to Spain. All the members of the Paris India Society left the country, except Cama and Rana. In October 1914 they were briefly arrested when they tried to agitate among the troops from the Punjab regiment who had landed in Marseilles on their way to the front. They were required to leave Marseilles, and Cama moved to Rana's wife's house near Bordeaux. In January 1915, the French government deported Rana and his whole family to the Caribbean island of Martinique and Cama was sent to Vichy, where she was interned.

By arrangement with the French authorities, all the letters of the Indian troops were submitted to the British Censorship authorities, whilst suspects domiciled in France were kept under observation by the Surete Generale. A circular was also sent to the medical officers in charge of hospitals in the U.K. for wounded Indian soldiers: 'It seems probable that efforts may be made to introduce seditious literature into the various hospitals occupied by wounded Indian soldiers either through the post or the medium of visitors to the hospitals.'[11]

The circular stated that the literature which had recently been seized in the post was designed to confuse the minds of the troops and incite them to mutiny. It listed the newspapers which needed to be confiscated by the censors. They included the *Ghadar* (Mutiny) published in Urdu, Gujarati, Gurmukhi and Hindi from San Francisco, the *Bande Mataram* published in English and *The Indian Sociologist* in English. The *Ghadar* was the party paper of the Pacific Coast Hindustan Association of San Francisco which was formed by Indian immigrants under the leadership of Lala Har Dayal, a nationalist Indian and Sohan Singh Bhakna, who became its president. Donations were raised from the Indian diaspora and particularly the Indian students at the University of California, Berkeley, and a printing press was set up. During the war years, it tried to influence the Indian soldiers with nationalistic articles. The organisation was later known as the Ghadar Party. *The Indian Sociologist* was an Indian nationalist publication which was edited by Shyamji Krishnavarma. It was originally published from London but moved to Paris in 1907. Subtitled *An Organ of Freedom, and Political, Social, and Religious Reform,* it aimed to look at how Indians fared under British rule from the perspective of the Indians. During the war, Krishnavarma moved to Geneva and was forced to suspend the publication.

The British authorities pointed out that the three publications were coming out from San Francisco, Rotterdam and Geneva respectively, and consequently all 'letters and wrappings coming from any of these towns are open to suspicion'. It further warned that the publications may come also from Brazil or through the towns of Avonmouth, Folkestone, London or Paris. 'The letters or wrappers may bear in print the name of a reputable firm, be marked "Circular" or be otherwise disguised in some misleading way. The literature is not likely to come from India,' the circular warned.

It was not just the incoming mail that worried the War Office. The British were concerned that the Indians may inadvertently divulge crucial operational data in their letters. They were also apprehensive that any negative letters written by soldiers from the frontline or hospitals would result in a fall in recruitment from India or spur the nationalistic forces in the country. The Mutiny of 1857 remained a constant reminder to the British about how things could spread like wildfire and they needed to put a lid on any hostile propaganda in the middle of the war. The letters to be censored also included those that incited crime, mentioned drugs or sex with white women and those portraying a negative view of English society. Even letters praising the treatment of Indian prisoners of war (PoW) in German camps were to be censored as they could lead to sedition.

Second Lieutenant E.B. Howell, an officer of the Indian Civil Service, was appointed censor of postal matters and all arrangements for Indians in France was placed under him. Howell had been attached to the Indian cavalry regiment as an interpreter and spoke fluent Hindustani. He took charge of the bureau at Rouen. Under him were a team of censors, mainly old 'India hands' or Oriental scholars. Originally there were four interpreters and this was later expanded to eight as the volume of letters grew to between 10,000–20,000 a week. The letters were written mainly in Urdu, Hindi, Gurmukhi, Bengali and Gujarati. With each set of letters, the censors wrote up a report summarising the contents and highlighting interesting ones. The censorship began with incoming letters but was soon applied to those written by wounded Indian soldiers from England and the frontline in France.

A list of suspicious addresses for incoming mail was submitted. It included New York and the Pacific Coast especially California for the USA, Zurich and Geneva for Switzerland, Rotterdam for Holland, various addresses in France and India and addresses in Folkestone, Avonmouth, Brighton and the sea ports and the whole county of Sussex for Britain.

The soldiers were told that they were not allowed to mention any war-time locations or operational details in their letters which they did not mind. However, they were quick to figure out that their letters were being read. Soon they invented code words and phrases for describing the soldiers and casualties. 'When you send a letter do not write about the war,' a Pathan (Afridi) sepoy in Hong Kong wrote to his friend in France. 'When you write say that so many walnuts have fallen from the tree, and we shall understand.'

The code commonly used by the Indian soldiers was 'black pepper' to describe Indian soldiers and 'red pepper' for their English counterparts. 'And there is an expenditure, too great for words, in this country, of black and red pepper,' wrote Khan Muhammad, 40th Pathans, from Brighton Hospital, to his friend Niyaz Ali, 74th Punjabis, Hong Kong. 'The black pepper which has come from India has all been used up, and to carry on with I will [i.e., they will] now send for more men, otherwise there would be very little red pepper remaining, because the black is hard and there is plenty of it. And the black pepper (here) is somewhat less than the red, and this water is not right without black pepper. Now you must understand, and what you can see with the eye, is written; you must multiply it all by 45.'[12] The censors, however, were quick to identify these codes and the appearance of words like 'black pepper' indicated that the feeling of despondency among the Indian troops was growing.

Indian sweets were becoming a major issue. The Indian soldiers in France and Belgium longed for Indian sweets and the Committee tried its best to accommodate this request. They even suggested that a man be brought from India to make them in France. The man could also order Indian ingredients like *misri* which was preferred to sugar. Such a supply chain from India would eliminate the need for sugar candy from England.

At a meeting of the Comfort Sub-Committee in London on 15 December 1914, it was decided that 30 lbs of Indian sweetmeats, prepared in two batches for Hindus and Muslims respectively, should be sent as samples by the Indian sweet makers, Messrs Veeraswamy & Company, to the General Hospital for Indian troops. Edward Palmer, the owner of Veeraswamy, was the great grandson of an English general and an Indian Princess and had come to London to study medicine. So homesick was he, that he set up a small company, E. P. Veeraswamy & Co., Indian Food Specialists, selling spices, chutneys and curry pastes. However, the sweetmeats supplied by them proved to be too expensive for the Comfort Committee which decided that of the sweets to be supplied to the Indian troops, three-fourths would be English sweets and a quarter Indian.

A few weeks later, the debate was still on. At a meeting on 5 January, the Committee considered whether it would be possible to procure a cheaper variety of Indian sweets that would satisfy the palate and be 'equally nutritious'. The Committee approved a sample called *pinnis* and asked the chairman for a quote. A supply of these would be despatched to the front if the price was reasonable.

By 18 January a decision had to be taken. The chairman gave an account of the interview with Sardar Basheshar Singh relating to the order of the *pinnis*. The Sardar had said that the price of *pinnis* would be 1/8s per lb. and that each man would require two *pinnis* per day. The cost would come to 7d per man per day. In view of this considerable expense, the Committee did not approve the supply.

The suggestion that a sweetmeat maker be imported from India and make fresh sweets for the troops in France was turned down by Hewett. Later another attempt was made to see if *sewai*, or *kheer* cooked with vermicelli and milk, could be prepared for the soldiers. But the sweetmeat maker refused to disclose all the ingredients and the committee thought it was too thick, so that too was discarded.

The Indians would just have to manage with the English sweets. Hewett ordered supplies of a special mint humbug as it was considered the most suitable.

By January 1915 the postal censorship department was working at full pace as a large volume of correspondence was passing through the Indian base. Howell had to request three more readers. The Indians were pouring out their thoughts and experiences in the West to their family and friends. Two more officers were appointed: Lt Col W. Donnan of the military accounts department and W.H. Wallinger, a retired officer of the Indian Forests Department. The former was an Oriental scholar and would look after the correspondence in Hindi. The latter would look at the letters in Marathi and other languages from Bombay Presidency.

The censors submitted a weekly report along with a series of extracts from letters to and from India. It gave them an insight into how the Indian soldiers were feeling. Also, any dissent could be quickly spotted. By the first winter of the war, the censors noted that the mood of the Indian soldiers was slowly changing from the initial enthusiasm to one of despair: 'It [the attitude] seems to be changing rapidly for the worse at present…Personally I am inclined to think that depression is spreading at the hospitals at home partly because the men who have recovered are now being sent back to the front. But I have only the letters themselves to go on for this view.'[13]

An official of the India Office commented that some letters conveyed a sense of despondency that the Indian troops were being sacrificed and asked to do more than their share. The censor board sent an example of a letter that appeared to be seditious. It was written by Jiwan Singh in Hong Kong to his brother Naik Nika Singh, serving in France. The letter in Gurmukhi praised the German Emperor and criticised the British:

> 'I am very anxious about you…The truth is that the German Badshah is a very great hero [bahut bahadur]…we hear that the German Badshah will win. The German Badshah said "I do not fight with the people of Punjab. I shall fight with the topi-walas." Doubtless this is true, but when the Punjabis came to fight what could the unfortunate man do, but kill all the regiments…And my brother, what do they give you? Eleven rupees, all told. It is a shame. The white soldiers get 100 or 80 or 70 rupees. Death would be better than this…My brother, the raja against whom is the fighting, is the country of the Germans. He is German emperor. He is very good. He has said, "You go to your own country and look after it. I have nothing to say to you." What else can I write? Now you know… There is no advantage in staying on…'[14]

The long letter was intercepted on the way from Hong Kong to France. The censor however remarked that the letter was harmless, it was probably meant in earnest as a warning to the brother, and that it showed that 'pro-German agencies' were at work in the Far East, but were not altogether successful.

He further added: 'It is certainly my impression, from the letters which have come under my notice, that there exists amongst the Indian troops, both here and in India, in more than one class, to no insignificant degree a spirit which would be favourable to disloyal agitation. That spirit is certainly not disloyalty yet, nor is it universal, but it exists.'[15]

4

First Blood

Khudadad Khan looked at the bleak landscape that lay before him. It was not what he had expected to see when he travelled to this war. The flat land was dotted with trenches and barbed wire. He was in a place South of Ypres in Belgium where the sky was grey and the land a sea of soggy brown. He had fought in the North West Frontier but that was different. There one could see the enemy. He had not yet seen a single German though he had been looking out for their distinctive pointed helmets. Everyone seemed to be living in an underground city, he thought. All they could see were the shells that exploded around them.

They had entered the trenches the night before and spent most of the time digging. All the while shells were flying over their heads. There were dead bodies too, more than Khudadad had ever seen in his lifetime. They lay strewn around the ground, half buried in the mud looking like sandbags. They were British soldiers. Occasionally one could see a flash of colour from their regimental uniforms and a young face. Apart from that it was a brown wasteland.

Until mid-October, the fighting had been 'hammer and tongs'[1] with alternate gains and losses on both sides, but on 21 October the Germans began an offensive from La Bassee in the South to Menin in the North. The Indians were soon to see their first action. They would be pressed in to defend the medieval town of Ypres and the area called the 'Ypres salient'[2]. The battle would result in 130,000 casualties.

The land around Flanders was low-lying as it was built on land reclaimed from the sea. Trenches criss-crossed the surface, with the soldiers occupying the 'dug-outs' which housed supplies and served as dormitories. Rows of barbed wire were placed by both sides in front of their lines. In between was no-man's land. The Germans occupied the higher ground and were able to dig deeper and build more secure trenches. As the British forces occupied the lower ground, their trenches quickly reached the water table. Consequently, they were shallow and did not provide much protection. At this time they were merely ditches with inadequate drainage. A few hours of rain left them flooded knee-deep in bog. Duck-boards were used to cross the trenches that often collapsed during shelling. The Allies had yet to learn to build the sophisticated trenches that they would later in the war.

It had rained through the night of 25 October and the next morning was grey and misty. There were gaps in the shallow trenches deep in mud and water, through which German snipers could come right through and shoot the British. The Allies were outnumbered and outgunned as there was no prospect of reinforcements. For the Indians, it was not just unfamiliar. Cold and uncomfortable, they were to be pushed to the edge.

The 57th Wilde's Rifles with Mir Dast and Gagna Singh in its ranks had marched to Wytschaete. The 129th Baluchis with Khudadad Khan in its ranks were also with them. Both were under the command of Major General Hubert de la Poer Gough of the 2nd Cavalry Division. Gough's regiments were battle-weary and he decided to split up the Indians into companies and use them to plug the gaps in the British line. The cavalry were in a desperate situation. The only wire they had was what they had taken from the farm fences. Even with the 57th Wilde's and the 129th Baluchis, the British could only muster a thousand rifles to a mile, including supports and reserves. If the Germans broke this line, they would reach the channel ports.

The British and Indian attack began on 26 October. Between 3 and 5.00 p.m. the first Indian war cries of 'Allah-o-Akbar' and 'Fateh' could be heard as the troops began their charge. It was the first offensive action by units of the Indian Corps on the Western Front.

It did not go smoothly. The 57th Rifles came under heavy shelling at Wytschaete and the first casualties took place that night. The 57th Rifles were occupying the trenches near Oost Taverne. For Sepoy Usman Khan, an Afridi, it was to be a night to remember. On the day of the offensive, Khan was hit by rifle fire but refused to leave though he was hit again. He claimed that he could fire his rifle perfectly well as long as he remained lying down. Finally, when a shell splinter blew away a large piece of flesh from both legs, he was carried back. For his bravery, Usman Khan was awarded the Indian Distinguished Service Medal, becoming the first Indian to win a decoration on the Western Front.

Meanwhile the 129th Baluchis found they had no cover and were totally exposed. The Germans, on the other hand, were able to mask their movements as they were in a small wood. Khudadad Khan was in the trenches when early disaster struck. Their first officer, Captain Hampe-Vincent, was mortally wounded by heavy shell and machine-gun fire. By nightfall they had lost nine soldiers, forty-eight were wounded and four were missing. It was a grim end to the first day of battle in Ypres.

Willcocks described how the two Indian battalions were suddenly 'dumped in a maelstrom'. They were depending entirely on their few British officers for guidance, but were split up into half companies, and attached to various British Corps – cavalry, infantry or artillery – and 'hurried from one trench to another, from one front to another, hardly realising the meaning or object of it all'. Then came the hardest trial of all, when the British officers who were guiding them, were struck down. When the Indian officers fell, the soldiers were left completely leaderless. 'The sepoys bewildered but faithful fight on', wrote Willcocks.[3]

The conditions were appalling; the ground was waterlogged and the trenches provided little protection. While the Germans had hand grenades, Khudadad Khan and the Baluchis improvised with 'jampot bombs', jam tins filled with guncotton and nails with a detonator and fuse pushed through the lid. The fuse had to be lit with a cigarette and thrown very quickly as it could explode in their hands. Pounded by German artillery fire, the Baluchis lost an entire division in a direct hit.

The fighting carried on relentlessly over the next few days. On the night of 29 October, the troops huddled in their trenches heard loud sounds from the German side. The next morning, the source of the noise became clear: the Germans had dragged heavy machinery through the night. Howitzers and field guns had been hauled into position. At dawn the Germans opened fire, plastering the trenches. By 6.30 a.m. both

Wilde's Rifles and the 129th Baluchis were under attack. The Company Commander, Major Humphreys, was killed.

For Khudadad Khan, thousands of miles from his homeland, it would be the day he would make history. Khan was handling the British machine guns under the command of Captain Dill. They had already been under intense German attack. Dill was determined to return fire. When one gun went out of action, Dill continued to fire with another gun till a German shell hit his head, killing him instantly. The relentless firing continued, the Baluchis holding on with few men and fewer guns. One by one all Dill's men were killed, the narrow trench choking up with the bodies of the dead. Only one man remained alive: Khudadad Khan.

The tall Pathan stood upright, determined to avenge the death of his comrades. There was no stopping him. Severely injured, bleeding profusely from his head, Khan screamed out to his God to give him strength and continued firing. All alone in his trench, he faced the German fire with fire. Images of his home and family flashed before him. This might be his last day, but he was not going to go down without a fight. Straining every muscle, Khan defended his trench. He continued firing till he could no longer stand and collapsed on the ground, numb with injury. Lying among the bodies of his dead colleagues, his life draining away, he heard the Germans entering his trench. Instinctively, he pretended he was dead. The Germans walked between the bodies inspecting them. Someone was counting the corpses. He could hear German numbers being shouted out. He even heard them fire a few bullets again. Barely taking a breath, Khan lay still waiting for the Germans to leave. What seemed like hours later, he managed to crawl out, joining the rest of the regiment who were stunned to see him alive. He then gave them a full account of the battle.

For his bravery in defending the trench single-handed, Khan was awarded the Victoria Cross, becoming the first South Asian to win the medal. His actions had held the Germans off long enough to allow the British and Indian Forces to get to the area. The news of India's first Victoria Cross recipient made it to the major newspapers in India and Britain. On 26 January 1915, when Khan had recovered from his injuries, he was personally presented the medal by King George V. By the end of the war Khudadad Khan would be a Subedar Major and return to Pakistan to lead a hero's life.

While Khudadad Khan earned himself the coveted medal, the action was not over for Wilde's Rifles. At about 3.00 a.m. on 31 October nine German battalions made a fierce onslaught on Messines. Shells rained over the evacuated ghost town. The Germans followed up the artillery attack with a charge of infantry resulting in several casualties. Despite the night-long bombardment, the Dogra Company of the 57th Rifles prevented the Germans from breaking through. Even as the shells fell around them, the commanding officer, Lieutenant Molony, asked his men to come out of the trench and into an open position. He asked them to fire till the ammunition ran out. It was about 6.00 a.m. and still dark when Molony was badly hit in the arm and dragged away by his men for medical attention. The 57th were left without a single British officer. Molony ordered Jemadar Ram Singh to hold the line.

The Indians were fighting without cover and soon nearly all of them were dead. They lay splattered around the soggy ground, a mangle of bodies, arms and legs. When Jemadar Ram Singh was severely wounded, the task of defending the line fell on Jemadar Kapur Singh. With ammunition running out and no one left to get more supplies, Kapur Singh faced the fire alone from nine German battalions. With singular determination, he kept going till the bullets ran out. And then, rather than surrender, the Indian officer took a pistol to his head and emptied the last cartridge. He thought it better to die in battle than be taken a prisoner by the Germans.

It was now up to Subedar Arsla Khan, the senior Indian officer remaining, to lead his company. He made a valiant counter-attack with the bayonet but was completely outnumbered. Recognising the hopelessness of the situation he succeeded in getting the rest of his men to Messines and was recognised for his gallantry with the Order of British India, 2nd Class, and the title of Bahadur. There was more to come. As the Dogras and Afridis came under fire, a determined attack was taking place on No. 3 Company north of Wytschaete. Havildar Gagna Singh, a former gymnast, was holding a portion of this trench with a few men, when the Germans burst upon him. Savage hand-to-hand fighting followed in which most of the 57th were put out of action. Gagna Singh fought it out, killing five Germans till his bayonet broke. He then picked up a sword and continued fighting. He finally collapsed after receiving six wounds.

When the trench was re-taken, Gagna Singh was found alive and was rewarded with a 2nd Class Indian Order of Merit.

Despite losing officers and men, the 57th and the 129th bravely fought on. They were next called out to a farm which had been taken by the Germans. The 129th were in their element for the hand-to-hand fighting that ensued in the building. They chased the Germans from room to room killing ten and wounding three. Those who had not bolted, surrendered. As one of the 129th remarked, 'It was a very good game.'[4] A few days later the 129th were ordered to hand over their trenches to the French cavalry and re-join the Ferozepur Brigade. Thus ended their role in the famous First Battle of Ypres. They had become the first of the Indian Corps to see action in the First World War.

The cost had been heavy. Of the 750 men of the 57th Rifles who entered the Salient, only 460 remained. The 129th also faced heavy losses: three British officers, three Indian officers, and 230 other ranks.[5] The majority had been shot or shelled, some had died under collapsing trenches and others by drowning in the dark water-filled ditches. Yet they had won several gallantry medals including the highest honour, the Victoria Cross.

As the news of the war filtered through to India, the poet Rabindranath Tagore wrote the poem *The Oarsman*:[6]

> Do you hear the roar of death through the listening hush of distance.
> And that awful call midst fire-floods and poison clouds and wrestling of
> earth and sky in mortal combat.
> The Captain's call to steer the ship towards a shore yet unnamed?

There was considerable coverage of the Indians' first engagement in the war in both the British and French media. The Paris newspaper *Le Temp* said that the Indian Army had proved itself to be equal to the British: that it was 'equally indomitable'.[7]

Congratulatory messages were sent to the troops from Sir John French, the Commander-in-Chief.

It was reported that the Kaiser himself was fighting in the trenches near Ypres, so determined was he to break through the Allied line. The Germans were in full force: 'Mounted troops are fighting in the trenches along with infantry, armoured motor cars with maxims and quick firing guns,' the Secretary of State informed the Viceroy. The British and Indian troops had successfully prevented the German effort to reach Calais.

Shortly after the Indians entered the trenches in Belgium, a German wireless message was intercepted. It directed the German Commanders near the Indian lines to 'take prisoner as many unwounded Indians as possible, to treat them with all possible courtesy and consideration, and send them into headquarters'. According to British officials, it was a 'cunning attempt to undermine the loyalty of the Indian contingents, but it never met with the slightest success.'[8]

German propaganda continued throughout the war. On one occasion when General Willcocks visited some Indian soldiers who had been brought back from the trenches for a well-earned rest, a German airship scattered leaflets with false news of the war claiming the proclamation of Jihad and alliance between the Afghans and Turks. On another occasion Indian troops noticed a sign sticking out of the German trenches, a white sheet fitted on to two poles with the following inscription: 'Indian Soldiers. The Holy War has begun. Come and join us. Death to the Hated British.'[9] The Indian soldiers ignored the leaflets and received the General with enthusiasm, chanting traditional songs of victory.

While the 129th Baluchis and 57th Rifles were in action in Belgium, the line in France – a distance of about eight miles in the area Ratinghem/ Aubers/Neuve Chapelle/Givenchy – was being held by the 39th Garhwalis, the 47th Sikhs, and the 9th Bhopal Infantry (who were nicknamed the Bo-Peeps). To the west of them lay the ports of Calais and Boulogne which Germany wanted to reach. Once again, it was going to fall on the Indian Corps to prevent this. In October the Germans had been attacking heavily along the whole line from La Basee to Messines. For most of the year this portion of the British line was a dismal sea of mud. On a typical winter's day a steady cold downpour turned the trenches into fetid, water-logged ditches and the communication trenches into bottomless muddy streams. Even the British troops, who were used to the weather, found the dreariness and discomfort appalling. To the Indian Corps it was the most miserable sight they had ever seen.

'The names of Givenchy, Festubert, Neuve Chapelle and Fauqissart sum up the story of our existence,' wrote General Willcocks. 'That short line holds more Indian dead than the whole of the rest of Europe combined." For nearly fourteen months the Indian Corps was allotted the same part of the front. General Willcocks wrote later that it was the best way to dishearten good soldiers. "Often did I urge that we might be given a change from the same bog and swamps to somewhere North or South, but it was not agreed to, and so for over thirteen months the men went up to the same old trenches and returned to the same monotonous billets..."[10]

On 21 October the Jullunder Brigade marched 19 miles to Metern. The men were issued with maps of France but had no idea where they were going. The 47th Sikhs were shown around the positions: a line of unlinked shallow trenches. There was no wire, no support line and no communication trenches. The Sikhs were warned that there were still bodies of the French soldiers in the parapets of a trench and that they should leave it undisturbed. A hand had been left sticking out so they could identify the trench. The Sikhs found that the French had left the trenches in a filthy condition. Yet they set to work digging more trenches in the water-logged ground.

On 24 October the 15th Sikhs with Manta Singh and Captain Henderson in its ranks, entered the trenches. For eight weeks the Germans tried to break through, but the Indians fought back, holding the line. When their ammunition ran out, the Indians used rifle and bayonet. The Indian Sappers and Miners invented the Bangalore Torpedo, a tube filled with explosives, which could be pushed under the barbed wire to blow a gap. They also supplied the 'jampot bombs'. The Indians were fighting the superior German army with homemade bombs, but they carried on.

Very often they had to manage without the food they were accustomed to, as the Indians did not like tinned food. But there were times when the Indian cooks valiantly cooked close to the trenches. The food would be brought through the supply tunnels in the trenches in the dark. Sometimes, there would be a follower who would make tea that kept the troops going in the cold. A cook of the Sikh regiment told General Willcocks: 'We like cooking close up to the trenches, or otherwise the government may refuse to give us a clasp for our medals…and then in India they will call us the Marseilles *walas* [those who managed to make it only to Marseille and not the frontline].' Many of the cooks and followers were killed in the frontline, downed by artillery fire, as they tried to carry hot Indian food to the soldiers.

The Indians were soon going to see action in Neuve Chapelle, a village some forty kilometres South-West of Lille. The village consisted of several large houses with walled gardens, a church and fields intersected with hedges and deep water-logged ditches. Portions of the village had been taken and retaken by the British brigades, but by 27 October the Germans had gained control over it. The 47th Sikhs were ordered to counter attack. Facing a heavy fire of machine guns and howitzers, the 47th Sikhs received 'their baptism of fire since raised in 1901' and pushed forward, not halting for one moment till they reached the farthest trenches.

Early next morning they were ordered to make a frontal attack in conjunction with the Sappers. Inexplicably, according to General Willcocks, there were no British troops at this stage. War cries of '*Wah guru ji ka Khalsa*' and the final yell of '*Fateh*' rang out as the 47th Sikhs and the two companies crossed the 600 yards from their positions and charged with their bayonets inside the village. The Germans who were in the houses around Neuve Chapelle kept up a steady fire but the Indians entered and engaged in hand-to-hand fighting, killing several of them. Such was the valour on display that a British officer remarked: 'I climbed up into a house and looked down the street, and the way those fellows fought was a sight to remember'.[11]

The Germans realised for the first time that the Indians were good fighters. A soldier wrote in the *Frankfurter Zeitung*:

'Today for the first time we had to fight against the Indians and the devil knows these brown rascals are not to be underrated. At first we spoke with contempt of them. Today we look on them in a different light. The devil knows what the English had put into those fellows. With a fearful shouting, thousands of those brown forms rushed upon us... In no time they were in our trenches and truly these brown enemies are not to be despised. With butt ends, bayonets, swords and daggers we fought each other and we had bitter hard work.'[12]

When the commander of the Sikhs was shot dead by a concealed German sniper in the middle of the village, the Sikhs immediately shot the German. Through a hail of machine-gun fire, the struggle continued and both Corps soon cleared the main street. A German prisoner remarked later that his people had been taught a lesson which they would remember the entire time they faced the Indian Corps. The Germans now brought in heavy counter attacks, sweeping the streets firing rapidly from heavy machine guns. The Indians had no reinforcements and no one to bring them through. They were forced to fall back crossing the 600 yards of open ground under heavy firing. In the space of a few hours the Indian Corps had taken 300 casualties. They had made a splendid attack, but unsupported, had lost all their officers.

'I felt wild with the General who had ordered it, who was sitting four miles back,' fumed Rex Benson of the 9th Lancers. 'The Ferozepur brigade which arrived first, was split up and sent to help various parts of the line and this Brigadier, I suppose he thought, "here is a battalion of Indians, let's band them at it". Anyway they did a jolly fine attack, which could never have succeeded, as they were never supported. But this is my private opinion,'[13] he wrote to Lord Hardinge.

There was considerable discussion after the war about the wisdom of sending the Indians into Neuve Chapelle without proper reinforcements. 'Had reinforcements been sent up, the Battle of Neuve Chapelle in March 1915 might never have been necessary; but in war it is so often an "if"', wrote General Willcocks.[14] He added, 'What is sure, and that is what concerns me here, is that the Indians fought in a manner which at once established their reputation as first-class fighting men.' The two companies of 47th Sikhs went into action with 289 men of all ranks. In the end they were down to half the number. Manta Singh had survived the action. It was at the next battle of Neuve Chapelle in 1915 that he would make his mark.

Lord Roberts had launched the Comfort Fund for Indian soldiers in London, but the retired general wanted to do more. 'I must go to see my Indian soldiers,' he told a friend. Within hours of making an appeal for donations, he set off on the ferry for France. After a night of heavy rain and wind, the morning broke bright and sunny as Lord Roberts arrived at the headquarters of the Indian Corps in France on 12 November. There was a flurry of excitement in the camp as the soldiers waited to see the famous General. He was welcomed by General Willcocks, inspected the guard of honour of the British and Indian troops, then went to the divisional headquarters and that of the cavalry and inspected two men from each unit. The Field Marshal spoke freely to the troops pausing to ask some questions in Hindustani which was much appreciated. In a stirring speech, he asked them to remember that the Indian Force had made the first Imperial contribution to the Empire's Field Army. He then conversed for a few minutes with his old friend, Sir Pratap Singh; he also met the Maharaja of Bikaner. Roberts visited an Indian hospital in France and spoke to the wounded. He left amid cheers from each Headquarter. A British officer described the event: 'This has been a day which will live in the memory of the Indian Army when its colonel in chief visited five Corps which is upholding the traditions in the fiercest struggle in its annals…news of his visit and his constant interest and sympathy will encourage and inspire force in the task before them.'[15]

The visit was, however, to prove costly for Lord Roberts. Seeing that the Indian soldiers did not have greatcoats, Roberts himself did not wear one, with fatal consequences. The following day, he contracted pneumonia and died on the night of 14 November. The news, communicated to the Indian Corps early next morning, was received with profound grief. 'No other English soldier has commanded such measure of human affection,' the Secretary of State wrote to the Viceroy. An Indian officer said that Lord Roberts was truly 'not only the colonel-in-chief of our army, he was our father, he was a pattern of the British officer under whom we gladly serve, brave, wise and full of sympathy...but thank God we saw him here at the last and if I live, we will be able to tell my children in Punjab that he shook hands with me and spoke to me in my own language. What death could have been more to his choosing than to die amid the sound of the guns, among us, the army he loved so well.'[16]

Tributes poured in in the House of Lords. Lord Kitchener declared that, till the end, Roberts took the keenest interest in India and Indian troops and it was to greet Indian forces in the field that he made his last journey. Lord Roberts' body was brought back to Britain where he was buried at St Paul's. King George V was present as were the Indian Maharajas and Princes. The Second Mountain Battery with Indian drivers and mules took part in the procession to the cathedral, the crowds watching as the Indian soldiers and Princes paid their tribute to their Commander-in-Chief.

Back in France Darwan Singh Negi and Gabar Singh Negi were getting used to the frontline. On the night of 29–30 October their regiments were ordered to relieve the British battalions. They had to hit the ground running. The downpour had left the trenches filled with water and mud. The Germans were relentlessly shelling them with 8-inch howitzers. The casualties were high, but they remained steady. A few days later they would face their first charge. They were ordered to occupy the German trenches and block them with rubble. About fifty Garhwalis, including Darwan and Gabar Singh Negi, were lined up in a drainage ditch. The Garhwalis daringly made their way to the German parapet where they could hear the soldiers speaking. As soon as they got the signal, they swarmed over the German parapet. The Germans fired only a few rounds and fled. The Garhwalis entered the trench taking six prisoners. The early victory fired them up.

Darwan Singh Negi's battalion spent twenty-one days in the trenches while Gabar Singh's spent nineteen. The men were exhausted. There had been no 'breaking in' to trench warfare, which was to become customary later. The men went in under adverse weather conditions with only the kits they stood in. They were not allowed to light even a candle, leave alone a fire.[17] Food was mainly bread and biscuits. It was enough to knock out even the toughest of men.

Though a seasoned soldier, Darwan Singh had not been prepared for the horror of the Western war. After a relentless three weeks in the trenches, his battalion arrived in billets at Le Touret on 20 November.

The mud and bog had drained his energy but he felt he had to keep his spirits up and help the younger Garhwalis of his regiment. Many of the men were delirious when they left the trenches. In the billets, they were kept in a hot room and given a bath. Slowly they would come back to the real world. He had helped some of them write letters home and knew how they felt. Most were certain they would not return. They were sorely in need of sleep, having been reduced to the lowest level that they could withstand. But there was hardly any rest. Barely two days later, the regiment was diverted to Festubert.

It had been snowing on the lines and the Garhwalis were going to be severely tested. The Germans had taken over sections of the British trenches in Festubert and were occupying about 300 yards. The British troops flanked them on either side. At 3.00 a.m. on 24 November the assault commenced with seven bombers from the 57th Rifles (who had headed down from Ypres to join them). When the bombs were exhausted, the Garhwalis were ordered to charge. Led by Darwan Singh, they jumped over the barricade and went into the trench 'like tigers'.[18]

It was going to be Darwan Singh's finest hour. The Garhwali soldier was a man on fire. He was the first to push round each successive traverse facing the full onslaught of German bombs and rifles at close range. Stabbing furiously with his bayonet, Darwan Singh took down several Germans. Despite bleeding profusely from two wounds on his head and one in the arm, he continued to push through, determined to defeat the Germans. Then, letting out a cry of victory as the last German was captured, he jabbed his bayonet in the air and claimed his trench. As dawn broke, Darwan Singh led the Garhwalis through the trench joining hands with the 107th Pioneers who were on the other side of the line. So charged up was he, that he did not even report himself wounded. His company commander noticed that he was streaming with blood from head to foot and sent him for medical attention. For his bravery, Negi was awarded the Victoria Cross, bringing honour to his remote village of Kefarteer in the Garhwal hills and putting it on the map. He became the second Indian soldier after Khudadad Khan to receive the coveted medal.

The Garhwalis had proved their mettle. The 1st Battalion held the recaptured trench till the night of 25–26 November when it was relieved by the 2nd Battalion. By then the trench was in a terrible condition with putrefying corpses in the front and rear. The mainly Hindu soldiers of the Garhwal regiment found the job of removing and disposing of the dead particularly repugnant, but they did it stoically. Moreover, the exhuming, removal and reburying of the corpses – German and Indian – had to be carried out under fire from the enemy fifty to two hundred yards away.

The awards buoyed the Garhwalis and made them even more determined to make their mark in the war. There were celebrations in the village of Kefarteer in the Garhwal hills. In the regimental headquarters in Lansdowne, they raised a toast to Darwan Singh Negi and to the other decorated soldiers. It was the first VC for the Garhwal regiment and they had received it within six weeks of their arrival in Europe.

The soldiers of 57th Wilde's were, however, not faring well in Festubert. On 24 November a volley of German shells rained down on the village, hitting a dressing station and wrecking it completely. Captain Singh of the Indian Medical Service, who was the officer in charge, was killed instantly along with Surgeon Hakim Rai, ward orderly Zaman Khan, sepoy Akbar Shah and Major P Atal, medical officer of the 129th Baluchis.[19]

In a separate firing, Sepoy Zaman Khan, who had survived falling off the train in France a few weeks ago, was also killed. The young Pathan's name would be carved on the memorial at Neuve Chapelle as his body was never found. In the remote village of Chakwal in the Punjab, his father Wahab Khan would forever mourn his death.

On 1 December the Indian Corps prepared to receive a special visitor. King George V was visiting Locon in France accompanied by the Prince of Wales. The Indian troops were drawn up on both sides of the road. Representatives of the cavalry gave him a guard of honour after which he visited various divisions. The two battalions of the Garhwal Rifles sent 100 men each. The King Emperor spent time with the ranks of all the regiments, speaking to the soldiers and asking after their welfare. He visited a hospital in North France asking the sepoys about the nature of their wounds. The King displayed his knowledge of the battles in which the Indians had fought and told them that he was impressed by the extraordinary hardiness and patience with which they bore their wounds. The visit delighted the soldiers.

The Royal visit was to be special for Darwan Singh Negi. On 5 December the modest Garhwali was taken in a car to General Headquarters. He was to receive the Victoria Cross from the King himself, becoming the first Indian soldier to have it pinned on him personally. Unfortunately, Khudadad Khan, still wounded in hospital, could not attend the ceremony. Asked by the King if he had a personal request, Negi wanted only that a school be built in Karnaprayag in Garhwal so that local children could be educated.[20] The school still stands today.

5

The Trenches

'London was horrid. Everybody busy knitting mufflers and visiting hospitals (both of which can be overdone) while the conversation was always of the war or of the invasion of England, which many seemed to think imminent,' complained Lt Rex L Benson of the 9th Lancers in a letter to Lord Hardinge, less than two months since the Indian Corps had joined the war effort.

Benson said that he saw little of the Meerut and Lahore divisions which had by now settled down and been given a small frontage to hold. He felt they were 'splendid fighters' but were lost without their officers. The officer described how he had to rally the relics of two companies of Wilde's Rifles, whose officers had all been shot: 'They were splendid in the trenches as long as their officers were there but afterwards did not know what to do… The poor 2nd Gurkhas had a bad knock, also the 8th. I saw them both arrive at Neuve Chapelle and they looked splendid, every man grinning.'

Benson met the Maharaja of Bikaner in London and had tea with him. The Maharaja was in fine form and was off to the front again. 'So many of my friends have been killed that one wonders if there will be any left. It is after the war that one will miss them so much,' said Benson.[1]

In the early days of November the scene on the frontline was an un-ending row of trenches dotting the landscape that had once been woods and flat farmland. Many of the Indian soldiers lamented that though they could hear the Germans, they had not actually seen the enemy. The Germans lay concealed in the trenches, a labyrinth of tunnels that wound its way like a rabbit's warren. They had a well-thought out plan. They would start digging and sapping their trenches in a zig-zag pattern approaching the Allied trenches, till they were barely fifty yards away. From this vantage position, the soldiers who were massed in front could rush the Allies as soon they got the signal. By the final stage, they would reach within a yard of the Allied trench. 'They are so close that our guns cannot harm them,' wrote Major R.A Steel in his regimental diary.[2] 'From the heads of these saps, bombs of all sorts are lobbed into our trenches'.

The bombs were not the only problem. With the rains came the flooding. Trenches turned into bog pits, the stench of decaying bodies mingling with the smell of burnt shells in the ever-present slush. Standing in the bog gave them trench foot. Frost-bite was common. Large rats ran through the tunnels causing infections and disease as they fed on corpses. Many of the soldiers had lice and fleas. If not killed by artillery fire, the soldiers died under collapsing trenches. This was an alien world for the Indians, an inferno of shell fire and bombing. They had never seen men blown to pieces. They were used to a different kind of war: hand-to-hand fighting with swords and rifles in the North West Frontier of India, an enemy they could see, a charge of cavalry and infantry. Instead they watched as the sky rained with artillery fire turning night into day.

'No one who has ever seen the war will forget it to their last day,' wrote a Pathan soldier. 'Just like a turnip is cut into pieces, so a man is blown to bits by the explosion of a shell… All those who came with me have all ceased to exist… There is no knowing who will win. In taking a hundred yards of trench, it is like the destruction of the world.'[3]

As the war dragged on through the harsh winter, the sense of despair grew even deeper. The rain water turned to frost and many lost all sensation in their legs as they stood for days in the biting cold. The soldiers soon realised that there was no getting away from the trenches. If they were injured, they would be sent immediately to the hospitals and convalescent depots in France. Once recovered, they would have to return to the frontline. This made them despair even more.

A wounded soldier described the war as the 'Mahabharat'. 'I have no hope of surviving, as the war is very severe,' he wrote to his family in

India. 'The wounds get better in a fortnight and then one is sent back to the trenches… The whole world is being sacrificed and there is no cession. It is not a war but a Mahabharat, the world is being destroyed.'[4]

An Indian staff officer wrote how hard it was for the soldiers to maintain their positions against the combined effect of artillery hand grenades, sniping and hand-to-hand assaults.[5] In the dark, the soldiers could not distinguish the German from the French. Moreover, they were often placed under the command of Allied officers who did not speak Hindustani, causing further confusion. The Allied trenches were sometimes marked with the names of London streets to aid navigation. None of this made sense to the Indians who could not distinguish Piccadilly from Regent Street or Trafalgar Square. To facilitate the Indians, trench maps were marked in Hindi, Punjabi and Urdu. Nevertheless, it was not easy for them to read the maps and find their way.

Even the followers were perplexed by the war of the trenches. A Gujjar follower describing the scene to his family wrote: 'In this war the rifle is useless. It is a scientific war. Poisonous gas, guns weighing 30 Bengali maunds, machine guns that fire 620 rounds per minute, bombs, mines in the trenches, aeroplanes throwing bombs, flooding of trenches with water, throwing hot liquids and other devices to cause destruction are being used… I am unable to fathom this war. The fighting is not in the open, but inside the Earth, which has been dug into…such a war has never occurred before and that it may never occur again is my prayer.'[6]

The soldiers had spent nearly two months in Europe. The initial enthusiasm of going to *Vilayat* and fighting in the Western war had begun to wane. They were missing their families and longed to return. But there was no way back.

The entry of Turkey on the German side from 28 October caused concern in the British administration that the Indian Muslims may pledge loyalty to the Ottoman Empire. The Governor of Bombay, Lord Willingdon, told the Viceroy that it would 'increase our anxieties here'. Willingdon was worried about a Reuters report which had appeared in the Indian newspapers. According to the report, the opinion in Berlin was that the

British reserved the Indians until hand-to-hand fighting was necessary and then pushed them in. 'Surely this is not a wise thing for the censor to pass in this country now. The unfriendly will at once say that the Indians are doing all the dirty work,' wrote a miffed Willingdon.[7]

The government kept a watch on potential areas where Muslims could revolt. The Governor of Madras was asked to prepare a report about the opinion of Muslims in the Malabar region, especially around Tellicherry. The Collector of Tellicherry, Mr Innes, said that the local Mappilas were loyal Muslims at heart and it was possible that they could support Turkey. He also noted that the leaders of the community such as Sultan Ali, the Raja of Cannanore, the Chowakkaran family of Tellicherry, and the principal tangals of Calicut, Ponnani and other Mappila centres, as well as the richer merchants who had a stake in the country, could probably be depended upon to exercise their influence on the side of the British government and many of them had already organised meetings to express loyalty to the British throne. The lower-class Mappilas, were the ones given to disloyal talk, but they had no leaders and with the help of the more influential men, could be kept passive. At the same time the possibility of trouble always remained, said the collector. Mallapuram was the centre of the 'fanatic zone' and disturbance, if any, was likely to take place there. The collector requested a strong armed police force to guard the area in case of an outbreak.

Lord Crewe, the Secretary of State for India, thought it important to publicise as widely as possible in the country, messages of support for the British from influential Muslim rulers like the Aga Khan and the Nizam of Hyderabad. He urged the Viceroy to spread the word that Britain would not attack any of the holy sites of Islam during the war. To boost the morale of the Indian Muslims, the Aga Khan's message was published in Indian newspapers:

> With deep sorrow I find that the Turkish government have joined hands with Germany and acting under German orders is madly attempting to wage a most unprovoked war against such mighty sovereigns as the King Emperor and the Tsar of Russia. This is not the true and free will of the Sultan, but of German officers and "other non-Moslems" who have forced him to do their bidding.[8]

The Aga Khan warned that Turkey would become a vassal of Germany and called on Muslims to 'remain loyal, faithful and obedient to our temporal and secular allegiance'.

The response of the Nizam of Hyderabad, Mir Osman Ali Khan, was also hopeful. He informed the Viceroy that he had decided to issue a 'clear pronouncement' of his attitude in the *Gazette Extraordinary* of his state, copies of which had been posted to leading Urdu newspapers and an English translation made available to the English newspapers. 'I have every hope that my co-religionists in India will not be misled into any seditious action, whether open or covert, against a government which all thinking men recognise to be the best friend and protector of Islam,' said the Nizam.

Turks in India were now listed as enemy aliens, except for the inhabitants of Cyprus and Egypt, and transit of messages from India to Turkey was suspended by order of the Director General of Post and Telegraphs, India. Efforts were made to see that Indian branches of enemy firms would not be used to remit money to enemy territory and two German agents charged with communicating news in Eastern waters were identified as Ernsthausen & Company in Calcutta and Behn Meyer & Company in Singapore.

Keeping the Indian Muslims satisfied with the war against Turkey was like walking on eggshells. Lord Willingdon shot off an angry telegram to the Viceroy on 12 November slamming Prime Minister Asquith's speech at the Guildhall where he had said, 'Turkey is to be wiped off the map of the world'. It was particularly distressing, as the speech was made before the Shia festival of Moharram, when the Governor was trying hard to keep the situation under control. 'Really, our politicians at home are hopeless,' grumbled Willingdon. 'They don't seem to know, or to care to try and realise, the true situation out here, and they make your task and that of your subordinates doubly difficult.'[9]

The presence of the German warship *Emden* in the waters of the Indian Ocean also aroused suspicion of possible secret agents. In the view of General John Nixon, General Officer Commanding in Chief, Southern Army, the *Emden* had some means of communication in Madras and Ceylon from where she gained information about the movement of British ships. Nixon was not convinced that the British had been stringent enough in rounding up Germans in Madras and Ceylon. Willingdon had found that removing the Germans from Bombay had certainly had a good effect, as the bizarre rumours were not nearly as bad as they were before.

The war had imposed another problem on the Indian administration. As the number of wounded Indian soldiers began arriving at the front hospitals and ships, the demand for ward boys, cooks, cleaners and bhistis, to serve them increased. General Sir Beauchamp Duff, Commander-in-Chief of the British Indian Army, wrote to the Viceroy in frustration from his Delhi office: 'We are doing all we can to scrape personnel together for the hospitals, but they increase their demands daily. All our trained ward orderlies have gone and the Corps we can hire in the bazaar are not fit for the work. It has even been seriously suggested to me that I should ask you to release the convict Corps from jails, murderers and other cheerful people on condition of their taking up this work. It may come to that.'[10]

Captain 'Roly' Grimshaw of 34th Poona Horse had just stepped on what he thought was a sandbag. It was 5.30 a.m. on 24 November and his regiment had been asked to enter the soggy trenches to relieve the 58th (Vaughan) Rifles near Neuve Chapelle. To his horror he found that he was standing on the corpse of an Indian soldier. Grimshaw quickly pulled the soldier's hand out of the mud to feel his pulse to see if there was any chance of life. There wasn't. Nearly 200 soldiers would have trampled on the soldier in the dark. 'There he was, almost submerged in the mud and slush. His face had hardly been injured, and I could see he was a young Pathan…Moving on, I tried to blot the hideous picture from my brain, but could not,' Grimshaw wrote in his diary. 'I thought of that youth in his home in the hills in India, probably the pride of his parents, and then to see him thus trampled into the mud like another piece of mud, of no more account than a fragment of offal.'[11]

Born in Dublin, Grimshaw was from an Irish Protestant family. He had been on leave in England when war broke out and joined his regiment in Egypt. The Captain's diary conveys the full horror of the action in the mud-filled trenches near Ypres and Neuve Chapelle in the harsh winter of 1914. Poona Horse, a cavalry regiment, had been asked to do infantry work, such was the pressure on the British Expeditionary Force. The sowars were handed a bayonet, a weapon they had not handled before as it was meant for the infantry. To their credit they adapted easily and were soon using it in trench warfare.

Under the command of Lt. Col. C.O. Swanston, a man of indomitable energy and leadership, they were the first cavalry division of the Indian Corps to see fighting on the Western Front. The 2/2nd Gurkhas had been heavily attacked in the trenches and their forward positions had been overrun. Poona Horse was asked to recapture these positions. They had to do so in daylight, under full enemy fire and without artillery support. Swanston, who was personally leading the attack, was killed. He had raised himself above the cover to search the ground and ascertain the situation. While preoccupied with his field glasses, he was fatally shot.

'The news made me reel,' wrote Grimshaw. 'So this war was, the very thing I had always longed for. What form of mental derangement makes one crave for one thing, which the moment one sees in its true light, raises a feeling of loathing?'[12]

The combined strength of the Indian Corps was little more than a British Infantry Division. Even though severely outnumbered, they carried on. On 24 November, as a blanket of snow covered the ground, Poona Horse was ordered back in the trenches to relieve the 58th (Vaughan) Rifles. Grimshaw described the horrific scene as the wounded were being removed at the same time as the frozen troops of the Poona Horse were entering. Dozens of corpses choked the trenches, most had been bayoneted, but some had their heads clean blown off. Grimshaw ordered all the corpses to be buried. Then about 8.00 a.m. the bombing started again. Almost immediately, a soldier was killed.

'The killed was Ashraf Khan, one of the nicest fellows,' wrote Grimshaw. 'Both his legs were blown off below the knee, and one arm, and half his face… Poor Ashraf Khan, an only son, and his mother a widow. He lived for forty minutes… I had him carefully put on one side where he would not be flung about or trampled on, till I had time to bury him. I moved him myself and was astounded at his extraordinary lightness…'[13]

The dead bodies in the trenches soon became part of the landscape as the relentless fighting continued, the soldiers recovering only slightly at night when some blankets, braziers and charcoal were provided to keep them warm. They sat huddled against each other, their feet frozen, trying to snatch a few moments of rest in the inferno of mud and the smell of rotten flesh. They watched as lines of rats, the size of small cats, scurried past them in search of food. They took turns to keep guard allowing themselves a snatched hour or two of sleep. The penalty for falling asleep on watch-duty was flogging, even death, and there were many who faced a grim end when they momentarily nodded off in sheer exhaustion.

On the night of 26 November, as snow fell on the trenches, Grimshaw could not sleep. He walked up and down the line trying to cheer up the soldiers and keep them warm with extra blankets.

'What my feelings were about our poor men I can find no words to express,' he wrote. 'Their almost dumb suffering was infinitely worse than if they were complaining… Here and there I sat down beside a soldier and chatted to him. It is curious how suffering draws us together. These simple minded men had hearts of pure gold. Never a complaint that they were half frozen to death…or that they were being called upon to fight as they had never in their wildest transports of imagination pictured, armed with a weapon they had never handled before they put a foot in France.'[14]

In the confines of the trenches a comradeship grew between the sepoys and their English officers. As Grimshaw sat out the night, a rescue party brought in a young Sikh from 58th Rifles. He had been shot through the temple with a shrapnel bullet and was almost dead from exposure. As the Captain gave the young soldier some hot rum and water and chafed his frozen limbs, the young Sikh slowly regained consciousness. The soldier had been found by four men who had been sent on Grimshaw's orders to search the 150 yards near the trench to bring back anyone who was alive. After searching for twenty minutes among the bodies, only the Sikh was found. The four sowars carried him back while under fire from the Germans. It was just another day in the trenches; there was no sign of any relief. Grimshaw was told that he would have to stay another twenty-four hours.

Though they despaired about not returning home, the soldiers continued to put up a brave fight.

Between 19 and 22 December the Indian Corps had lost sixty British officers, fifty Indian officers and 2,600 British and Indian soldiers. They had spent fifty consecutive days in the trenches. By the end they had no resisting power left. 'In the attacks on enemy trenches they had displayed splendid courage and keenness, but *in* the deep mud-laden, water soaked trenches, attacked by the best European troops they had no chance,' wrote General Willcocks.[15]

Meanwhile, after the first few weeks of intense fighting on the front, Lord Crewe wired the Viceroy: 'Lull maintained last few days. Eye witness says cold great. Many men in firing line so stiff from cold they have to be lifted out the trenches on relief. Artillery bombardment continues night and day. Hundreds of shells burst along the length of each line. Men being continually killed and wounded…'[16] It was clear by now that the war would not end by Christmas.

Gabar Singh Negi had been standing in the trenches for nearly forty-eight hours. He was watching the full moon in the sky, the light reflecting in the pools of mud and water. There was an eerie silence that night. What was he doing in this devastated land, he thought? His feet were frostbitten and he could not feel them anymore. He was up to his waist in mud. He was used to the cold in his village in the hills of Garhwal, but he had never seen anything like this. His regiment had been on call continuously in the area around Neuve Chapelle. He missed his family and wondered how his wife Satoori was. This war seemed to have no end in sight. He had already seen many of his regiment die and watched with a numbing sadness the sight of bodies of young men lying in the tangled barbed wire. The dead lay in the same soil – English soldiers next to German soldiers – enemies going to a common grave. He could not understand why the white people were fighting the white people. All he knew was that he had to continue as he had eaten the salt of the *Sarkar*.

The mud in the trenches had left a permanent impression on the Indians. Letter after letter recalled the horror and nature of the underground war. A Garhwali wrote to his family: 'The war is going on as usual, the rain has begun to fall heavily and there is so much mud that men sink in it and are drowned. Such are the scenes that take place in this stupendous war.'[17]

On 20 December, the Germans began relentlessly shelling Gorre. The rain was slashing down as Poona Horse were ordered to march to the town. Grimshaw described the apocalyptic scene: 'Little Gurkhas sloping through the freezing mud barefooted; Tommies with no caps and plastered in blood and mud from head to foot; Sikhs with their hair all down and looking more wild and weird than I have ever seen them; Pathans, all limping or reeling along like drunken men, some helping an almost floundering comrade'.

Grimshaw asked some of the Gurkhas why they were walking in bare feet. They replied: 'Sahib, our feet hurt us terribly, but in boot we hurt worse.'

At Gorre the trenches were half full of icy water and Grimshaw could not bring his men to enter them. Finally he lined it with some straw to give some relief. The same night two men from the 8th Gurkhas drowned in the dangerous marshy trenches. Another slipped and fell into the marsh, but Grimshaw managed to haul him out with great difficulty, massaged him trying to bring him back to life and eventually managed to send him off in an ambulance. About midnight Grimshaw's unit was ordered to Festubert. They were so frozen, they could barely walk and several men dropped on the road.

'The crashing of the enemy's howitzer shells over the town…all brought the hideous reality of war home to me,' wrote Grimshaw. 'I asked myself, is that what civilisation means? If so, what a mockery it all is.'

Grimshaw was severely wounded in Festubert and had to be removed from the front. Back in England, he spent time in the Indian hospitals raising the morale of the soldiers. The cavalry officer, who had developed a real bond with the Indians, returned to India in 1915 to take command of an Indian Cavalry War Depot and wrote a book about their bravery.[18]

As the war looked likely to stretch into the New Year, an extraordinary event was to occur in the trenches on both sides of No Man's Land. War-weary soldiers paused for a moment and thought of Christmas and their families and the warmth and love that they were missing. As they looked around the sea of mud and the incessant rain, they could not bring themselves to fire.

To the astonishment of the Indians from the 1st and 2nd battalion of the 39th Garhwalis, holding the line around Givenchy, about a hundred Germans climbed out of the trenches opposite them at about 2.30 p.m. on Christmas Day. They stood up unarmed on their parapets, and shouted across an invitation to come out and speak to them. The offer was accepted first by some British cavalry machine gunners who were in the line, and then (after the necessary precautions) by a few officers and men of the two battalions. The Germans laid stress on their not being Prussians, but Saxons (apparently of the 16th Saxon regiment).[19]

Christmas greetings were exchanged and there was some hand-shaking, while the Germans offered cigars, cigarettes and brandy. The exchange took place about halfway between the two lines, and the soldiers on both sides took permission to recover or bury some of the bodies lying in No Man's Land. When news of the fraternisation spread, orders were received for everyone to return to their trenches. The temporary truce was strongly disapproved of, and measures were taken to prevent any further recurrence. However, scarcely any firing took place in the area over the next few days.

Captain W.G. Bagot-Chester of the 2/3rd Gurkhas in the Garhwali Brigade recorded the incident in detail: 'One German from his trench raised the butt of his rifle. No fire from our side. He then put his helmet on the butt. No fire. He then commenced to climb out of the trench. Still no fire from our side. So he began to advance towards the 2/39th Garhwali trenches, carrying a bottle of beer in one hand and a box of cigarettes in the other. One from our side went out to meet him and he pointed to the dead lying about. The first arrivals were followed by others from each side until there was quite a collection of Germans, or rather Saxons, and Garhwalis in No Man's Land. The burial of the dead proceeded, meanwhile the remaining fraternized, each giving the other cigarettes etc. After this had been going on for some time the 39th thought the informal armistice had lasted long enough, so they fired two shots in the air, whereupon the Germans retired and fired a shot and the armistice ended. Some of the Garhwalis went into the Hun trench and said they were very comfortable, with Christmas trees burning with candles.'[20]

The days following Christmas saw a fall in the level of fighting. Both sides found that they could just about manage to keep warm and dry. The Indian Corps spent the days training in bombing, wiring, construction of proper trenches and dugouts, learning the routine of trench relief and the use of telephones. The King sent a Christmas present for the soldiers, a box filled with barley sugar, fruits, nuts, raisins, spices and other treats. A pair of socks was also included, something the soldiers welcomed, as they did the box of cigarettes. The box would be a memento, that those who survived would bring back to their villages. On New Year's Day, the soldiers received a special souvenir, a signed photo of 'Jarj Parcham' (George V) himself. Freezing in the trenches and billets they told each other that the King always thought about them.

Supplies of warm coats had finally begun and the Indian soldiers would no longer have to face the bitter winter in their tropical khakis. Sadly though, they came too late, as many had already died of cold and frostbite.

The long winter was wearing down the soldiers. The ground was covered in snow and the men found it difficult to work in the trenches. A wounded Sikh soldier wrote to his friend in India on 20 January 1915: 'A lucky man escapes and a very fortunate man will meet his brothers again. Countless canons and machine guns are firing… In the trench the snow rises from the feet to the neck, and the feet and hands are frostbitten… It rains and snows day and night. The sun is never seen. On all sides men were fighting with swords and bayonets. Corpses lay at every step and the blood ran in little rivers. Since we arrived the Lahore and Meerut Divisions have been constantly fighting. They came 72,000 strong. Of these 42,000 have been killed or wounded. The commander of the Lahore division says that until both divisions are killed the third division will not join in.' There was a general feeling in the Indian Corps that they would never return to their homeland. Only those who had lost an arm or a leg or an eye were likely to go back.

The news of the hardship the Indian soldiers were facing had reached Tagore. Filled with sadness, he paid tribute to his countrymen who were fighting on foreign soil, in *Summer's Pioneers*:

> You were the first to march to the breach of death
> Your clamour of colour and perfume troubled the air
> You laughed and pressed and pushed each other
> Bared your breasts and dropped to the ground in heaps.

The poet wrote to his friend, the artist William Rothenstein, on 9 February 1915 requesting him to publish the poem and 'out of its proceeds buy something for our soldiers in the trenches'.[21]

6

Winter

While the soldiers were putting on a brave fight in the trenches, the Royals on both sides showed their willingness to get involved in the action. The Kaiser was reported to be fighting in the trenches and the Prince of Wales had gone to the front. The Indian Maharajas had come to their first European war, determined to make their mark. Sir Pratap Singh of Jodhpur was in his seventies and raring to strike. Rex Benson wrote tongue in cheek to Lord Hardinge: 'I believe everything is running smoothly [with the Indian Corps], except that they are having great trouble in looking after Sir Pratap, who is asking every shell to hit him. What a gallant man he is.'[1] Much to Sir Pratap's delight, the Jodhpore Lancers had brought down a Taube aeroplane a few days back.

When the war began and the overwhelming feeling had been that it would be over by Christmas, Maharaja Ganga Singh of Bikaner had been one of the first to leave for the front. However as the war dragged on, he felt uncertain as to what to do. From the Headquarters of the Meerut Division in France, he wrote to the Viceroy:

> This war is the most extraordinary war that has ever taken place. The two armies sit facing each other for several days – pounding away at each other before we get the Germans to move on... But it seems very uncertain how long exactly this war will last… I am writing now to be on the safe side. I hope YE will not think I have already wearied of this show. I am as you know really very happy to be here and you may remember, I had asked YE at Simla not to send for me while the fighting was going

> on – that was on the assumption that the war might be over by Xmas. Much as I am happy at being here I am not sure, in view of several "big fats" we have in the fire in Bikaner – if I might be permitted to use such an expression – whether, should the war last a year or so, I ought not to return for a few months to India in between, and it is on this subject that I am venturing to turn to Your Excellency for your advice and wishes.
>
> 1. Of course, if the war is likely to be over by Xmas or Jan 1, I should like to stay on and see the thing through, please God.
> 2. If not should I stay on here or return to India say about the middle of Jan and come back here after about four months or less
>
> If after my return to India – in the event of YE thinking it advisable – the war is likely to come to an end sooner than perhaps I might be permitted to return here earlier than four months?
>
> If YE thinks I ought to return, I hope you will allow me to go over to England for a week or two and pay my respects to HM before starting for India. My regiments in Egypt (I hear they are going there) is also likely to have some fighting there. If so – in such an eventuality – might I also spend a few days with them and join the fighting there also on my way back?[2]

The Maharaja of Nawanagar, Ranjitsinhji, who had played Test cricket for England, volunteered for the war effort and was honoured to be called to the front. On November 18 he received communication from the Commander-in-Chief asking him to join the 2nd Indian Cavalry Division sailing from Bombay. 'Nothing could have given me greater pleasure than being allowed to take part in the stupendous effort the empire is putting forth for the vindication of a righteous cause and to serve His Gracious Majesty the King Emperor on such an occasion,'[3] wrote the 42-year-old. His nephew, K.S. Sawai Sinhji, who had recently graduated from the Imperial Cadet Corps, had been given a commission in His Majesty's army and was wounded in East Africa. The Maharaja told the Viceroy that he was proud to think that a member of his family had fought well.

The Maharaja of Gwalior sent a ship called *Loyalty* for the troops and contributions were made by the Maharajas of Jaipur, Jodhpur, Rewa, the Nizam of Hyderabad, the Begum of Bhopal, the Maharaja of Kashmir, the Maharaja of Kapurthala, the Holkar of Indore and the Maharajas of Benares, Dholpur and Darbhanga.

General Willcocks kept the Viceroy updated about the progress of the Maharajas on the Front. The Maharajas had been carefully selected and he felt it was important to let the Viceroy know his honest assessment of them. The General was all praise for Sir Pratap Singh and his Lancers who had taken their share of trench work as infantry soldiers, as well as done ordinary cavalry work. 'They are doing very good work indeed and all fine fighting men…they dig trenches or do any other manual labour with the greatest cheerfulness. The King, the Prince of Wales and Prince Arthur have all seen them with the other troops of the Army Corps. Sir Pratap is a very fine man and a fine soldier,' he reported. Willcocks also appreciated the young Maharaja of Jodhpur and described Bikaner as a 'first class fellow, a real soldier and now ADC to Sir John French'.[4]

Despite the high praise from Willcocks, the Maharaja of Bikaner was getting increasingly anxious. He had already been away from his state for over two months. He had been appointed as ADC to Sir John French and had taken his post on 7 December. Yet there was little he was seeing of the actual fighting as they were stationed a few miles from the frontline. The Maharaja of Kishangarh was also with him. Both felt they were simply whiling away the time, living in luxurious chateaus away from the action. Perhaps the British felt that it would not be a good idea to throw the Indian Maharajas into the trenches with the regular sepoys. Maharaja Ganga Singh felt he needed to touch base with the Viceroy again. On 10 December 1914, he wrote from the headquarters of the British Expeditionary Force in France:

> We are staying in a fine big house here, with beds, furniture, a bath, (a rare luxury in this part of France)…and you would hardly think there was any fighting going on here. As in my former place I have practically no work to do, so time hangs very heavily; and though we are away further from the firing line, I hope to be able to yet manage to get about and see what little fighting there is to be seen in this most extraordinary warfare!… It is more like siege warfare and *dull* doesn't half describe the situation. Though I have on some occasions been under fire – both shell and rifle – I haven't had a single opportunity of loosing off my Mannlicher rifle or revolver and the worst of it is that there seems no immediate prospect

of things livening up; the general view seems to be that it will be a long war and one of wearing out the Germans.

The Maharaja was clearly frustrated. Having realised that the war in England was likely to drag on, he now felt there was no point in going back for a few months and returning again as he would not be able to undertake any projects in his state. Instead it would be best to return to India and attend to his state affairs. The Maharaja decided to explain to the Viceroy why he had changed his mind:

> Even if I return here in the spring there is no knowing of when the war will end and it will not look nice for me to be going backwards and forwards even I got YE's permission to come again, and I could not *conscientiously* leave my state frequently for several months at a time especially as we have many very big schemes in hand of vital importance to my state.
>
> The time taken in three voyages to India and again to Europe and back would alone mean a waste of at least one-and-a-half months.
>
> And this same kind of dull and uninteresting warfare may be in progress when I did return!

The Maharaja also revealed that his daughter was unwell. She had developed a tumour in August and needed to have it removed. He had earlier given the doctors full permission to carry out the operation in his absence, as he was leaving for the war, but the doctors had said that no operation was without risk and if there was any problem, then he would regret not being present. He also said that he was greatly disappointed that he could not see the war to its end:

> As YE can imagine, [it will] be a great disappointment to me not to be here at the end of the war, but perhaps I must look at it philosophically... Others may see more lively and interesting things, but at least I shall console myself with the knowledge that I came here as early as was possible...

The Maharaja signed off, apologising for the length of this letter and the stylo pen ('we have no facilities about pen and ink and paper even at HQ, in spite of other luxuries').[5]

A few days later the Viceroy received a letter from another Maharaja, Sir Pratap Singh. He too pointed out that he had not seen any real action yet.

> "My esteemed friend,
>
> Much pleasure in informing you that Sumer Singh [Maharaja of Jodhpur] and I are enjoying the best of health. The other day our regiment was inspected by the PoW and also HM the King. The regiment has been doing very well although this trench work is quite new to them. We have not had a charge yet, but live in the hopes for one at least. All our men are very well and in good spirits and I hope that they will keep them up.
>
> Pratap Singh"[6]

In January, the Maharaja of Kishangarh suffered from a prolonged attack of bronchitis and severe influenza. Doctors recommended that he return to India. The Secretary of State wrote to the Viceroy: 'I hope you will agree with my view that he should leave before his illness assumes a more severe form.'

Meanwhile, the Maharaja of Bikaner's troubles showed no signs of easing. He wrote once more to the Viceroy that he had received a cable that his daughter's symptoms had worsened and that he needed to be in his state as the purdah system made it difficult for doctors to proceed in his absence. He said he would go to Bikaner in February. The Viceroy however told him that he should return to Europe when he could, as the war would go on.

If the Maharajas were proving a handful for the Viceroy, General Willcocks had other problems to deal with. It was reported that the Brahmans in the Brahman regiment were refusing the rations that were issued to them. They were suspicious that the biscuits supplied to them may contain animal protein. Moreover they were influencing the Rajputs and Sikhs of the regiment not to eat the biscuit and bread rations either. The same classes had accepted these rations in other regiments. Willcocks dashed off a note to the Viceroy that it would be preferable if Brahmans were not sent to the frontline. Though brave fighters, their dietary requirements made it difficult for them to fight, he said.

As the year was ending Willcocks wrote to the Viceroy. The brief Christmas break was over and further trench warfare beckoned in the cold months of the New Year. The General was feeling despondent. He felt that the progress of the Indian Corps had not been reported accurately by the press. 'When we did things by no means out of the common, they were glorified into great deeds (generally by "Sikhs and Gurkhas", the only two classes some papers appear to think; though this has now been set right in the press), when we fail to come up to the expectations of the popular reader, then we have done badly,' he wrote on 30 December. The real truth, felt the General, was that they had done neither, but had done their duty well.[7]

According to Willcocks, the Sikhs did well but the Gurkhas had disappointed. 'I may be wrong,' he said, 'but I prefer many other classes now. Punjab Mahomedans – frontier men especially – they do well always.' The General had clearly been impressed by the 129th Baluchis and the 57th Wildes, the frontier men he wrote about, who had battled bravely in Ypres and won many gallantry medals. The likes of Khudadad Khan, Mir Dast, Jemadar Kapur Singh, Gagna Singh and others were principally in his mind.

The General was also critical of the British generals and commanders in the Indian Army. 'Our generals and commanding officers are too old or not in sufficient good fettle,' he wrote. Gen Watkis of the Lahore Division was a 'good soldier,' commanded well, but his health was indifferent and he had to go. Generals Carnegy, Macbean, Johnson, Brunker all had to go owing to the fact that they were over the age when they should be in command of brigades. Willcocks saw this as a 'serious matter for India.'

The General also felt that many of the Indian officers, who were reservists, were 'too old' and 'quite useless'. He felt they should never have been called to the front. 'They have been kept because the Indian government *will not*, as I have recommended for years, acknowledge that a native soldier after 18 years' service is useless for war. Why! Our batches of reservists have been in some cases a pitiable sight. Men almost weeping in the ranks and asking why they have been sent to die. It is very painful, YE, to me as their Commander and I have sent all I could, back again. The officers who passed these men as fit for service should go before a court martial.'

'Think of an old Sikh man who probably in his day was a good soldier, having to come out here merely because his pension was held up, to face the VII German Corps in the trenches! It is too cruel and I cannot write too strongly about it.'[8]

The General was clearly in no mood for niceties. He told the Viceroy: 'The empire is engaged in a mighty struggle in which Indians are giving their all, and we in return should do justice to the men who are giving it.' The General ended urging the Viceroy to alter all these things.

Following the General's complaints, the Secretary of State wrote to the Viceroy about the quality of troops saying that 30 per cent of the reinforcements were declared unfit for service by the British officer commanding the base depot at Marseilles. Moreover, the Medical Board had pronounced sixty-eight soldiers unfit for service in Europe on medical grounds, thirty-two temporarily unfit, due to old age and weakness. 'Despatch to France of reservists of over 15 years' service should be prohibited,' said the Secretary of State firmly.

Willcocks was a prolific writer. He enjoyed filling in the Viceroy with the details of life on the front. He told him how the Germans had tried to win over the Indian soldiers to their side by dropping propaganda pamphlets in Hindustani from the clouds on to the Indian lines. 'We captured an aeroplane one day and the officers' haversacks were full of them. By German laws we might have shot them, but instead we gave them tea and cakes and put them under guard. They are still alive!' wrote the General.

The Viceroy in turn praised the bravery of the Indian soldiers and welcomed the fact that they had thrown themselves into the battle: 'It is, I think, a good thing that they should be well blooded,' he wrote to Willcocks. 'It will improve their self-respect and probably their fighting qualities.' He believed that the Indian Army had proved its merit over the other colonial armies and that Britain would not have achieved what it did in France without them: 'That is where India beats all the colonies, for even now the colonial contingents are still unfit to go to the front, while our Indian troops have been there for three months,' the Viceroy said proudly.

Recruitments he said were going 'wonderfully', adding that 'the Sikhs and the Punjabi Mahomedans are tumbling over each other.' The Indian Corps was getting an average of over 8,000 recruits per month, whereas their normal intake was usually 15,000 over the whole year. The campaign for recruitment continued in the provincial towns and villages. Those already in the service were sent back to the villages to bring in fresh recruits. Village headmen would also coerce the farmers using a mix of pressure and persuasion. Good food (three meals a day), a steady pay (Rupees 11 a month) and the hope of bravery awards and glory were used to convince the villagers to sign up for the war. Most needed little persuasion. Facing a future of failed crops and uncertainty, they opted for what they thought would be a life of adventure and steady income.

Meanwhile in France, more Indian soldiers had arrived, disembarking at Marseille and making their way to the frontline in February 1915. Among them was a Sikh cavalry soldier. He described the scene in a letter home: 'The front is 1,200 miles from here. The fighting is now not so violent as it was said to be at first. Its violence began to decline from the day on which our Punjabi brothers joined in the fray. The cold is the greatest hardship. It is so severe that a man can neither open hands nor feet, and it rains every day. The sun is never seen.'[9]

As the soldiers arrived they made their way North by train and were put up in camps or farmhouses along the way. The initial wonder of seeing Indian troops for the first time as they had in September may have worn off, but the French wanted to give a warm welcome to every shipload of Indians who arrived to help them in their war. The soldiers, on their part, were full of admiration for the French who received them warmly into their homes: 'The women of this place are very pleased to see us, like opening flowers. They shake hands with our men when they disembark, and attempt to feed them from their own pocket. There are people here of all degrees and they are of the same colour and complexion as our English from England,' the soldier wrote. The Indians also noted how the

French treated the troops from their own colonies: Morocco, Tunisia and Algeria. They felt that the French showed far less racial prejudice than the British. An Indian soldier wrote home to his family that he now had a 'French mother' who looked after him.

The attitude of the Indians to the French was noticed by Walter Lawrence, commissioner for Indian troops. 'The Indians have acquired a liking for the French people,' he noted.[10] 'The French have made more of them and treated them more as equals than we do… In Marseille the Indians compared the strict discipline with which they were treated with the greater liberality which is accorded to the coloured troops of race.'

The War Office noted that some Indian soldiers might be mixing with hostile agents and a strict memo was sent by Sir John French urging that the activities of all British subjects (Indian, Egyptian etc) of suspicious character be monitored by the British Consul and the Indian Criminal Investigation Department. Passports to France, he said, should not be handed to anyone of 'doubtful loyalty'. All Indian ranks except officers were confined to their camps at Mousso, La Valentine and La Barasse and strict rules of discipline were invoked around them. The Indian Mail Censors also noted that 'It would appear from the tenor of certain letters passing between the Base Camp at Marseilles, where the scum of the Army has naturally tended to collect, and the front, that the Indian soldiers in camp at Marseilles have been able in some cases to obtain access to the women of the neighbourhood and that a certain amount of illicit intercourse with them is going on.'[11] The War Office felt that this had to stop immediately.

The Indians wrote in detail describing the new land they were visiting, the customs and the cultural differences. Since most of the soldiers came from peasant stock, they took a keen interest in the crops and farming methods of the French. They were full of praise for the French women who worked the farms and offices as the men had gone to war. A letter written by a Punjabi soldier to his brother in India, listed the finest things about the French:

> First, unity, second knowledge or ability; third, obedience to orders, fourth, absence of jealousy with regard to women, fifth, the cleanliness of everything, in house, in person, in clothes, in dress. Throughout the

> country there is one style of dress with no caste distinctions. You cannot tell the prosperous rich from the poor. In the evening every young man goes for a walk. It is the same for men and women. Both men and women please themselves. They cannot forbid one another. That is the way of the country.[12]

The Sikh cavalry soldier described the generous rations they were given: 'Twelve 'chittaks' of 'atta', one and half of 'gur', and the same amount of 'ghee' every day. Meat we get twice a week and rum… I have had a larger issue of clothing here than I got at Delhi. When we go to the front we take with us only the clothes that we stand up in and two blankets and a waterproof sheet, all the rest are left behind here in charge of the government… The troops are changed every twenty four hours and each regiment takes its turn once a week… When they go they are fresh and fit, when they return they are senseless and drowned with rain. Warm clothing heated by a machine is put ready for them and the men are shut up in a warm house; after four or five hours they come back to their senses. Every man wears three pairs of socks and warm boots, but even so it appears their hands and feet sometimes fall off. Nowadays there is snow a foot deep or even more, the rain never ceases. It is said there will be a great attack at the end of March. As God wills so it will be. Do not be nervous. Whatever is fated will happen to me.'[13]

Soon India would feel like a place very far away as the 'great attack' scheduled for March would be upon them. Soldiers from all units would be called upon to face the battle of Neuve Chapelle. It would be the first battle the Indians would fight as a single Corps, both Lahore and Meerut Divisions in action together.

In a hospital in New Milton in England, a proud Pathan soldier, was polishing his shoes and smartening up his uniform for a rare honour. He was to be driven to Buckingham Palace that day for a special function. 26-year-old Khudadad Khan, the first Asian to win the Victoria Cross, was to receive his honour personally from the King. The gunner from the Chakwal region of Punjab had continued firing in the first Battle of

Ypres till he was the last man left. Severely injured, he had been taken to a hospital and had been too ill to receive the Victoria Cross when the King had visited France in December. Eventually Khan was sent back to England to the New Milton Hospital in Hampshire where he made a slow recovery. On 25 January, cheered by his fellow Pathans of the 129th Baluchis and other soldiers, he left for London with some of his comrades to be presented before the King. The King congratulated him on his bravery and asked him about his recovery. Khan spoke through an interpreter, barely believing that he was in the King's Palace receiving the highest honour from him. The military band played a jolly tune and crowds of people pressed their faces against the gates of Buckingham Palace to see the brave heroes being honoured. Khudadad Khan held back his tears of pride. Afterwards he was photographed with his medal, and his picture carried on the front page of *The Daily Mirror* under the headline 'The First Indian to win the Victoria Cross.' The caption read: 'This is Sepoy Khudadad of the 129th Duke of Connaught's Baluchis. He was the first Indian soldier to win the coveted honour of the 'V.C.' through gallantry on the field of battle. He worked a gun single-handed although wounded. All his comrades were killed.'

By mid-January the soldiers were back in the trenches. In a hospital in Rouen a wounded Pathan was longing to play his flute. He wrote a letter to his friend to send him one: 'I have no need of anything, but I have a great longing for a flute to play. What can I do? I have no flute. Can you get me one from somewhere? If you can, please do, and send it to me… For I have a great desire to play upon the flute, since great dejection is fallen upon me. You must, you simply must get one from somewhere. Make a small wooden box, put a little cotton wool in it, and put a flute to play on in the middle of the cotton wool. Then put a little cloth over it… I shall be very grateful. I have no need of anything else, but I do want a flute to play on.'[14]

The letter was probably read by the Censors and the Pathan's wishes passed on. Sir Walter Lawrence heard of the injured Pathan and forwarded the request to the Comfort Committee. The Committee purchased an excellent flute from Boosey & Hawkes in London and posted it to the Pathan. Meanwhile, some sympathisers in England hearing of the case, had sent the Pathan a penny whistle. Thinking it was the Committee's response to his request, the Pathan wrote a letter to them explaining the uselessness of a penny whistle, which puzzled the Committee. When he finally received the flute that the Committee had posted, the Pathan's delighted letter of thanks cleared the confusion.

Soulful tunes from the flute soon filled the hospital ward in Rouen reminding the soldiers of the land they had left behind.

7

Bandobust Sahib

The arrival of the Indian soldiers in Europe had left Sir Walter Roper Lawrence, civil administrator, travel writer and veteran India hand, feeling that he should do his bit. After all, the 57-year-old had been based in India from 1875 serving in the civil service. If anyone knew about organisation and management, it was Lawrence. As a specialist in the revenue and agriculture department, he had been appointed to the post of settlement commissioner in Kashmir in 1889. He had loved his time there and written an account of it in *The Valley of Kashmir*[1]. So popular was he that the Kashmiris had given him the name 'Bandobust Sahib' (the Sahib who organises). They had even expressed their wish to erect a memorial for him for his work as settlement commissioner and wrote to him for suggestions. The request, which was forwarded to Lawrence, stated: 'Your memory here is not likely to fade…think of a means which would also be of real benefit to the people on whose behalf you toiled so hard and with so much success.' The letter touched Lawrence deeply. He wrote to his wife Lilian, who had travelled with him extensively in India, that it was a great honour to be remembered in the East after twenty years. He suggested that the Kashmiris could perhaps have a caravanserai in his memory for the villagers who came to Srinagar, and if funds permitted, a modest reproduction of his head with the words, 'Walter Lawrence, Bandobust Sahib. 1889–1895.'

Lawrence had left Kashmir in 1896 not wishing to take any more administrative jobs in the provinces and went back to England. In 1898, however, he returned to India as private secretary to Lord Curzon. It proved an exhilarating but exhausting task as he had to balance Curzon's reforming zeal with a resentful bureaucracy that wanted to slow him down. In 1903, thinking it foolhardy of Curzon to stay on for a second term, Lawrence resigned and returned to England, where he wrote for *The Times*. But his return was short-lived. In 1904 the Prince of Wales asked him to organize a royal tour of India in the winter of 1905–6. Lawrence's delicate management of the tour, widely regarded as a success, laid the foundation of a lifelong friendship with the future George V, for whom he later wrote a number of speeches. Walter and Lilian had friends among both Indian royalty and the British establishment. Their circle included the author Rudyard Kipling, with whom Lawrence shared a common interest in writing about India.

In the summer of 1914, three days after England entered the war against Germany, Lawrence decided to write to Lord Kitchener offering to work for him as civilian private secretary. Kitchener offered him the job of commissioner for the sick and wounded Indian soldiers in France and England. Lawrence would have to organise the field hospitals, ensure proper transport for the wounded and look into their comforts and needs. He would report directly to Kitchener. The 'Bandobust Sahib' had been given a job that was dear to his heart. For the next two years, he would travel every fortnight to France. He would also tirelessly survey the hospitals in England in Brighton and Brockenhurst and the convalescent homes in Barton-on-Sea and Netley, and report back to Kitchener about the arrangements as well as the mental condition of the Indians. He wrote detailed letters to Lilian and his son Henry, describing the Indians on the frontline and how they were coping in this alien conflict. Sympathetic to the Indians, whom he understood well, Lawrence was determined to ensure that they were well looked after in Europe. An empire builder to the core, Lawrence was equally determined to ensure that everything was run according to proper English norms, and that the line between the English and their Indian visitors was not crossed. English nurses would play a supervisory role in the hospitals and not actually nurse the Indian patients; English women weren't allowed to visit the hospitals to see the Indian soldiers unless there was a special case; officers of the Indian Army were welcome to visit and women would be admitted only if they were related to the men in the hospital. Every visitor would require a pass to visit the Indian hospitals. Lawrence did not want any illicit romances between white women and the Indian soldiers and laid down strict rules.

Hospitals for Indian soldiers in France had been set up in Boulogne, Hardelot, Montreuil, Rouen and Abbeville. The worst cases arrived straight from the front; men with their faces blown off and limbs missing. They lay groaning on stretchers outside the huts in the freezing weather, crying out for their loved ones and begging for relief from their pain. The sea of wounded soldiers became all the more overwhelming after an attack. Often they had to wait for hours before they could be given a bed. Many of them had frostbite. Lawrence had quite a task on his hands. He reached Montreuil, a military school that could house 750 Indians, when the wounded of the Lahore Division were arriving in large numbers. 'I saw it at its worst,' said Lawrence. 'But the wounded were brought in quickly and were comfortably installed.'

In the clearing hospital at Lillers, he met a sick prisoner who had tried to take his life and been sentenced to death, the sentence later commuting to fourteen years. The wounded soldier, a Sikh, had been so depressed by the war and his own injuries that he had lost the will to live. There were two British soldiers on guard outside his room. Lawrence felt, on reflection, that it would have saved everyone a lot of trouble if the first sentence had been carried out.

Lawrence suggested that the fit men convalescing in England could be sent to Marseilles for a bit of sunshine before proceeding to the fighting line via Rouen. 'Sunshine makes all the difference to the Indians,' said Lawrence. 'A few days sunshine will greatly change their outlook.'[2]

The supply of ghee for the troops had also run short and Lawrence sought an assurance that this would not happen in future. He requested that 20,000 lbs of ghee be sent over for the use of Indian hospitals in England and asked the India Office to arrange for a continuous supply. To make the Indians feel at home, Lord Kitchener had suggested that they be given Indian-style *rezai*s (quilts) in the ambulances and hospital trains. But Lawrence discovered that the *rezais* became bug-infested. 'What the Indians like are red blankets,' said Lawrence. 'We have *rezais* at Hardelot, but both Indians and the Indian Medical Service officers prefer the red blanket, which brightens up the wards and is easier to keep clean and sweet.'[3]

Having spoken at length to many of the Indians, Lawrence found that the climate and the two months' work in the trenches had greatly depressed them. 'They regard the frostbite as a visitation of Providence and not as an incident of warfare,' he told Kitchener. 'As they put it, "We are not fish..." They got absolutely numbed standing in cold water and when they are in this numbed condition they put their feet into the fire of the braziers. The pain of this frostbite seems intense, and no one seems to have a remedy for it... No one seems to know how long it will take before these frostbites can be cured.'[4]

Another troublesome issue was the disposal of the dead bodies. At Boulogne the Hindus were buried as there were no facilities for cremation. Hindu corpses were brought from Hardelot and Montreuil to Boulogne for internment. A Hindu medical officer and Brahmin sub-assistant surgeon had been consulted and they had recommended that if the body could not be burnt or cast into the sea or river, burial was the only alternative. At Lawrence's request arrangements had been made for a burning ghat at Hardelot where Hindu corpses from Boulogne and Montreuil were taken. Talking to some Dogras on the subject of burial for Hindus, Lawrence was told that although they would prefer cremation, they accepted burial as a necessary evil, and only stipulated that 'their boots should be left outside the graves'. Attempts were made where possible to record the names on a headstone. A fatally injured Sikh soldier told his regiment that if he could not have a gravestone for his ashes, then he would rather be buried, even if it was against his religion, as he would prefer to have a headstone and be remembered.

There was also a suggestion that a Moulavi be attached to each brigade in Europe to attend to the dying and conduct funeral services. The Secretary of State wrote to the Viceroy that General Willcocks was being consulted on this. 'It would be appreciated by the Mussalmans. This war is regarded by them as peculiar as it is being waged in a Christian country,' wrote Lawrence.[5]

Lawrence felt that the wounded Indian soldiers fared better in France than in England and recommended that fewer be sent across the Channel:

'the fewer Indians who come to England the better for the Indian Army now and in the future,' he recommended.

The wounded soldiers who arrived in Britain were taken to hospitals in Brockenhurst, Netley and Bournemouth. When the soldiers disembarked from the hospital trains, they carried a piece of paper naming their caste. The patients were then sent to the hospital and kept with people of their own caste. At Brockenhurst in the New Forest, two hotels had been converted into hospitals for the Indians and could accommodate 280 patients. At Bournemouth, the Mont Dore Hotel was converted into a 500-bed hospital. The Royal Victoria Hospital in Netley mainly accommodated soldiers suffering from gunshot wounds, frostbite or trench back. Netley had its own railway station. By November there were 880 patients in the hospital and 224 in the Red Cross Huts.

By December the Lady Hardinge Hospital in Brockenhurst opened with space for 500 patients. Lawrence reported that both the English nurses and the patients seemed satisfied with the arrangement. 'The English nurses all said that they liked the work and that the Indians were fine gentlemen. The Indians *salaam*ed the nurses and told me that it was an honour to them to be supervised by English women,' said Lawrence. In Brighton he advocated that English nurses would be in a supervisory role with English orderlies attending on the patients. There is no choice. There is [sic] no Indian personnel available, and that most essential person, the sweeper, is not forthcoming,' moaned Lawrence. 'It is remarkable that no sweepers have arrived. We do not want bhistis, barbers, tailors etc, we only want sweepers and cooks for the convalescents.'[6]

As the Indians needed to have Indian cooks (Hindu and Muslim) and servants, men were engaged from The Asiatic Home on West India Dock Road in the East End in London, which housed unemployed lascars and provided shelter and food for foreign sailors. Also known as Strangers' Home for Asiatics, Africans and South Sea Islanders, it was built in 1857 on the initiative of Henry Venn, Secretary of the Church Missionary Society, and other missionary societies in the East End. Its foundation stone was laid by Prince Albert on 31 May 1856 and the first donation

Mir Dast amongst his colleagues, Royal Pavilion, Brighton.

Manta Singh (*top row, fourth from left*) and George Henderson (*top row, fifth from left*) enjoyed a friendship that would last over three generations. Nowshera, NWFP, 1913.

Darwan Singh Negi.

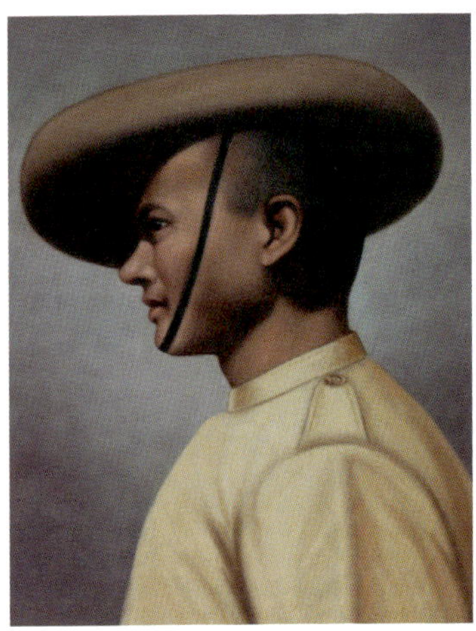

Gabar Singh Negi.

PRIVATE COLLECTION

Report in the *Daily Mirror* on Khudadad Khan receiving the Victoria Cross.

COURTESY OF GARHWAL RIFLES REGIMENT

Satoori Devi, widow of Gabar Singh, wears the Victoria Cross at the Memorial in Chamba.

© THE ROYAL PAVILION AND MUSEUMS, BRIGHTON & HOVE

Mir Dast receives the Victoria Cross from King George V on the grounds of the Royal Pavilion, Brighton.

COURTESY OF GARHWAL RIFLES REGIMENT

Darwan Singh Negi receives the Victoria Cross from King George V as Queen Mary looks on, Locon, France, 1914.

COURTESY OF INDIAN AIR FORCE MUSEUM

Hardit Singh Malik (*left*).

COURTESY OF INDIAN AIR FORCE MUSEUM

Indra Lal 'Laddie' Roy (*right*) and his drawing of a Sopwith Camel (*below*).

COURTESY OF INDIAN AIR FORCE MUSEUM

COURTESY OF JAMES WHITTAKER

General James Willcocks, Commander-in-Chief of the Indian Corps in France 1914–16 (*right*).

PRIVATE COLLECTION

Postcard: General Douglas Haig, Commander-in-Chief of British Expeditionary Force 1915–18, introduces Maharaja Sir Pertab Singh of Jodhpur to General Joffre, Commander-in-Chief of the French forces on the Western Front (*left*).

Postcard: An Indian camp in France, 1914.

Life in the trenches.

Indian soldiers in their newly issued gas masks, 1915.

Infantry digging trenches, 1915.

Painting of the trenches in winter, December 1915.

PETER BANCE COLLECTION

Postcards: Indian soldiers arrive in Marseilles (*above*). A Sikh soldier receives a rose (*below*), Paris.

PETER BANCE COLLECTION

Injured Indian soldiers in France.

Soldiers from the 20th Deccan Horse in the Carnoy Valley shortly before their unsuccessful attack at High Wood during the Somme offensive, 14 July 1916.

The entrance to the Royal Pavilion, Brighton (*above*) and inside the Music Room (*below*).

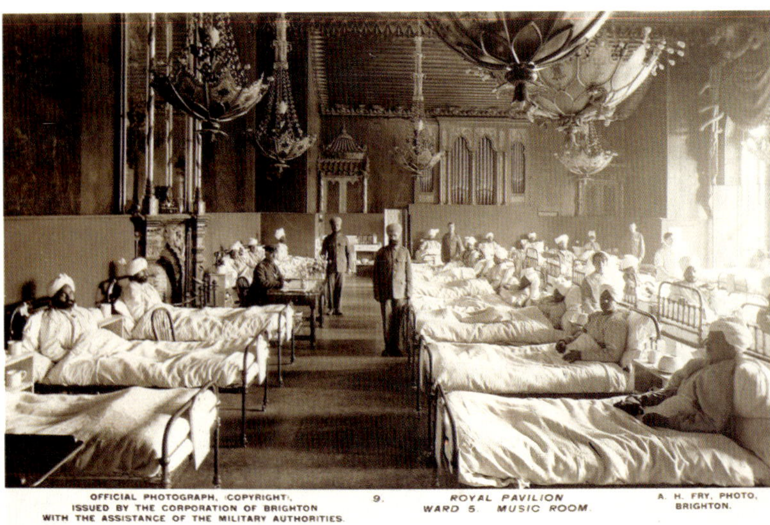

The four worst cases in the Brighton Hospital.

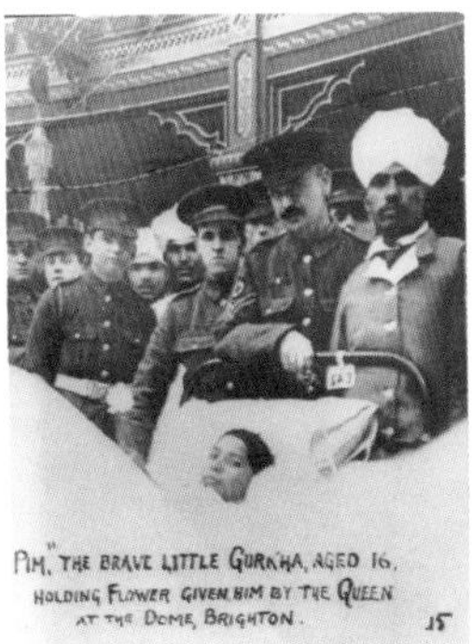

Pim, a sixteen-year-old Gurkha boy, convalescing in the Brighton Hospital.

Wounded soldiers write letters home, Brighton.

PETER BANCE COLLECTION

Postcard: Soldiers from Britain and the colonies.

Postcard: A dapper Sikh soldier impresses the French ladies. The artist did not realise that Sikhs don't smoke.

Postcards: Separate slaughter houses for Hindus and Muslims (*above*) and Indian soldiers with their 'little English friends' (*below*), Brighton.

Postcard: 'A good French lady is happy to offer some refreshment to our Allies'.

British and Indian troops being transported to the frontline in France on a London bus.

The Indian Memorial at Neuve Chapelle, France.

Sukha's grave, St Nicholas Church, Brockenhurst, Hampshire.

Chhatri Memorial at Patcham Downs, Brighton (*left*).

The graves of Muslim soldiers, Brookwood Military Cemetry, Surrey (*right*).

The graves of Indian soldiers, Bedford House Cemetery, Ypres (*left*).

The Imperial War Conference, London. *Top row*: Lord Sinha of Raipur (*first from left*), Ganga Singh, Maharaja of Bikaner (*sixth from left*); *Bottom row*: Jan Christian Smuts, Prime Minister of South Africa (*third from left*), Sir Robert Laird Borden, Prime Minister of Canada (*fourth from left*).

Detail from William Orpen's painting *The Signing of Peace in the Hall of Mirrors, Versailles, 28th June 1919*. The Maharaja of Bikaner can be seen standing in the centre.

Milford-on-Sea had told Lawrence that apart from the Gukhas, all classes claimed more pay. Sepoys were paid Rupee 11 per month during the war. Later this was raised to Rupee 19. While this was a small amount, it was regular pay, which most of the Indians did not get back home. There was also the hope that if they won gallantry awards, the *Sarkar* would give them land grants and increased pensions. Another source of discontent was the discrepancy in salaries between those recruited in England and those in India. Lawrence calculated that a 'sweeper [recruited in England] gets a pay three times larger than that of a sepoy, and an Indian ward orderly gets more pay than a havildar.'[10] The soldiers also complained that it was not fair to send them back to the trenches until fresh regiments from India had been sent first.

The direct interaction with the Indian soldiers taught Lawrence a lot about their character. Despite serving twenty-one years in India, he felt he had never really heard first hand the views of the ordinary villagers. In India these were always filtered through the village headman or a British official. But in the field in France and in the hospitals in England, Lawrence felt for the first time that he had managed to reach out to the heart of the Indians and understand them. He knew why, in the bleak midwinter of their first Western war, the Indian soldiers had reached breaking point, and he felt he needed to let Kitchener know about this. When Lawrence first met the injured soldiers in hospital, they were 'hazy and distorted'. They had gone through great strain and suffered severe shock. At this stage, they were prone to exaggeration and had very little notion of proportion. But after they had been in hospital for some time, Lawrence found that their ideas became more coherent and what became clear to him was that the strongest emotion the Indians – both the officers and sepoys – felt, was their 'intense love for their homes'.

'They are a very domestic people, and it is clear to me that they are not suited for long campaigns at any great distance from India,' Lawrence told Kitchener. 'When war broke out there is no doubt that there was a great wave of enthusiasm in India. And that it would have been a political mistake to have chilled this enthusiasm by not allowing the Indians to take part in the war... Unfortunately the conditions of warfare in Flanders were most uncongenial to the Indians. The climate was against them, and the style of warfare was utterly opposed to their ideas and former experience… Their suffering from frostbite and the moral and physical shock caused by "trench back" when a man is buried and crushed under the falling clay of trenches – were especially resented by the sepoy.'

In December 1914 the soldiers had reached a peak of depression. The first three infantry battalions who went into action were the hardest hit. Some of the soldiers suffered from hysteria and the phrase 'hysterical spine' was used to describe their condition. In New Milton these cases were called *langra-lulas* (lame-useless) and Lawrence thought these patients should be separated from the rest. He also concluded that it wasn't the fighting that bothered the Indians, it was the constant shelling.

'They enjoyed the attack, but what they cannot stand is the shelling day after day in the trenches... I should say that the Pathans were least able to stand the strain of long and severe bombardment. I saw four young Mahsud Pathans, all from the same village, all insane from the horror of the bombardment: they had not been wounded or touched… the men who came best through the mental strain of bombardment were the Jats. In talking to the sepoys I formed the idea that a great deal of the early depression, which was so marked in December last, hinged on what happened to the first three battalions of native infantry who went into action.'[11]

To provide a space for the convalescent soldiers an Indian Soldier's Club was opened in a building facing the sea in Barton-on-Sea. It was paid for by the Laymen's Society[12] composed mainly of Englishmen who had served in India and those who were grateful to the Indians for the service they had rendered in the field. Supervised by retired Indian officials, the Club provided a place for the soldiers to meet, play cards and socialise. There was also a shop selling watches, pocket knives and other articles which the Indian soldiers wanted to buy before returning to France or being invalided back to India.

The Club opened on a wintry English day on 16 Feb 1915. William Coldstream, ICS, Retd, addressed the gathering with hearty salutations of 'Sat Sri Akal' and 'Salaam':

Six months ago one could never have expected to see hundreds of soldiers from Hindustan in England, all gathered together as you are here... It is true that you have come from a distant land, but we do not call you foreigners; rather, I should say that you have come, as it were, to your second home,' said Coldstream. 'You have come to the country of your Sovereign. And just as we English, when we go to your country of Hindustan, consider that country as our own country, so we wish you to consider that, having come to England, you have come to a country of your own.

We have the fullest confidence that you men of the Punjab, of Hindustan, of Rajputana, of Nepal, of Maharashtra, and of the Deccan – men of the fighting races of India...will not cease to fight until you have conquered the foe... Then, when the war is ended, and each of you is at rest in his own village, sitting on his own dalan in his own house, with wife and children around him, cows and bullocks standing by the stall, you will sometimes, while you thus sit at ease, remember in your hearts the days when, in this Club House at Barton-on-Sea, you found a place of comfort and recreation, and met with kind friends and brotherly treatment in the far-off land of England.[13]

The enthusiastic Coldstream then proceeded to make the speech in Punjabi, reading from a Roman script. The soldiers, who were soon to return to the front, clapped and cheered for the English surgeons and doctors who had taken care of them and had got them back on their feet. They looked around the room with its views of the sea, inspected the shop and the recreation room and felt proud that their Sahibs had built this for them. Copies of the speech were printed out in Urdu, Gurmukhi, and Roman Punjabi and distributed. For the English, it was important to make the Indians feel comfortable and looked after. Anything less would be a public relations disaster.

There was nothing that depressed the soldiers more than the absence of letters. News from home written by a loved one or a friend was what kept the soldiers going as they lay in hospitals, uncertain about what the future held for them. Lawrence was quick to sense this. He once came across two Sikh officers who were continuously grumbling about the arrangements made for them in the hospital in Bournemouth. Puzzled by this, as the officers were staying in relative luxury – they had good rooms, were attended by two Indian sepoys and had a motor car at their disposal – Lawrence tried to get to the root of the problem. He discovered that the reason for their melancholia was that they had not received any letters from home. The sepoys, he realised, were always anxious about India and news from home. These letters often brought news of plague, cholera, famine, disputes about land and domestic concerns about marriage and infidelity. Lawrence came up with the idea of starting a regional language newspaper for the soldiers that would carry news from home.

The newspaper *Akhbar-i-Jang* was printed in three languages, Urdu, Hindi and Gurmukhi. Published weekly from Devonshire Square in London, the paper was edited by old India hand, Sir David Barr, who had recently resigned from the India Council. Lawrence asked Barr to focus on news about rainfall, crops, prices and general health. The paper provided a platform for the Indian soldiers to talk about their experiences in the hospitals and publish their poetry and articles. Usually they praised the treatment in the hospitals or invoked the soldiers to fight for their King Emperor and defeat the Germans. Sometimes there was a query to the editor of the paper. Soldiers considered it a privilege to be published in the *Akhbar*, many turning into reporters as they recollected events. Barr was quite overwhelmed by the number of articles he received.

In early February the Indian Corps had their first experience of desertion. Major Barstow, 41st Dogras, was shot at and severely wounded by an Indian soldier who then deserted to the German side in the early dawn. 'I never knew a Dogra do the sort of thing before and it is the first case I am glad to say of desertion in the Corps,' said Willcocks. The General hoped he had been shot before he reached the German trenches but was not sure. The deserter had carefully concealed his arms and ammunition before he started and then probably put his hands up near the German trenches and got through the lines.

'Crimes have been very rare and the Indian Army has earned a high name for discipline, both from our troops and from the French', the General informed the Viceroy. There were practically no cases of Indian soldiers annoying women, even though 'low-class women and Belgian refugees' had haunted their billets about three miles behind the battle mines. The General said he had to shoot three Gurkhas in February for deserting their posts in the advanced trenches. 'I hate doing it, but it is absolutely necessary as an example and so I had them shot on parade of Indian troops just behind the trench supports,' said the General. 'Discipline of this kind is very rigorously enforced in this army and several British soldiers have paid the penalty. It is, sir, a really big struggle and one has to harden one's heart when it comes to battle discipline.'[14]

The desertions did not worry the British too much. In early February, the Viceroy wrote to the Secretary of State that the desertions were high amongst the Pathans, especially those from the transfrontier. 'The war with Turkey has undoubtedly affected transfrontier Pathans in whose case disinclination to fight against co-religionists is evidenced. This is the primary cause of desertion and is affecting recruiting of these classes seriously which shows strong signs of ceasing.'

On 15 February 1915, the first and only mutiny of the First World War occurred in Singapore. Incited by the Ghadar Party and local Muslim propaganda following the entry of Turkey in the war, the 5th Native Light Infantry, comprising Muslims of Rajput origin and Pathans, mutinied when they were ordered to shift to Hong Kong. They feared that they may be asked to go to Turkey to fight against fellow Muslims. Two British officers of the regime were killed. The mutineers were joined by German prisoners of war including crew members from the *Emden* and went on a rampage killing Europeans and local civilians. The mutiny lasted seven days and resulted in the deaths of forty-seven British soldiers and civilians. More than two hundred sepoys were court-martialled and forty-seven executed publicly at Outram Road in Singapore.

Despite the mutiny and desertions, recruitment remained high amongst Punjabi Muslims and Muslims from Central India. The Viceroy noted that total recruitment in January had been higher than in any previous month. He was more worried about the economic situation in India. Famine conditions were leading to discontent, especially in the Punjab. The ruling chiefs were calling for strong measures. Under the circumstances, the Viceroy felt that a total prohibition of food grain exports to Britain should be imposed at the earliest. 'Until prices have fallen here it is useless to consider at present how far we can meet the demands of the market in England,' he wrote to the Secretary of State on 24 February. Exporters were exploiting the situation by forward buying food grain at high prices and adding to the popular unrest. His Council felt it was imperative to take action at once. There was also 'disquieting' news from the provinces. There had been some serious incidents in Lahore which involved murder of policemen and arrests of conspirators with bombs. The leaders of the Ghadar movement were telling the people that the high prices were due to the grain being exported in order to supply the allied armies in the field and to feed England.

The Viceroy wanted prohibition of exports announced immediately from 1 April. 'Grain riots in Peshawar are anticipated by Sir George Roos-Keppel which will react across the border unless action is urgently taken,' said the Viceroy. 'The Indian Army is considerably affected by the high prices,' wrote the Viceroy, 'for though the men themselves receive compensation, their families are suffering to the same extent as the rest of the population. Necessity of action is being urged in the press and at public meetings by representatives of all classes and interests.'[15]

The Viceroy's warning was noted at Whitehall. With hundreds of thousands of Indian soldiers fighting in the frontline, it was the Empire that was at stake.

8

Neuve Chapelle

Gabar Singh Negi had been in the trenches for what felt like a lifetime. His boots were heavy with mud that was impossible to scrape off. He huddled with his fellow Garhwalis next to a small coal fire. Cups of weak tea kept them going. He thought of his family in their village in Manjood and hoped they had got through the winter without any problems. Being illiterate, he had not been able to write any letters home. Someone had offered to write them for him, but he had felt shy dictating his thoughts. Gabar Singh hadn't received any news from his village. His family, too, could send a letter only if someone wrote it for them. The soldiers who managed to read the *Akhbar-i-Jang* talked about a famine back home. Did his family have enough to eat? Did they have to sell their goats? He missed the warmth of his village home and his wife Satoori.

The long winter had not quite turned to spring. The Indians had spent over five months in France and Belgium. They had survived Ypres, Festubert and the first attack on Neuve Chapelle. They had lived through their baptism of ice. As the winter had closed around them, they had sat it out – numb and frozen – clinging to a frail hope that this too would pass. By mid February they were holding a line which was 'very wet and sodden'. The trenches were still filled with water, making mining and sapping impossible. The shell and rifle fire continued despite the wet and cold. General Willcocks wrote to the Viceroy that he was losing about fifteen to twenty-three soldiers per day. The Germans, it seemed, had an unending supply of ammunition.

It was time for the British forces to act. The intention was to make a fresh attack on Neuve Chapelle, which formed a German salient in the British line, and if possible, the high ground of Aubers Ridge, an important observation post overlooking the plain. It was to be the first offensive of 1915, and was part of the plan to push the German line which had been maintained through the winter. Field Marshall French hoped to cut off the portion of the German troops that held the line between Neuve Chapelle and La Bassee. Ultimately he wanted to get behind the German front and threaten the defences of the city of Lille. Lieutenant General Douglas Haig, the General Officer Commanding, 1st Army, had the task of carrying out the operation.

Haig believed that a prolonged attack would produce results in the end, even if it meant taking high casualties. The Oxford-educated, Sandhurst-trained general had served as Inspector General of Cavalry in India in 1903 and had returned there as Chief of General Staff in 1909. He had a reputation for being relentless and at the end of the war would emerge as one of the most controversial British generals.

On 28 February 1915 a 'secret' preliminary order marked G-757 was issued to both the divisional commanders. Special reconnaissance was carried out by the intelligence section who noted the nature of the surrounding country, the obstacles and the enemy's defences. Aerial reconnaissance mapped out the position of the trenches. Engineers prepared the cover under which the assaulting Brigades would line up. Communications, too, had to be improved. Ration depots were established at La Couture and Richebourg St Vaast holding in all 6,000 and 10,000 Indian rations. If chapatis had to be cooked in the frontline, the provisions had to be taken care of. A team of Hindu and Muslim cooks also took up their positions. It was important to ensure that the Indian soldiers fought on full stomachs.

The Indian Corps had its headquarters at Richebourg St Vaast. On the night of Feb 28 the Indian Corps extended its position from the Chocolate Menier Corner to Port Arthur on the La Basee-Estaires Road. This front was occupied by the Meerut Division with one brigade in reserve. Gabar Singh Negi was in position here with the Second Division of the 39th Garhwalis. Like his fellow Garhwali, Darwan Singh Negi, who had received the Victoria Cross, he too wanted to bring honour to his regiment. Their commanding officer had told them how crucial this offensive would be. The Lahore Division was in the area Calonne-St Venant-Busnes-Robecq. Braving the chill here was Manta Singh of the 15th Ludhiana Sikhs.

For the first time, both divisions of the Indian Corps – Lahore and Meerut – were to be part of the attack. Infantry, cavalry, artillery, sappers and miners and the followers had all been given their duties and positions. The wounded would be collected at the existing regimental aid posts in Ruedes Bercaux. The ambulance would be at Vielles Chapelle and Zelobes. Prisoners would first be passed back to troops of the Bareilly Brigade who would hand them over at the Brigade Report Centre. From this point they would be marched to Locon.[1]

The attack on Neuve Chapelle was to begin on 10 March. Gabar Singh Negi was in the trenches, ready for assault. The instructions were clear. On the night of 9 March the preparations would begin. The Bareilly Brigade would cut the wires in front of their trenches under cover of darkness and put bridges in position over the ditches between the British and the German lines. Troops were to be in position by 4.30 a.m. It was a sleepless night for Gabar Singh. Crouching in the trenches with his colleagues, the only thing on his mind was the action they would see the next day.

The village of Neuve Chapelle comprised a school, rows of houses and a few narrow streets. At the centre of the village was a church with a large cross outside. The village had been evacuated of all civilians. Most of the houses bore the signs of the bombardment and heavy shelling of October. The Germans occupied a vantage position in the village. Their snipers were already in key locations.

The morning of 10 March broke cold, damp and misty, although the night before had been cloudless.[2] Precisely at 7.00 a.m. the Germans began a heavy bombardment of Port Arthur, causing a number of casualties. The British replied half an hour later. Three brigades of 18-pounders fired at German entanglements for the first ten minutes demolishing them completely.

The Garhwal Brigade was the first to 'go over the top'. As the bagpiper started playing, Gabar Singh and his regiment rose collectively from their trenches with an almighty roar of '*Jai Badri Vishal*' and swarmed over the parapet to attack the German positions. The 1/39th Garhwal Rifles attacked from the right and the 2/39th Garhwal Rifles from the left. They virtually tore through the barbed wire and reached the German trenches by 8.30, the adrenalin well and truly flowing in the men from the hills. They were through to the road joining Port Arthur with Neuve Chapelle. The Germans had been struck badly. Mangled bodies lay in the collapsed trenches. The 2/39th Garhwalis pressed through the first trench and took the second. The Germans were retaliating with heavy gunfire but the soldiers charged on, their bravery on full display. Next they took the third trench, and made for their main objective, the fourth line.

The day would belong to Gabar Singh Negi. Bayonet in hand, his senses on high alert, he was the first to go round each traverse, facing the full onslaught of the German attack. Letting out a fierce war cry, he charged at them bayoneting and killing several Germans as he swept through the trenches. In the clash of steel and helmets and relentless fighting, his officer was killed. The 22-year-old Garhwali, who had once tended goats on the hillside of his remote village, took command and carried on, driving the Germans on despite his injuries. As the shells rained down around him, Gabar Singh fought his way through, not stopping till he had forced the Germans to surrender.

He had taken the call and secured the trench, but Gabar Singh's war was soon to be over. Fatally injured, he drew his last breath. He died in the rubble of his hard-won trench, still clutching his bayonet, a soldier to the last. His body was never recovered. For his gallantry, Gabar Singh Negi was posthumously awarded the Victoria Cross.

Thousands of miles away in her village on the hills, Satoori Devi, barely fourteen, would be informed of her husband's death by an officer from the headquarters at Lansdowne. Her heartbroken cries filled the silent hills. She had barely known her husband and now he had gone, leaving her to face the rest of her life alone. Gabar Singh's mother joined her daughter-in-law, wailing a Garhwali song for the dead and circling in a trance for the son she would not see again. The lamps burnt low in their Garhwal home that night. The family huddled under blankets in the chilly March night and prayed for their loved one. Their only consolation was that he had upheld the honour of his regiment and would be awarded the Victoria Cross.

Satoori Devi would never remarry. She would look after the extended family, tend the cattle and carry firewood, wearing the Victoria Cross pinned on her sari all her life. Villagers would salute her as she passed by. The family would eventually move to the mofussil town of Chamba, a ninety-minute trek through the hills, where they would build a house on land given to Satoori Devi by the British government. The original house in Manjood would lie deserted. Satoori Devi would never see the memorial in Neuve Chapelle where Gabar Singh's name was carved.[3]

Queen Mary sent a personal letter with a photograph of herself to the Garhwal regiment after Gabar Singh's death. 'In sorrow and in sympathy my thoughts fly across the seas to my sisters in India, that beautiful land which I have twice visited and love so much. I send you this to do honour to a very brave Indian of the Empire who died for you and for us in the glorious fight for truth and freedom against tyranny and broken faith.' It was signed 'Mary R.I.'. The framed letter hangs in the museum at Lansdowne.

Meanwhile, the Battle of Neuve Chapelle was still raging. The 1/39th Garhwalis were hopelessly lost. Their trench map had not been accurate and they had gone a bit too far right. Finally they managed to reach a point of the enemy's trenches where the wires had not been cut and burst through the passage capturing 200 yards of the German frontline. However, they faced the full force of artillery fire and suffered many casualties. Several Garhwali officers were lost in this raid. The survivors of the assaulting party of the 1/39th Garhwalis were now completely isolated and were left without a single British officer. They were also short of guns and ammunition. Repeated attempts were made by small parties to reach them, but it was futile. All those who tried to cross were killed or put out of action. However, despite the continuous attacks by the Germans, the Garhwalis held their position.

While their comrades were stuck in their position, the 2/39th Garhwalis had pushed on into the village and started searching the houses for snipers. The battalion took up position in a line South East of Neuve Chapelle facing the Bois du Biez. The Jullunder and Dehradun Brigades were also ordered to push on to Bois du Biez. They moved steadily along the road and by 6.30 p.m. a portion of the Brigade had reached the Western edge of the wood. It was nearly dark by the time the troops reached the line of the river.

The 15th Sikhs had spent the day advancing under heavy fire. Manta Singh was in the trenches with his friend Captain Henderson. They had survived the first attack on Neuve Chapelle the previous year and the shelling of the last two days. There was an uneasy calm as the soldiers strengthened the trenches they had gained from the Germans. There was to be no sleep that night. At 1.45 a.m. on 11 March the Meerut Division received their orders. They were to continue the advance at 7.a.m. through the Bois du Biez and Eastwards. However, the early morning mist made it difficult for the artillery to fire and the attack was held up.

As daylight broke, the Sirhind Brigade reached Richebourg St Vaast. The Indian Corps took up their positions. By now they were in the thick of battle and the enthusiasm was high despite the heavy attack from the Germans. All through the night Neuve Chapelle was heavily bombarded by the Germans and the Jullunder Brigade alone sustained some 300 casualties while moving up into the village.

On the third day of the Battle of Neuve Chapelle the objective was the capture of Bois du Biez to be followed by an advance on the line of La Cliqueterie Farm. The capture of the Bois du Biez was assigned to the Indian Corps and of La Cliqueterie Farm to the 4th Corps. Yet, once again, the hour of the attack had to be postponed due to the low-lying early morning mist. For the eager soldiers, there was nothing to do but wait.

The Germans continued to fight back with heavy bombing and artillery fire. General Haig was not prepared to stop. At 3.15 p.m. the 1st Army sent out orders to carry the Bois du Biez. The Garhwal Brigade held the line under continual heavy bombardment at Neuve Chapelle and Port Arthur. An officer described this experience as a 'foretaste of hell'.[4] It was estimated that 3,000 shells fell in the latter section on the 12th alone.

Among the stories of bravery in the battle of Neuve Chapelle, would be that of Manta Singh of the 15th Sikhs. On the afternoon of 12 March, he and Captain Henderson were part of the assault party that was advancing towards Neuve Chapelle. The night before in the trenches they had had a brief chat. Henderson had encouraged the young Sikh and told him that they would get through this together. They began moving through the woods towards Neuve Chapelle in the morning. However the 1st

Army had not been able to provide enough cover and a Geman bullet hit Captain Henderson. Manta Singh saw him lying on the ground writhing in pain. Without a thought for his own safety, he took a wheelbarrow and went to rescue him. Placing Henderson in it, Manta Singh pushed him through the open ground. But a German bullet now hit Manta Singh on his left leg. His leg bleeding heavily, Manta Singh kept going, eventually bringing Henderson to safety in the trenches. Gasping and struggling, the two friends waited in agony to be rescued. It was an act of sacrifice for his comrade that would become one of the most enduring stories of the First World War.

Henderson survived. The badly wounded Manta Singh was sent to England to Kitchener's Hospital to be treated. But his leg had developed gangrene by then and the brave Sikh soldier succumbed to his injuries. He was cremated on the South Downs. Years later his name would be carved on a commemorative plaque at the spot. The story didn't end there. Captain Henderson was determined to do something for the family that Manta had left behind in India. When he returned to India after the war, he ensured that Manta's son, Assa Singh was given a position in the army. Assa joined the Sikh regiment and served in the Second World War with Henderson's son, Robert, who had become his friend. The two of them served together in France, Italy and North Africa. The Henderson and Singh family friendship continued into the next generation. Robert's son, Ian Henderson and Assa's son Jaimal Singh Johal remain friends and attend the memorial service at the Chattri in Brighton every year.

Despite the high casualties over three days in Neuve Chapelle, General Haig was determined to continue. He ordered the 1st Army to carry on the attack through the night. All three brigades of the Lahore Division were ordered to begin their attack at 10.45 p.m. But General Willcocks did not wish to push the troops any further. On hearing of the command, the angry general immediately ordered the operation to be cancelled. He did not consider it feasible to carry out at the attack at night, over un-reconnoitered ground with such a large body of troops.

At 10.50 p.m. orders were received to stop further active operations. 'This brought to an end the battle of Neuve Chapelle,' noted a weary Willcocks. The toll had been high. The number of casualties in three days of fighting amounted to 4,233 including 133 British officers.

'We had not done all that was hoped for,' said Willcocks. 'We had not captured the Aubers Ridge (nor did we succeed in doing it until three years later), but as far as the Corps was concerned we had shown that Indians will face any enemy.'[5]

The victory at Neuve Chapelle sent a flurry of excitement down the corridors of Whitehall. Congratulatory telegrams flew between the offices of the secretary of state for India and the Viceroy. Sir John French also wired the Viceroy on 15 March:

> I am glad to be able to inform YE that the Indian troops under Gen Sir James Willcocks fought with great gallantry and marked success in the capture of Neuve Chapelle and subsequent fighting which took place on 10th, 11th, 12th and 13th of this month. The fighting was very severe and the losses heavy, but nothing daunted them. Their tenacity, courage and endurance were admirable and worthy of the best traditions of the soldiers of India.[6]

The Viceroy received a detailed update from General Willcocks. The General, clearly delighted with the outcome of the battle and the performance of the Indians, especially the Garhwalis, wrote on 15 March:

> Today an extraordinary calm succeeded four days of hard fighting. The guns only intermittent now, and my division are enjoying comparative peace. You will, sir, by now have heard with delight how well our brave Indian troops fought at Neuve Chapelle… I am more pleased than I can tell you. I have served my life with them and I knew their value. They advanced over the withering fire – swept fields like veteran soldiers; the Sikhs, Mahomedans, Gurkhas, Dogras, and last but first the brave Garhwalis, such toppers those 1st and 2nd battalions of the 39th. They are magnificent fellows and I should like 5,000 of them. Hard to beat. The 2nd Gurkhas retrieved all they had lost. They faced the shell fire without flinching. The 9th ditto and so on…47th Sikhs did very well.

Today all were walking about with their heads held high. Well done the Indian Army![7]

For Willcocks, the most important gain from the Battle of Neuve Chapelle was that the Indians had taken part in it as a whole body. 'It marks the beginning of a new era in the history of that wondrous land; it proved the solidarity of our Empire in the East; it opened new fields to the people of Hindustan, and it was a living proof of the genius of our race to weld into one Imperial whole, people so diverse in colour, race and creed.'[8]

The British were comforted by the fact that the German casualties had been far higher than their own. The Secretary of State informed the Viceroy that the number could not have been less than 17,000 to 18,000.

General Haig sent his own congratulatory message to the troops and informed them that nearly 2000 German prisoners had fallen into British hands and that the village of Neuve Chapelle had been captured.

'The absolute success of the operation…has proved beyond question that our forces can defeat the Germans where and when they choose, no matter what mechanical contrivances or elaborate defences are opposed to their advance.'[9]

There was no mention in Haig's congratulatory letter about the contribution of the Indian troops and books written subsequently about the battle of Neuve Chapelle would barely mention the stellar role the Indians played in taking control of the village and the heavy losses they endured. It was as if they had been all but forgotten.

The Official History later claimed that Neuve Chapelle was to show the French the attacking ability of British troops. It was the first time that the German line had been broken. The advantage gained by the first rush was however neutralised as the Germans had retaliated strongly, destroying British telephone lines and disrupting communication and back up. British artillery power had not been able to match them. After four days of intense fighting and thousands of casualties, the British divisions had penetrated only to a depth of 1,500 metres.

Despite the celebrations, a dark cloud hung over the Battle of Neuve Chapelle. It was the issue of deserters. Shortly after the battle, Lord Crewe sent the Viceroy a list of deserters from the Indian Corps: Havildar Banat, Naik Saiyid Kasim, Naik Skahi Shah, Sepoy Gul Hasan, Sepoy Yar Shah, Sepoy Gulab Shah, Naik Sher Akhmad, the last suspected of being in sympathy with deserters; the rest being relatives of deserters. Havildar Guli Jan and Rana Sahib were also being sent back as 'undesirables'.

But even before the battle, a famous desertion had taken place that would go down as one of the most significant rebellions on the Western Front. It was the desertion of Jemadar Mir Mast, a Pathan from 58th Vaughan's Rifles (Frontier Force), and brother of Mir Dast. The story of the two brothers was one of the most intriguing stories of the war. Both were known for their bravery. In the winter of 1914, both were in the trenches in the area around Neuve Chapelle and Festubert. Yet on the chilly night of 2 March, a few days before the Battle of Neuve Chapelle, Jemadar Mir Mast, worn out and despondent, climbed out of his trench with fourteen men and crossed over to the Germans. All he wanted to do was go home. Only a few days earlier he had been awarded the Indian Distinguished Service Medal. By the time the news of the honour was published in the *London Gazette* on 10 March 1915, Mir Mast was with the Germans. On 1 April 1915 the *London Gazette* announced that the award to him and to his colleague Sepoy Azam Khan had been cancelled.

Mast was taken by the Germans to Lille where he was interrogated. To prove his credibility, he drew a map of Afghanistan for the Germans showing them the number and dispensation of the British and Indian troops along the Khyber Pass, the main corridor between India and Afghanistan.[10] From Lille, Mast and his other Pathan colleagues were transported to the Half Moon Camp for Prisoners of War in Zossen outside Berlin. The camp, which had a purpose-built mosque, had become the base for a grand German plan to build a small army of jihadi warriors to take on the Allies. The jihadis would be plucked from the Muslim PoWs from India and Africa in the camp. Mast – who had already proved himself a brave warrior – was recruited for a daring mission to Afghanistan. The purpose of the expedition would be to persuade the Emir to switch sides and join the Germans against the British. Getting the British out of India had always been one of the prime wartime aims of Kaiser Wilhelm II. In July 1914 he had stated: 'If we are going to shed our blood, England must at least lose India.' Mast is rumoured to have been presented with the Iron Cross by the Kaiser.

Wearing the uniform of the Turkish army, trading his regimental conical kullah headgear for a fez, he joined the delegation comprising German and Turkish diplomats and volunteers from the Half Moon Camp. His local knowledge of the frontier was considered invaluable for the Germans. The group started out from Berlin and went through Turkey to Baghdad, then through the mountains of Persia to Afghanistan reaching their final destination, Kabul, in May 1915. More than half of the group died of exhaustion along the way. But Mast survived, his sole mission at this time to get back home. In Kabul, the Emir was not swayed, preferring to stay with the British. The Germans and Turks were disappointed. Mast cared little for the outcome. The British secret file on deserters noted that Jemadar Mir Mast, along with two other colleagues, had been part of a 'Turco-German mission to Afghanistan and reported to have returned to their homes in Tirah in June 1915.'[11] His main aim had been fulfilled.

Mir Mast's trench notebook lies in the National Archives in Delhi in an envelope marked 'His Majesty's Office'.[12] Along with maps and sketches it contains a list of English words with the Urdu meanings next to them. The words – a seemingly random collection – paint a picture of an Afridi from the North West Frontier trying to cope with the alien world of the Western Front. Military words like 'retreat' and 'retire' sit next to everyday words like 'haversack' and 'blanket'. The word 'please' is listed; Mir Mast clearly keen to learn British politeness. Mir Mast's Urdu-English phrasebook also lists words like 'newspaper', 'university' and 'pronounciation' (sic). Was the Pathan, whose English handwriting was reasonably good, thinking of his education? Was he trying to improve his English? The fact that he was clearly missing his family is reflected in words like 'nephew' and 'honeymoon', an untold story about which we can only speculate. The word 'hungry' appears on his list. How often would he have needed to say this? The notebook also reveals another side to life in the trenches. Mir Mast listed words like 'testacles' (sic), and 'brest' (sic). Why would he have needed to learn these? The notebook does not provide answers. The words hang like pieces of a jigsaw puzzle that contain within it the life of Mir Mast in his first winter in the trenches. But connect the dots and you get a glimpse into the world that led a brave Pathan, who set out to do his best, to reach breaking point.

Mir Mast was not alone in his desperation. Demoralised British soldiers also gave up and walked away: 346 of them were shot at dawn for desertion, cowardice, sleeping at their post or casting away their arms between 1914 and 1918.[13]

Back in India, the Viceroy took a lenient view on the reason for the desertion of the Afridis under Mir Mast. 'I cannot help thinking that it was simply that they could not endure the dog's life. And they thought it preferable to surrender and enjoy a quiet life as a prisoner of war,' he wrote to Willcocks.[14] 'I cannot help think that "cold feet" was the cause of that somewhat discredited incident.'

In the cold trenches in Neuve Chapelle, Mir Dast heard about his brother's desertion. He felt Mir Mast had disgraced his regiment but at the same time he was worried about him. What had prompted him to take such a step? Why had he not tried to contact his brother and take his advice? He pictured his brother with the Germans and hoped they treated him well. Mir Dast knew it would fall on him to save the family honour. He knew he would have to do something extraordinary.

Three days after the battle of Neuve Chapelle, work continued on the frontline. The weather was slowly improving, allowing for the trenches to be dug down to about three feet. The trenches were deeper now and provided more protection unlike the shallow ones of the first winter. General Willcocks felt the Indians were now 'thoroughly blooded' and enthusiastic after their successful campaign. The new arrivals, instead of hearing only of the damp, horrible trenches, heard the tale of how their brethren charged and won. The victory at Neuve Chapelle had made an extraordinary difference to the appearance and demeanour of the Indian soldiers.

However, Willcocks also felt that it would not be right, despite their bravery, to keep the Indians in Europe indefinitely, should the war drag on for another winter. The General thought it important that some healthy soldiers go back to tell the tale and inspire others, rather than only the injured returning from the battlefield. He told the Viceroy that when he had met the soldiers of the 1/39th Garhwalis – his 'best battalion' – on the third day of the fighting at Neuve Chapelle, and praised them for their valour and endurance, they had said, 'We have done our duty as your own, and only sixty of us original Garhwalis remain (this was true). When will you allow us to see India again? We should love to see home whilst still unwounded and well.'[15]

The Indian soldier had told Willcocks, "If we could see home again, we would be ready to return and fight hard for the *Sarkar.*"

The General made a final plea to the Viceroy: 'These were no laggards, but our very bravest and best… They see British soldiers go home and return and do not realise the distances of their own homes. The policy of "they have enlisted and must stay till the end" does not appeal to me, but I do not know how YE looks at it.'

The General's wishes about sending the soldiers on leave, however, fell on deaf ears. Most of the Indian troops stayed for the whole duration of the war, with some of the sappers and miners even remaining after the war to clear the fields. They watched their British counterparts go home on holiday but were told that the journey for them was too long and expensive and that they could not be spared. It was March 1915. The end of the war was still a long way away.

9

Clouds

In the weeks following the Battle of Neuve Chapelle, Jemadar Mir Dast nursed a heavy heart. The desertion of his brother, Mir Mast, had cast a shadow over him. Mir Dast had been a soldier for most of his adult life and was proud of his Afridi heritage and achivements. Born in December 1874 in Maidan, Tirah, in the North West Frontier Province, he had enlisted in the 1st Punjab Infantry at the age of twenty. In 1908 Mir Dast had displayed conspicuous gallantry in the Mohmand expeditions and was promoted to the rank of Jemadar, the junior-most Indian commissioned rank. Since arriving on the Western Front, his regiment, 57th Wilde's, had been holding the line in France till Christmas and he had played a minor role in the Battle of Neuve Chapelle. As he worked in the trenches over the next few weeks, the forty-year-old thought of his family in Peshawar and wondered whether he would see them again. Would he ever be able to return to his village with his head held high?

In the early spring of 1915, Hill 60 was playing a crucial role on the Western Front. It wasn't really a hill at all but a mound of earth excavated and dumped when the Ypres-Lille Railway was being constructed. Two hillocks were on the west side – a long irregular mound on the ridge called 'The Caterpillar' and a smaller mound down the slope towards Zillebeke, known as 'The Dump'. On the East side on the highest point of the ridge, was a third mound known as 'Hill 60'. The Germans had occupied it in December 1914 and it had provided them a vantage point for observing the area around Zillebeke and Ypres. On the night of 17 April 1915, the

Allied Forces exploded seven mines below Hill 60 taking several German casualties and occupying the Hill. For the next few weeks the struggle for possession of the Hill continued. According to the regimental diaries, the Second Battle of Ypres officially began on the evening of 22 April around 5.00 p.m. when the Germans attacked a French Colonial Division with a terrific bombardment. It was the day the Germans made their first gas attack in the trenches.

The French soldiers were holding the line from Steenstraat to the East of Langemarck. It was to all effect a 'glorious spring day'[1]. Suddenly the nozzles of what looked like fire hoses appeared over the German parapet and thick yellow smoke started coming out of the trenches. At first the French colonials, mostly from Algeria, did not quite comprehend what it was. Within minutes the North-Easterly breeze had started blowing the smoke down the French line and the impact was lethal and immediate. Hundreds of men started writhing in pain from the poisonous fumes of the chlorine gas, going blue in the face, choking and retching. Within an hour the position was abandoned by the French colonials who had faced the gas without any protection. As they lay suffocating, the Germans swept over the French trenches and bayoneted them.

The retirement of the French led to confusion, opening up gaps in the defence. Over the next few days the situation East of the Ypres canal became critical for the British forces. There was the danger that Ypres might fall to a German follow-up assault. Determined to check the German advance, Sir John French felt compelled to bring up the Lahore Division from the South and send them straight into the battle.

On 24 April, still exhausted from the Battle of Neuve Chapelle, the Lahore division set off for Ypres. They marched thirty miles North without a break on rough, cratered roads carrying loads of nearly 50 kg on their back, arriving at La Manche on the Belgian border at midnight. Barely had they prepared for a night halt when they were asked to march nine miles further to Ouderdom. Most had not eaten since breakfast the previous morning and none of them had had any sleep. Some were limping from the strain. By mid morning next day the entire Division was in place. Soon they would be facing heavy German bombardment and another gas attack.

Marching with his regiment, the 57th Wildes, was Mir Dast. Drained but determined, he carried on. It had been barely a month since his brother had defected to the Germans. The family honour rested on Mir Dast's weary shoulders.

The situation in Ypres was grim. All the roads leading to it were under heavy artillery fire and there was confusion everywhere. There were parties of men, with and without officers, in bits of trench or ditches. A heavy haze of smoke and gas lay over the battlefield. The birds had dropped dead. Even the giant rats in the trenches had succumbed. The smoke made it difficult for the soldiers to read the maps.

On 26 April 1915 the Lahore division was ordered to counterattack in conjunction with the French. The infantry attack began at 2 p.m. Mir Dast was in the centre of the Ferozepore Brigade's front-line, with the Connaught Rangers on their left, and the 129th Baluchis to their right. The Indian soldiers had suffered heavy losses from German shells and machine-gun fire. Undeterred, Mir Dast carried on with a few men, taking cover behind farm buildings. Soon they were able to creep to within 40 or 60 yards of the German trenches.

At about 2.20 p.m. the Germans launched their second gas attack. The thick yellow smoke blew South-West in the wind and covered the left of the Lahore Division. The men had no gas masks, but being warned of what to expect, dipped the ends of their turbans in chloride of lime, tied them over their mouths and kept their faces pressed against the parapet. They were even asked to urinate on the turbans first if possible. The improvised measure offered little protection. Within minutes the ground was covered with bodies of men writhing in pain, their eyes protruding, eventually dying of asphyxiation. The Germans followed the gas attack with an infantry charge.

His mouth and face wrapped with his turban, Mir Dast had passed out briefly under the effect of the gas. As he began recovering, he rallied a small group of survivors. Although wounded, he held on until nightfall, when he was ordered to retire. As he withdrew he led to safety some other men, whom he had found taking shelter in old trenches and kept them under his command. There were no British officers left at this time. After dark, he risked his life once again. Despite heavy firing, Mir Dast went out in the open and helped to carry back eight injured

British and Indian officers who would otherwise have died. While doing so he was wounded for a second time.

For his extraordinary courage Mir Dast was awarded the Victoria Cross becoming the fourth Indian to be recommended for this honour and the second Pathan after Khudadad Khan. His award was announced on 29 June in the *London Gazette*. He was also promoted to the rank of Subedar. Mir Dast was shifted to the Pavilion hospital in Brighton where he received the award from the King in August 1915.

The gas attack on the Allies had been deadly. French, British and Indian troops streamed back, many of the men reaching La Brique. Only a small band held on, about fifty men of the Manchesters, a few from the 40th Pathans, 47th Sikhs, 129th Baluchis and 57th Rifles.

Describing the event later, a soldier wrote: 'It was cold and damp with a sharp wind blowing, rain clouds in the sky and rain coming down, our boots in a fearful state with the awful mud, and our fingers shrivelled up with the intense cold... Corpses were lying in front as they fell, in their uniform and boots, with their rifles in hand, as in the act of assault… If anyone had been in the kneeling position, he remained exactly as he had been. No one went to raise them up. In the air aeroplanes were flying and throwing down bombs… If the wind blows from the front, the enemy discharge the fumes of gas which asphyxiates men, but we tie bandages over our faces and so protect ourselves...'[2]

The German bombardment carried on turning Ypres into a city of the dead. The sound of the German projectiles hurtling through the air sounded to the Allied troops like an express train and they were soon named 'the Wipers Express'. The smell of the gas on a clear night could be felt as far as Popperinghe, seven miles from Ypres. During the course of the Second Battle of Ypres which lasted till 1 May, the bodies of two Indians were seen suspended by the neck, hanging from a tree near the German lines, an outrage that was added to the list of German crimes. Despite being under heavy fire and gas attack, the safety of Ypres was secured and on 3rd May the Lahore Division proceeded to rejoin the Indian Corps, having taken part in two major battles of the war within two months. Total casualties of all ranks including British and Indian officers amounted to 18,573. Sir Herbert Plumber commanding the division, wrote to General Keary saying he 'deeply regretted the very heavy casualties they have suffered.'[3] Special praise was reserved for the 47th Sikhs, the 57th Rifles and the 40th Pathans though all brigades were praised for their contribution.

'Please convey to all ranks of Division my own and all their other comrades' best congratulations on having taken part on the battle near Ypres. We are proud of you all. Well done,' said General Willcocks. The Lahore division had lost 3,888 of its 15,980 men, killed, wounded, or missing in the Second Battle of Ypres. There was to be no rest for them. Two days later they had to relieve the Meerut Division in the trenches.

Meanwhile in France, the lesson of Neuve Chapelle had been learned and detailed instructions were now issued for quick arrival of reserves, as delay could prove fatal. On 18 April (before the Lahore Division were ordered to march to Ypres), secret orders were issued by General Willcocks for the operation of the Indian Corps. The Meerut Division would attack the front of 600 yards reinforced by the artillery of the Lahore Division. The object would be to capture the Ferme du Biez and eventually advance on La Cliqueterie Farm.

On 4 May a heavy thunderstorm during the night converted the trenches into quagmires and thick mist led to further postponement of the advance of the 1st Army. Finally on 9 May the morning broke fine and clear and the Dehradun Brigade prepared for the assault. It was not an easy task. The Germans had bombarded the trenches beyond recognition.

Merewether and Smith recorded: 'It was a most pathetic sight to watch the poor remnants of this magnificent battalion, before the action over 1100 strong with 26 officers, returning to billets a mere skeleton, with a solitary piper marching at its head.'[4]

On the night of 18 May the battalion found the trenches in a shocking condition: 104 corpses and wounded were still lying there; mangled remains were trodden into the deep mud at the bottom of the trenches and it was not till some days later that they could be extricated. The Battle of Festubert in May ended with heavy casualties.

According to Merewether and Smith, the Indian Corps had failed not because of any fault of theirs, but because the Germans were in a far stronger position. The defeat, after the glory of Neuve Chapelle and Ypres, was hard to take. The Allied forces had gained only 600 yards. The total casualties including dead and wounded of all ranks was almost 26,000.

On 22 June when General Willcocks visited the trenches South East of Neuve Chapelle, he was informed that Naik Ayub Khan of the 129th Baluchis had gone missing. He had been ordered to go on a patrol and was last seen near the German trenches. Naik Ayub Khan was a courageous soldier and his colleagues would not accept the theory that he could have defected. They wanted to go out and search for him, but were dissuaded as it was too dangerous. Two nights later Ayub Khan returned. He had an adventure to relate.

The plucky soldier had decided to enter the enemy trench and pick up information at the risk of his life. Standing near the wire, he held up both hands and said 'Mussalman'. The Germans appeared over the parapet and after some speculation allowed Ayub Khan to enter the trench. As they conducted him through the trench to the Bois de Biez and further to the divisional headquarters at Marquillies, Khan made mental notes of all provisions and facilities, even noting the shoulder strap numbers of the German soldiers. In Marquilles he was met by the General and an officer who spoke poor Hindustani. He was asked about the troops, particularly the 69th and 89th Punjabis, who had recently arrived. Khan cleverly provided correct answers to unimportant questions and gave incorrect information when it mattered.

Giving the impression that Muslims were upset about fighting against Turkey, Khan gave the Germans to understand that a large number of Indian soldiers were prepared to defect. The Germans believed him. They thought that Khan would – like Mir Mast before him – return with twenty men, and offered him 400 Marks as an incentive. Khan feigned greed and readily accepted. He remained in the headquarters through the night and was well fed and cared for as the Germans tried to prove that they looked kindly on Indians. On the night of 23 June he was taken in a motor car to Bois de Biez, and then back through the trenches to the spot where he had originally entered. Not certain of his fate till the last minute, his life still hanging by a thread, Khan finally escaped the German lines.

Back in the Allied trenches, he gave a detailed account of the German enforcements, listing ammunition dumps and supply routes and reported that there were no gas cylinders in trenches near the Bois du Biez, information which was crucial. In order to deceive the Germans, the Allies put up a notice announcing Ayub Khan had been shot for being a traitor. Whether the Germans believed the story or not was never discovered. For his bravery and intelligence, Ayub Khan was promoted to Jemadar and awarded the 2nd Class of the Indian Order of Merit.

As the summer progressed, the soldiers continued work in the trenches. In July, Willcocks asked Field Marshal French to allow the Muslims to carry on their fast of Ramadan in the frontline, while doing re-organisational work. The request was granted. It was to be the last thing Willcocks did for the Indians.

On 3 September 1915, while attending a meeting of the First Army Corps in a chateau at Hinges, Willcocks was abruptly and unceremoniously sacked by Sir Douglas Haig, commander of the First Army. Only a few weeks before, he had been honoured with the GCMG by the King, and praised for his work with the Indian Corps. It was a terrible blow to both Willcocks and his beloved Indian Corps. He had not dreamed that he would not be with his men till the end of the war. 'I had gone to the Conference in high spirits,' he wrote in his memoirs. 'I was leaving it, little caring whither I went. I should have to depart before even I could shake the hand of many brave Indians, officers and men, my lifelong friends. I felt I must perforce go without saying a word, lest any spark of ill feeling should be revealed.'[5] Willcocks never revealed the details of the sacking or the full extent of his feelings. It seems Haig considered him to be lacking in 'initiative and tactical skill'.[6]

Lord Kitchener saw him a few days later in London and said he had asked for the official report. However, Kitchener died in June 1916 when his ship *HMS Hampshire* was struck by a German mine West of the Orkney Islands in Scotland while he was making his way to Russia.

'Had Lord Kitchener lived, I think I may safely say I should not have been cast on the scrap heap; with his death vanished the last hope of re-employment in the war, and what other employment was worth having?' wrote Willcocks. He remained faithful to the Indian Corps and chose to return to India in 1922 after retiring as Governor of Bermuda. He died in Bharatpur in 1926 and was given a full state funeral with elephants and soldiers in procession presided over by his friend, the Maharaja of Bharatpur. Willcocks was cremated on a sandalwood pyre according to Hindu custom and a memorial was erected over his ashes to honour and remember the General who was devoted to his Indian troops.

James Willcocks was replaced by Lt General Sir Charles Anderson, who had spent long years in India and knew the sepoys well. He would lead the Indian Corps in the Battle of Loos. It was the battle in which the British decided to use poison gas against the Germans. Unknown to the Germans, the British transported around 160 cylinders to the firing line. Full orders were given on 20 September. Every soldier now wore a balaclava and had two smoke helmets, one in the haversack and one on the top of his head. During the day of the 24th the wind had been blowing in the direction of the German trenches, but by night the direction had changed. At 4.40 a.m. the German shells burst on the gas cylinders, sending the smoke billowing, incapacitating several soldiers instantly. The remaining soldiers quickly put on their gas masks preventing further damage. But worse was to come. The Royal Engineers had not been given any discretionary powers about whether to turn the taps on. Despite the wind having changed direction, and blowing now towards the Indian trenches, they turned on the tap. It took some time before the cylinders could be turned off, but by then there was smoke everywhere. Merewether and Smith concluded that the gas attack was a failure on the Indian Corps front 'causing no inconvenience to the enemy and very seriously interfering with the movements of our troops'.[7]

A dense cloud of smoke hung over the German trenches for days. On 24 September rain and mist added to the problem. The infantry assault which began under these circumstances was to prove costly. The barbed wire before the trenches had to be cut under heavy firing. Grenades, machine guns, trench mortars rained down on the soldiers as they tried to push through. Many soldiers and officers of the 2/3rd Gurkhas were killed before they could even penetrate the wire. Those who managed to get through to the German trench faced an equally grim end. All of them were killed except for one soldier, Rifleman Kulbir Thapa of the 2nd Battalion, 3rd Gurkha Rifles.

Thapa had barely entered the German trench when he saw a badly wounded soldier of the 2nd Leicesters. The wounded soldier begged Thapa to leave him and save himself, but the Gurkha refused to do so. He stayed with the soldier all day and night comforting him and shooting any German who approached them. On the morning of 26 September, Thapa carried the wounded soldier through the trench and barbed wire fencing and put him in a shell hole where he could be under cover. He then returned to the enemy trench and found two wounded Gurkhas of his own regiment. He picked up one of the Gurkhas and carried him back to the 39th Garhwalis, who were further back. Then he returned for the second. By now it was broad daylight. Despite being under fire, Thapa returned to the German trench and brought back the 2nd Leicester to the Allied trenches. For his selfless act of bravery towards his wounded colleagues, Thapa was awarded the Victoria Cross. Kulbir Thapa survived his injuries, went to Egypt with his regiment, and eventually returned to Nepal. He died at the age of sixty-eight in Nepal on 3 October 1958. Like many other Gurkhas he had added a few years to his age in order to sign up and had joined the army very young. He had been no more than twenty when he had arrived in France.

The Battle of Loos was one of the major operations undertaken by the Indian Corps on the Western Front. The battle would carry on for a fortnight, but no further gains were made. The Indian Corps remained in the same position they had been in since arriving in France: the line stretched for six-and-a-half miles from North of Neuve Chapelle to the La Bassee canal. The casualties were high, most battalions reduced to fewer than a hundred. Hardly any of the original officers remained. The 47th Sikhs had only twenty-eight sepoys left. There were no British or Indian officers. The 39th Garhwalis had lost all their officers and were down to sixty. Scinde Rifles had only seventy-five sepoys and four Indian officers.

The Indian Corps were soon to face the second winter in the trenches. A signaller in France wrote to a Dafadar in Gurmukhi: 'On the 19th of November I began writing a letter and found that the ink was frozen in the inkstand. I broke the inkpot, took out the ice, melted it over a fire and wrote the letter to you…'[8]

The remainder of the Indian Corps were now told that they would be moved to the other theatres of the war – The Middle East, Gallipoli and Africa. Only the cavalry would remain, along with the Sappers and Miners. The cavalry would remain in the Western Front till 1918; the Sappers would still be there in 1919, clearing the mines after the war.

In a prisoner of war camp in Germany, a group of Indian soldiers sat huddled in a room watched over by German soldiers. One by one they were led to a strange machine, asked to put their heads close to it and speak or sing into it. Terrified, they followed orders, observed by German scientists. The prisoners were in the Halfmoon Camp in Wunsdorf, near Berlin in Germany. The gathering of prisoners of different countries and ethnicities had sparked an idea in German linguist and sound pioneer Wilhelm Doegen, who felt that it was an opportunity to record the different voices of the people as an academic study. He convinced other linguists, musicologists and anthropologists, and soon thirty scientists from the Royal Prussian Phonographic Commission (RPPC) began recording the 'voice museum of all people' in the prison camps. Between December 1915 and 1918, Doegen and his team made 1,650 wax records in the wooden barracks. The frightened Indians stood with their heads near the large funnel of a gramophone and anxiously spoke into it. They spoke of legends, folktales, religious texts, ghosts, but most of all they spoke about their longing to go home.

Through the crackling sound of the Shellac recording, the high-pitched voice of Mall Singh speaking in Punjabi could be heard. He spoke of himself in the third person and said:

> There was once a man.
> He ate one *ser* of butter in India. He drank two *ser* of milk.
> This man then came into the European war
> Germany captured this man
> He wishes to return to India.

He will get the same food as in former times.
If this man has to stay here for another two years – he will die.
If God has mercy, he will make peace soon.
This man wishes to go away from here.

'*Hindustan mein khana milega* [He will get food in Hindustan]', wailed Mall Singh into the machine. '*Hindustan jayega* [He will go to Hindustan]', he ended, his voice filled with desperation.[9] Mall Singh made the recording on 11 December 1916, his second winter in the war. Born in 1892 in Ranasukhi in Ferozepore in Punjab, he went to Regimental School, Naushera in Peshawar, and was only 24 when he was incarcerated in the prison camp in Germany.

'I do not wish to live in Europe. Please reach me to India,'[10] pleaded Jasbahadur Rai, a 23-year-old Gurkha soldier. Rai did not make it back to his country. He died shortly after he made the recording on 6 June 1916.

Bhawan Singh, a prisoner who spoke Khas, Hindustani and English and had even learnt some German, believed in ghosts and claimed to have seen the ghosts of his dead comrades strolling up and down the training ground in the moonlight. On December 8, 1916 he recorded, 'When a person dies, he constantly roams about as a ghost. It is the soul that roams about. The roaming soul is like air. So a ghost is like air. It can go everywhere.'

The recordings housed in the Sound Archive at the Humboldt University in Berlin bring to life the desolation of the prisoners in the war camp. Two thousand Indian soldiers were detained in Halfmoon Camp and 700 recordings made. The uncensored voices of the Indian prisoners of war recorded for academic study is testament to the loneliness and isolation they felt in an alien land.

In the summer of 1916 General Douglas Haig decided to amass over one million soldiers in the Somme for a major onslaught on the German lines. The Indian Cavalry would bear the brunt of the operation. On 1 July 1916, the first day of the Battle of Somme, it was on Haig's orders that 110,000 British infantrymen went 'over the top' climbing out of the trenches for what they had been told would be a walkover. It was a moment frozen in time, as the soldiers, many of them barely in their twenties, faced a terrifying barrage of heavy German artillery that blew them to bits, dotting their bodies around the fields and farmlands of the French countryside. The Indian Cavalry, Sappers and Miners were also in the thick of the battle. They were photographed on the first day sitting on their horses, doffing their helmets and smiling for the cameras, confident of victory. Nearly all were blown to bits by the German shells. In the first few hours alone British troops took nearly 60,000 casualties with 20,000 dead. Tens of thousands more would die from their wounds or never be found, their bodies slowly rotting in the trenches and in the treacherous barbed wires of no man's land. Despite the casualties, General Douglas Haig ordered the action to continue. The action earned him the name of the 'Butcher of the Somme'. Never had such a beautiful summer day seen so many dead.

By October, the weather had changed and torrential rains turned the battlegrounds into a sea of mud. 'It is certainly very cold here and you cannot keep warm with two or even three pairs of socks on,' a Muslim soldier wrote to his Hindu friend in Farrukhabad. 'Even two pairs of gloves will not keep you warm. …At first Nabi Alam, Tufail Ahmad and I went to one trench in which there was about 3 foot [sic] of water; we sat in dirty water for 24 hours; our hands and feet swelled. Many people are taken from here to hospital in motors. Any number of people had their feet amputated.'[11]

By mid-November the Battle of the Somme was over. The Allies had advanced only six miles. The British suffered around 420,000 casualties, the French 195,000 and the Germans around 650,000. The total number of dead was 1.3 million. Though the newspapers of the day carried the list of the dead for months, few remembered the Indian cavalrymen and their horses fallen in the battle.

While the Indian soldiers fought in the trenches, flying above them in the skies was a young Sikh pilot, dodging German planes. He was twenty-five year old Hardit Singh Malik, the first Indian to join the Royal Flying Corps.

It had been a tough fight for him to get to the skies. Malik had not been allowed to join the war effort in 1914 when he was in his second year at Balliol College, Oxford, and had watched in dismay as all his colleagues left for the frontline. But he was not one to give up. After graduating from Oxford in 1915 he got his chance. With the help of his tutor, Sligger Urquhart, Malik received an offer from the wife of the French Military Attache in London to join the French Red Cross as an officer ambulance driver. The determined young Sikh immediately took driving lessons, improved his French and set off for France at the wheel of an ambulance that he was instructed to deliver there. Driving through the picturesque countryside of Normandy and Chateaux, Malik finally reported at the Hopital Auxilaire No. 5 in Cognac in central France, where seeing him in turban and beard, the staff thought he was an Indian prince.[12]

But Malik was soon frustrated at being just an ambulance driver. It was planes that he dreamt of flying. He asked his French friends in Cognac if he could join the French Air Force and found that they were open to the idea. When Malik wrote to his tutor about this, Urquhart was outraged. He immediately went to see General Henderson, Commander of the Royal Flying Corps (RFC) and told him that it was 'scandalous' that although Malik was a British subject, the British Armed Forces had no time for him whilst the French were willing to enlist him. The protest had immediate effect. Malik was asked to call on the General on his next visit to London. In 1917, after a personal interview with General Henderson, Malik bid adieu to Cognac (and the brandy that he had developed a taste for) and his colleagues at the French Red Cross. He joined the RFC as a cadet at Aldershot in Hampshire, becoming the first Indian pilot in the forces.

Hardit Singh Malik nearly lost his job on his first day. He appeared on parade duty, wearing his turban, which he had dyed a khaki colour. 'Why aren't you in uniform?' roared his Sergeant Major, 'Where's your hat?'[13] Malik explained that as a Sikh he had to wear a turban and an argument ensued. Finally, the Adjutant intervened and said he would refer the matter to the Commanding Officer. Malik was allowed to keep his turban. As the first Sikh in the RFC, he was in a unique position. Eventually Malik wore a specially designed helmet over his turban, earning himself the nickname of 'flying hobgoblin'.[14]

Malik was a natural. After ground training at Aldershot and Reading, he was sent to a flying school in Vendome in France where he flew his first 'solo' after only three hours instruction. Soon he was posted to Filton, near Bristol, and flew the Avro 504, the Royal Aircraft Factory B.E.2, the Sopwith Pup, the Bristol Scout, the Neiuport and finally the Sopwith Camel, which was considered the most advanced fighter of all time.[15] He got his wings in under a month and was posted to Yatesbury in Wiltshire with No. 28 Squadron. In 1917, Malik finally left for the frontline, flying his Sopwith Camel in a formation to St Omer in France, and then to an airfield in Flanders near the village of Droglandt to join the No. 8 Naval Squadron. Here, living in wooden Nissen huts, sharing with three other officers, Malik prepared for the job he had dreamt of doing. His Flight Commander was a Canadian, Billy Barker, who would later be awarded the Victoria Cross. Barker had joined the RFC in 1916 and become a legend, flying two-seaters and fighters. Seeing a spark in the young Sikh, Barker personally trained Malik in the art of aerial combat.

The first day he took Malik over the German lines, the young Sikh realised how close it could get. Almost immediately after they had entered enemy territory, Barker signalled to Malik and asked him to look back. Malik saw that a number of German planes were diving at them. Fortunately they targeted the more experienced Barker, and Malik watched as Barker immediately did a climbing turn. As the German plane continued to dive, Barker's plane gained height. Within seconds Barker had the vantage position and he fired on the German plane and shot it down. It was a practical lesson for Malik in actual combat.

The young Sikh was quick to learn. Proudly flying his plane, with 'India' painted on its side, Malik shot down his first German Fokker and had a remarkable eight aerial victories. He even went into action against the legendary German flying ace, Manfred von Richthofen, known as the 'Red Baron', who was credited with over eighty air-combat victories. At the Battle of Passchendaele in November 1917, when many pilots lost their lives, Malik survived and managed to bring down some German planes.

Barker was always looking for action, and often got impatient when they were grounded in bad weather. On one such cloudy day in November 1917, Barker decided to fly out to compass the German airfields, taking

Malik and two other pilots with him. After fifteen minutes they flew into a gap in the clouds only to discover that there were about a dozen German aircrafts in the same space. Almost immediately a dogfight ensued. As Malik tried to turn his aircraft back, the Germans fired continuously at him, a bullet hitting him, piercing his right leg. As he fired back at the Germans surrounding him, Malik smelled petrol. A German bullet had gone into the fuel tank beneath his seat. There was a real danger that his plane could explode. Malik saw that Barker was also in a struggle surrounded by German fighters. As Barker disappeared into the clouds, Malik knew that he had to somehow get back. He had only a small amount of fuel in his reserve tank, his leg was bleeding profusely and he was forty miles away from the RFC base. With four German aircraft firing continuously at him, a bullet in his leg and a fuel tank on reserve, Malik managed to fly back to base and landed his plane with an adrenalin-fired yell of victory. His colleagues pulled him out of the aircraft. His plane had been hit by 400 bullets but he had survived. 'Miraculously, they didn't hit me again and they never got a vital part of the plane,'[16] said Malik. Barker had also survived and the two were united once again in hospital.

After recovering, Malik took to the air again in December and was sent to Northern Italy, where he developed an allergy to castor oil. Recommended that he fly stationary engines that did not use castor oil, he was posted to No. 141 Squadron at Biggin Hill near London, a specialist unit that was defending London against the Zeppelins and Botha bombers. The dapper and charming Malik became one of the most popular officers at Biggin Hill where he flew the Bristol Fighter.[17] He remained on duty till the end of the war returning to France with No. 11 Squadron stationed at Bapaume and finally Nivelles near Brussels where he received the news of the armistice.

Hardit Singh Malik had cleared the way for other Indians to join the RFC. Impatiently waiting to finish school in London was Indra Lal 'Laddie' Roy. His brother, Poresh Lal, had joined the Honorary Artillery Company, bidding farewell to his mother, Lolita, and his five siblings, and leaving the house in Kensington for service in France. Laddie was impatiently waiting for his break. Even while he was in school, Laddie wrote to the War Office sending a drawing of a trench mortar that he had designed complete with notes about its advantages, which included 'rapidity of firing'.[18] He had won a scholarship to Oxford with the purpose of eventually taking the ICS examinations, but the bright teenager, who had a passion for speed and loved sports cars, had only one dream: flying a fighter aircraft. Laddie applied to the Royal Flying Corps but was rejected by the military optician on grounds of 'defective' eyesight. So determined was he to become a pilot that he sold his motorbike and paid for an alternative opinion from one of the country's leading eye specialists. Laddie cleared the eye test, the decision was overturned,and on 4 April 1917, joined the Royal Flying Corps.[19] Lolita said goodbye to her second son. She was proud to be sending two sons to the front, doing her bit like all the other mothers in England, but she could not help her tears as the young boy left.

In less than two weeks Laddie joined as a cadet and began training at Farnborough and then Oxford and Winchester.[20] By July 1917, the eighteen-year-old was commissioned as a Second Lieutenant and posted to Vendome with No. 56 Squadron. Laddie's ready smile, his youthful cockiness and verve had already made him popular. His only ambition was to knock the German fighter planes out of the skies. He was soon proudly flying the Curtiss, the Royal Aircraft Factory B.E.2, the Sopwith Camel, the Avro and the SE.5A, whirling in the skies doing daring loops and manoeuvres far beyond his age and experience.

On 6 December 1917, while on a flight over France on his SE.5A, Laddie's plane was shot down by a German fighter and crashed in no man's land. He was taken to the local hospital where he was left for dead. But the young Bengali regained consciousness, banged on the door of the morgue and woke up the terrified hospital staff calling out in his school-boy French. He was immediately sent back to Britain for treatment. While recovering, Laddie made numerous sketches, replacing his passion for sketching sports cars with that of drawing aircraft. Carefully titled and dated, his sketches included the De Havilland V and Sopwith Camel, planes he flew himself.[21]

Following his accident, Laddie was declared unfit to fly. He was told that he could only work as an equipment officer in Farnborough. But the young boy who had come back from the dead would not take 'no' for an answer. He watched the other officers take off on their planes and was determined to return to the skies. With all the stubbornness of a teenager, Laddie continued to pester his officers until they finally gave in. In June 1918 he cleared the medical test and joined No. 40 Squadron returning to France as temporary Lieutenant. This time he was determined to make his mark. Under the guidance of Captain George McElroy, Laddie trained hard and soon proved to be an excellent fighter pilot. On July 6 he brought down his first German plane over Arras in Northern France recording it in one of his sketches with the inscription: 'July 6, 1918. 5.45 a.m. N.E of Arras, Hannoveraner; 2-seater shot down by I.L.Roy'. Standing in the mess, cheered by his colleagues, Laddie was on top of the world. There was no stopping him after that. Between 9 July and 19 July, he knocked down nine German aircraft, becoming India's first flying ace in just over 170 hours of flying time. Flying his SE.5A No. B180, he shot down three German aircraft on 8 July and two each on the 13th and 15th.

On 22 July 1918, only four months before the end of the war, Laddie flew a daring sortie over the trenches in Carvin in France. Almost immediately his plane was attacked. Four German Fokker planes surrounded him and a hard battle followed. Not ready to be cornered, Laddie fought back bravely, taking down two German planes one after the other. But in the heat of combat, his plane was shot, bursting into flames and coming down over German-held territory. It was to be his final flight. Laddie was only nineteen. In the wreckage of the aircraft lay the body of a young boy from Bengal who had wanted to prove that Bengalis were good fighters. Even in his last battle, he had gone down in style, taking two enemy planes with him. Laddie was declared 'Missing in Action', and the news conveyed to his heartbroken mother in London.

Laddie's commanding officer wrote to Lolita: 'He went up on a patrol with three other fellows and they met four German aircraft. Two of these were seen to fall and one of our own, which was the machine your son was flying… From the time he came to the squadron, his one aim of life was to shoot down the Huns and through his skill as a pilot and wonderful dash, he succeeded in bringing down nine enemy machines. For the time he was here, that is a wonderfully fine record. I am sure he was very happy here; he was admired by all men and officers in the squadron and was very popular in the mess. I am sure he will be rewarded for the brave deeds he had done.'[22]

It was only in September 1918 that the RAF confirmed Indra Lal Roy's death and made it official. Three days later he was awarded the Distinguished Flying Cross for his bravery, becoming the first Indian to win the DFC. The citation read: 'A very gallant and determined officer, who in thirteen days accounted for nine enemy machines. In these several engagements he has displayed remarkable skill and daring, on more than one occasion accounting for two machines in one patrol.'

Flight magazine carried his obituary: 'He was one of a band of young Indians studying here who, precluded until recently from any chance of obtaining commissions in the Army, found scope for striking a blow for the Empire in the new arm of our forces.'[23]

Laddie's body was found and buried in Estevelles Communal Cemetery in France. His grave bears an inscription in French and Bengali. The Bengali words read: '*Maha birer Samadhi; sambhram dekhao, sparsha koro na* (A valiant warrior's grave; respect it, do not touch it.)'

10

Brighton

The injured soldiers from the Western Front were arriving in their thousands. The docks at Southampton were overflowing with a continuous stream of Indians, borne out of the ships on stretchers, many of them shell-shocked. Walter Lawrence, the 'Bandobust Sahib' had realised within the first few months of the war that more hospitals would be needed as the war looked likely to drag on. The special hospitals for them in Brockenhurst, Netley and New Milton were packed to full capacity. Patients were sleeping on mattresses on the floor in the Lady Hardinge Hospital in Brockenhurst and by 11 November 1914, there were over 1,000 wounded soldiers in the 500-bed hospital.

On 21 November Lawrence visited the seaside resort of Brighton looking to secure two hotels to be converted into hospitals. He met the Mayor of Brighton, John Otter, who made him a proposal. Instead of the two hotels, which were profitable businesses in the town, he offered Lawrence the York Place School, the Brighton Workhouse and, finally, the Royal Pavilion. The school was soon converted into a 550-bed military hospital while the Brighton Workhouse was transformed into the Kitchener General Indian Hospital with 1700 beds, and provision for 1,000 more in tents or huts if necessary. The Kitchener Hospital became the largest hospital for Indian soldiers in England. But it was the Royal Pavilion which would attract the most publicity.

The former Royal Palace with its oriental domes, opulent Chinoiserie interiors, and charming gardens set against the Brighton seafront was a perfect setting for recuperating soldiers. A delighted Lawrence telegraphed King George V to say he had procured the building. The King was equally pleased with the news. Originally built as a seaside holiday palace for the flamboyant Prince of Wales (later King George IV) between 1815 and 1822, Brighton Palace reflected the fascination of the time for all things exotic. With its India-inspired exterior and Chinese-influenced interiors, the Pavilion was Brighton's main tourist attraction. Queen Victoria, however, did not take a shine to it as the summer holiday crowds bustling along the pier and peering into the Pavilion gardens left her with little privacy. She bought Osborne House on the Isle of Wight, accessible only by ferry from the mainland, moved her summer retreat there, and, in 1850, sold the Pavilion to Brighton Council. Though it was no longer a Royal Palace, the War Office continued to propagate the myth that the King had personally given up his house for the Indian soldiers.

In the final week of November, the job of transforming the former Palace into a working hospital began. The opulent Ballroom, Music Room, South Drawing Room and Saloon filled up with over 700 bed-frames brought in by troops from the local Sussex Yeomanry. An army of surveyors and builders rolled up the carpets, took down the heavy curtains and pelmets, and lay down linoleum to create sanitary floors. The stone-flagged Georgian kitchen was converted into an operating theatre. Protective covers were erected over the paintings of peacocks and Chinese figures. Only the imposing chandeliers remained, hanging grandly over the beds of the soldiers, making the Pavilion one of the most exotic hospitals of the First World War. The neighbouring Dome and the Corn Exchange Buildings were also transformed into wards. The Dome, a 1500-seat theatre, was stripped of the chairs, the floor covered with khaki coloured linoleum and beds arranged in a radial pattern with a tropical foliage display embedded in the centre. The rooms upstairs were fitted out for the officers, and a mix of Indian and British Soldiers could be seen standing around the grand balcony, looking down at the hundreds of Indians lying on their beds with nurses and orderlies walking between them.

The arrangement ensured that the soldiers could follow their religious practices. There were separate taps for Hindus and Muslims along with separate milk churns and jugs. Nine field kitchens were set up to cook meals according to the religious requirements of the Hindus, Muslims and

Sikhs. A large tent on the ground was erected as a Sikh temple, another spot found for the Muslims to say their prayers facing Mecca. A temple tent for the Hindus was also provided. A butcher in town organised halal meat and the Indians' preference for goat over lamb was attended to. Segregated Indian-style bathrooms were also set up for the soldiers' comfort.

On December 14 the first train arrived with 112 patients, mostly seriously injured, who had to be carried out on stretchers. The second train had 233 soldiers on board. It was a cold wet winter day when the trains pulled into Brighton station, but people had gathered to give the Indians a warm welcome. Cheering crowds stood around as the soldiers were received by the Mayor and other town officials. It had been a long journey from the frontline. Many of the severely wounded died on the way as it took nearly four days to reach England. Alighting at the seaside town must have seemed almost bizarre, a world so different from the trenches and shelling. This was the soldiers' first view of the mother country. The *Brighton Gazette* reported the arrival:

> At last the wounded Indians are duly installed at Brighton. They arrived under rather mournful conditions. A drab day, rainstorms, and a fierce sea running in the Channel, mud-laden streets, and vista of dripping umbrellas and macintoshes. That was the first impression the warriors got of Brighton, and it was rather chilling.
>
> But crowds assembled to voice public welcome, and the reception undoubtedly cheered the brave fellows.

Two hundred of the soldiers were sent to the Pavilion and 145 to the York Place Hospital. Those admitted to the Royal Pavilion could not believe their eyes. In the Banquet Room, a fire-breathing dragon suspended from the ceiling seemed to be holding the giant chandelier in its claw. Dragons curled around the elaborately carved pillars and the walls were covered with Chinese paintings. In the Music Room, the soldiers lay under gilded lotus-shaped chandeliers. To the Indians it was a Chinese wonderland. One soldier thought he was in paradise and wrote home: 'If on Earth there is a paradise, it is this, it is this, it is this', borrowing the famous words of the poet Amir Khusro which the Mughal Emperor Shah Jahan had inscribed on the Diwan-e-Khas at the Red Fort.

A Sikh soldier from 59th Rifles wrote to his friend in India:

> Our hospital is in the place where the King used to have his throne. Every man is washed once in hot water. The King has given a strict order that no trouble be given to any black man in hospital. Men in hospital are tended like flowers and the King and Queen sometimes come to visit them.[1]

A letter written in January 1915 from a Subedar Major of the 6th Jats to a friend in India echoed the sentiment:

> Everything is such as one would not see even in a dream. One should regard it as fairyland...there is no other place like this in the world… A motor car comes to take us out. The King and Queen talked with us for a long time. I have never been so happy in my life as I am here.

The censor board realised the publicity potential of such letters and took full advantage. Nearly 120,000 postcards of the Indians in Brighton were sold locally during the war. Carefully constructed photographs were taken of Indian soldiers sitting in the grounds of the hospital playing cards, the domes of the Pavilion providing the exotic backdrop. Others showed them going for walks to the seaside. Photographs of the soldiers lying below the grand chandeliers in the Music Room were sold as postcards to tourists as propaganda for the war. Later a souvenir – *Royal Pavilion Brighton: A Description of it as a Hospital for Indian Soldiers* – was published in English, Gurmukhi and Urdu and nearly 20,000 copies shipped to India alone. The booklet was given to every Indian patient as they left the hospital. It had photographs of the grand buildings, the soldiers, the kitchens and the prayer rooms, to establish without a doubt that those recovering were being given the best treatment. To be treated by 'Dr Brighton' was common parlance among the Indian soldiers returning from the Pavilion Hospital.

King George V and Queen Mary also maximised the photo-opportunities the Pavilion Hospital provided. They visited the Brighton hospitals twice. Princess Mary and Queen Alexandra, the Queen Mother, were also among the royal visitors. The Queen Mother noticed a young Gurkha boy – no more than twelve – in the hospital and gave him a rose.

During her visit, one of the soldiers shouted out to her saying that the Sahib was his 'mai-baap' (mother-father). It showed the devotion and complete trust that some of the soldiers had in their British officers.

The War Office ensured that the Royal visits were reported extensively in the media and every impression was given that the King had himself opened up his palace to the Indians. In a letter to Walter Lawrence, Col J McLeod, the Commanding Officer of the Royal Pavilion, admitted: 'I tried to bring out that the Pavilion was a Royal Palace and that the initiation of all that was done came from the King. To bring the Corporation [Brighton officials] more prominently into it I thought would confuse things in the eyes of India.'

The sheer wonder felt by the King's visit is captured by a sepoy from the Sappers and Miners, who wrote from the Kitchener Indian Hospital in August 1915: 'The King and Queen have been here three times... Such a famous and great King came here and spoke as follows: "Well done, you soldiers of India, who have come here and rendered me so great assistance. You will recover and do your duty well again".'[2]

Visitors to the hospitals in Brighton also included Lord Kitchener, who spoke a few words in Hindustani to the soldiers, and Austen Chamberlain, the new Secretary of State for India. No effort was spared to keep the soldiers in good humour. Cigarettes were presented to them by the British generals as a symbol of the camaraderie in the field. The image of the soldiers standing in a queue, some with their arms in slings and others on crutches, waiting to receive the cigarettes, was captured by photographers and used for publicity purposes.

The military authorities running the hospital thought some music would help the soldiers to relax and sent out a letter to the organists of the town. The response was immediate and the Brighton and District Organists' Association and its energetic secretary, Seymour Pile, selected twenty-four performers. It was proposed that two musicians should play every day. This proved too much, and the recitals were rescheduled to twice a week and greatly enjoyed by the patients. The *Brighton and Hove Graphic* reported that the way 'in which the Sikhs beat time and asked for more, left no doubt as to the success of the experiment.'

Over the next few months the patients would also receive gramophone records of Indian music provided by the Comfort Committee. The voice of Gauhar Jaan, India's melody queen, would float across the room singing of love and parting as the soldiers listened with sadness and joy to music they could call their own. Hazrat Inayat Khan, the Sufi preacher and musician, performed for the Indian soldiers with his brothers and sang patriotic songs bringing tears to their eyes.[3] The soldiers were also visited by Princess Sophia Duleep Singh, daughter of Maharaja Duleep Singh, the last ruler of the Punjab. Her presence delighted the Indians, specially the Sikh soldiers and many asked for her autograph and wrote letters home about how Maharaja Ranjit Singh's granddaughter had spent time with them in the hospital. In 1915, determined to do more for her countrymen, Princess Sophia volunteered as a nurse and worked at the Lady Hardinge hospital in Brockenhurst, giving the soldiers signed photographs of herself and gifts of specially carved ivory shaving mirrors.[4]

The Indian Gift House was set up especially for the soldiers. The shop was started in December 1914 at the request of Colonel Neil Campbell who found the gifts at the hospitals too numerous to cope with. Soon a committee was set up by a group of formidable ladies with the Countess of Chichester as the President and Gertrude Brailey as the secretary.

Unable to work in the hospitals as there was not enough room, the ladies managed to secure a small house in North Road in Brighton. The rooms were fitted with shelves which quickly filled up. One room was for hospital requisites, two for clothing and the fourth for miscellaneous articles. The ground floor was used for receiving and unpacking parcels and a second room functioned as the committee room.

All the things were packed and marked in large hampers before being sent to the soldiers. The Indian Soldiers' Fund contributed to the Indian Gift House as well. The King and Queen sent a present of eight dozen mangoes for the officers, while Queen Alexandra, after her visit to the hospital, sent 2000 photographs of herself and the late King Edward VII. Flowers were sent by the Aryavarta Fund every Tuesday and the ladies of the committee made sure these were arranged in the hospitals. Everything from brahmanical threads and miniature Qurans to tooth powder and neem sticks were sent out to the soldiers from the Brighton store. If the soldiers had a sweet tooth, they would not be wanting: 5,898 lbs of boiled sweets were sent to them between 20 December 1914 and 20 January 1916 alone, along with 840 lbs of Indian sweets and 4,300 lbs of coconut candy. Jars of honey, jams, pickles and curries also arrived at the busy North Road address. The soldiers went through around 1,500 pencils, 1,500 pipes and 2000 bars of soap which were sent as gifts.[5]

Caste committees were appointed in each hospital to supervise religious observations. Muslims kept the fast of Ramazan. When it was pointed out to them that they need not fast as they were on a journey, they protested saying that they were not on a journey but honoured guests in their King's country and 'in their own King's Palace'[6] Sowar Abdul-Rehman, Ressalah No. 6, described the facilities for Ramzan at Brighton:

> The Mohamedans who keep fasts during the sacred month of Ramzan are kept in a separate ward. Every evening for the breaking of the fast, interesting arrangements are made. Every soldier is served two bananas, one pound of milk, sugar, one orange and other fruits which are produced in England. This is Iftari (the refreshment for breaking fast). Afterwards, supper is served which is comprised of meat, bread and rice. Every two persons are provided with a white Jai-Namaz (a white sheet of cloth to offer daily prayers upon).[7]

The Indians were taken for trips to London in an open-top mini bus, and many wrote of visiting Buckingham Palace, Madame Tussauds, the Tower of London, the British Museum and the Zoo. Passersby got a chance to see men in turbans and got to cheer the soldiers. An ecstatic Garhwali sepoy wrote to his family: 'I am here in England. The people are taking a great deal of trouble about teaching me, and are forcing me to learn. I go about in motor cars and see cities. The things which we used to hear about from our old Pandits, I have seen here with my own eyes, such as the sky carriages in which the gods used to go about. How can I tell you, too, of what I have seen being done under the Earth?'[8]

An Indian officer wrote to the court munshi in Karnal about his visit to the Tower of London and the Houses of Parliament: 'Inside the fort all the Royal crowns, diamonds, precious stones, pearls, rubies etc...in this country, on account of this war, the men and women are exceedingly fond of Indians. So, whenever I go out for a walk, because I am a foreigner, all these people recognise an Indian officer, and they are delighted whenever he speaks to them in English. They take us to their houses and entertain us kindly. There are many of them who have lived many years in India.'

The officer was taken to a house by a lady who had three sons and her husband at the war and a little girl ill in bed. 'She entertained me most cordially and made detailed enquiries about my family and sent her salaams to them all. She sends her best salaams and says "good morning" to you too,' said the officer.[9]

In Brighton, the Indians were a natural curiosity, and it was quite clear that the English women were drawn to them.

Another soldier wrote in Urdu: 'I had read about fairies in storybooks, but here I see them with my very eyes. Wherever I go, I see crowds of them. In this place the natives of Hindustan obtain great attention, but only those who wear turbans.'[10]

The most famous event at Brighton Pavilion was the day the King himself presented the soldiers with gallantry awards. Grainy footage showed the King pinning the Indian Order of Merit on Gagna Singh, who was wheeled out on his stretcher for the occasion, the soldiers standing by and cheering.

It was also the day that Jemadar Mir Dast would be presented with the Victoria Cross. Postcards of Mir Dast receiving his VC would eventually be used to shame the British youth who had not volunteered for the war effort.[11]

Severly injured after the German gas attack during the Second Battle of Ypres in April 1915, Mir Dast had been sent to the Brighton Pavilion for treatment along with several wounded soldiers. On 12 July 1915 he wrote to his friend in the 55th Rifles in Kohat: 'I am in England. I have been twice wounded. Once in the left hand, of which two fingers are powerless. The other injury is from gas – that is *dhua* [smoke]. I suppose you know about that. It gives me great pain and will go on doing so… The men who came from our regiment have done very well and will do so again. I want your congratulations. I have got the Victoria Cross. The Victoria Cross is a very fine thing, but this gas gives me no rest. It has done for me.'[12]

In early July the Secretary of State for India, Austen Chamberlain visited Brighton and met Mir Dast on the lawn outside the Pavilion. The two men shook hands and exchanged a few words. As Chamberlain withdrew, he was delighted to see all the Indian officers taking turns in saluting Mir Dast, 'shaking him by the hand, and congratulating him on the honour he had won'.

Mir Dast had become a celebrity among the Indian soldiers. Many fellow Pathans included a greeting from Mir Dast in their letters home. 'Subedar Mir Dast sends you greeting. He has got the Victoria Cross and the King has sent for him. He wonders how he is to go to the King, because he is wounded; but he is going to make a very urgent request of the King, that a man who has once been wounded ought not to be sent back,'[13] a Pathan in England, wrote to a soldier serving in France.

The day before his presentation, Mir Dast received a telegram from the King telling him to make any request he might have. Mir Dast asked the King: 'I have no son that you might give him a Jemadari or a Havaldari. But this is my request, that when a man has once been wounded, it is not well to take him back again to the trenches. For no good work will be done by his hand, but he will spoil others also.'[14] He was echoing the feelings of most Indian soldiers and their families who believed that, once an Indian soldier had been wounded, he had 'done his bit', and therefore should not be returned to the trenches to risk death a second time. Indian soldiers recovering in Brighton had petitioned the King on the same subject in May 1915. Mir Dast's request to the King earned him the admiration of his fellow soldiers making him even more of a hero.

On 25 August 1915 Mir Dast was presented his award by King George V on the grounds of the Brighton Pavilion. With him were Queen Mary and their daughter, Princess Mary. After the ceremony, Mir Dast wrote ecstatically to a colleague in the 55th Rifles. 'By the great, great, great kindness of God, the King with his royal hand has given me the decoration of the Victoria Cross. God has been very gracious, very gracious, very gracious, very gracious, very, very, very, very, very to me. Now I do not care. I want the kindness of God. If I go to Egypt, I do not regret it. The desire of my heart is accomplished… Show great zeal in your duty, and be faithful, and eat the salt of the government with loyalty.'[15]

At the time Mir Dast was being honoured in Brighton, his brother Mir Mast was back in his village in the North West Frontier after a dramatic journey from Berlin to Kabul.

But beneath the grand domes of the Pavilion and behind the high walls of the Kitchener Hospital, all was not well. Though the carefully propagated image was that of happy soldiers relaxing in the Pavilion grounds, being visited by the King and Queen and treated like special guests, there was another story which was carefully supressed.

Many of the soldiers resented the heavy restrictions placed on them. Walter Lawrence had imposed a strict regime ensuring that no one was allowed to visit the Indians without a pass. Nor were the soldiers allowed to go out on their own.

The British feared that Indian nationalists may infiltrate the wards and ask the soldiers not to fight. There had been an incident of an Indian student who had been inciting soldiers telling them that their pay was too low. The War Office had a list of 'undesirables' who they did not want employed as orderlies, or be given permits to visit the soldiers. In another incident, some soldiers under the charge of a Havildar, got into a public house and had a little too much to drink. Steps were immediately taken to prevent such a recurrence.

The authorities were also apprehensive of the Indian soldiers starting liaisons with English women, who showed a great deal of curiosity towards the Indians, often approaching them on streets and giving them gifts. Some even invited the officers home. Contact with English women was frowned upon and every effort made to ensure a safe distance between the lonely women whose husbands and fiancés had gone to war and the wounded Indians who were equally lonely and more than happy to befriend them. Efforts were also made to ensure that the Indians did not write back home giving the impression that white women were 'readily available'.

When the Indian storekeeper of the Kitchener Hospital wrote to his friend about the women of Brighton, the last line of his letter was deleted: 'This place is very picturesque and the Indians are liked very much here. The girls of this place are notorious and are very fond of accosting Indians and fooling with them, they are ever ready for any purpose and in truth they are no better than the girls of Adda Bazar of Indore.'

A soldier from the Kitchener's Hospital in Brighton wrote to his friend in India: 'The people here are most friendly and liberal minded, but we have no freedom. The real reason is that some Indians who were here before, disgraced us by doing things which have led to a general prohibition. Government really has our best interest at heart and wants to spare us trouble. There is a museum here and many other fine buildings, and we get a pass to go along to the bazaar with others to make our purchases.'

A far angrier letter was written in Marathi by an Indian sub-assistant surgeon from the hospital he described as the 'Kitchener Hospital Jail':

> Being ourselves warrant officers, we are allowed to stay out at night until 8.30 p.m. but it is only on condition that we sign our names in the book at the door when we go out and when we return. The book is watched over by a European havildar, and there is a European guard at the door. The walls are protected by barbed wire, and we are kept as prisoners inside. We are altogether 20 sub-assistant surgeons, the remaining 150 residents are not allowed to go out at all. Under special orders, accompanied by one sub-assistant surgeon and one European, batches of six men are allowed to go out for one hour…the condition of the remaining residents may well be imagined. They have not left the buildings for months together. Even assuming that six are allowed out daily, it will take 71 days and the individual gets out once in 2 and a half months, and then only for one hour during which time he is not allowed to speak to anyone in the streets. A complaint was made which led to enquiries but it was pointed out that the hospital was provided with everything the men could possibly desire, including hockey, football, phonographs and free cinema games of all kinds etc. This satisfied the higher officers, but this is besides the point and does not provide for the liberty of the individual to go about as he likes. Has not God given the individual a right to go about and talk to others as he likes?[16]

The officer went on to say that he did not know the condition in the two other hospitals in Brighton, but he knew that thousands of sepoys who were sick, but able to get about, were in the same condition.

'These men have left their country and come here to die for the sake of the Kingdom,' wrote the officer. 'This may well be called ungratefulness and yet our Indians are upright, and go on their way without giving this matter weight. They commit no atrocities for such is Hindu civilisation.

Today thousands are dying the in the war, and those who live after them will reap the reward. Albeit thousands die, yet many join the field of battle.' Unsurprisingly, the letter was withheld by the censors.

There was another complaint from a soldier at Kitchener Hospital, which seemed to be having more trouble than others. The letter written in Gujarati by a Parsi soldier to his friend in Bombay revealed: 'The supervision over us is very strict, and we are not allowed to go anywhere, and are hard pressed, and we do not like it. At first the *salas* [bastards] allowed us more freedom and we acted according to our pleasure and stayed out – sometimes all night. We were even placed outside in billets; but some men abused the privilege, and it was entirely stopped. We had plenty to eat wherever we went and the people were greatly pleased, not ever having seen natives before, and they thought we had come to save them. Some became diseased and some were flogged. If God releases us from this soon it will be well...'

The resentment against the strict discipline at Kitchener Hospital even resulted in an attack on Col. Bruce Seton, the commander of the hospital, by an Indian officer. Incensed by the high walls, barbed wire and lack of freedom to travel around, an Indian sub-assistant surgeon walked into the Colonel's office and fired a revolver at him. In the cross fire was another Indian soldier who described the event to his friend: 'By the grace of god the revolver missed fire and I immediately caught hold of the man. I will let you know in due course what happens in this case, also what reward is given to me.'

Lawrence, however, did not feel the restrictions were too severe. In his report to Kitchener, he said that the men from the hospitals were taken out in small parties through the town and on the whole 'their conduct had been exemplary'. The discrepancy in salaries, he pointed out, was a cause of discontent. A sweeper recruited in Peshawar was getting Rupees 10 a month, while those recruited at Poona and Bombay were being given Rupees 24. There were differences in salaries of cooks and other orderlies as well. It had led to trouble between the personnel recruited in Peshawar and those from Bombay and an 'outbreak had occurred in which knives were used.'[17]

By August 1915 the nurses in the Pavilion and York Place Hospitals at Brighton were removed leading to immediate protests from the Indians.

Sir Shapurji Broacha wrote two long letters to Lawrence urging that the sepoys be entitled to the care of English nurses. One Indian volunteer from the Indian Medical Service said, 'You take our men and money and yet deny us good nursing.'

Further tension broke out at the troubled Kitchener Hospital in July 1915. A wounded sepoy from the 129th Baluchis was lying in Block J along with Havildar Karim Ullah Khan, a Pathan from 58th Rifles, who was recovering from an arm injury. Supervising them was an orderly called Kali Charan. The sepoy told the orderly that he wanted some milk, to which the orderly replied: 'After placing your backside at the disposal of the Germans, you have come here to drink milk, have you?' The comment made Havildar Karim Ullah fly into a rage and he grabbed a stick which was lying near his bed and attacked Kali Charan, wounding him. The incident was immediately reported and Karim Ullah and the sepoy made to narrate what had happened to the Chief Doctor and the Colonel. When Karim Ullah was told he might be court-martialled, he declared he would write a petition to 'General Wil Kak Sahib Bahadur'.

Meanwhile about twenty Indian officers went to the Colonel and made a plea on Karim Ullah's behalf. Eventually the commanding officer came to Brighton and on hearing that a Havildar was to be court martialled, sent a telegram to London. An enquiry was resumed and the court martial dropped. The orderly was demoted from first class to second class and Havildar Karim Ullah was given ten rupees by General Willcocks and moved to an officers' room for the rest of his stay. Karim Ullah recovered from his injuries and returned to the front, after first making a trip to London.

There were also a few complaints from other hospitals. A wounded soldier at the Lady Hardinge Hospital in Brockenhurst wrote to his family: 'There is no fireplace, we are not given milk…it is very cold. We have to call the nurses "mother" and the European soldiers "Orderly Sahib" – if we do not, we are reported. The five Brighton hospitals are good. The others are not good. We are not given soup. We get nothing.'

A wounded sepoy in Milford-on-Sea sent a petition to the King saying no one except he should open it.

'No British Officer nor Indian Doctor cares for us. They deal hardly with the sick… Your Majesty's order was that a man who had been wounded once should be allowed to return to India; or that if he had recovered he should not be made to serve again. The heart of India is broken because they inflict suffering on the sick. Blessed King, what can I say?... We do not get new clothes. In the morning only…tea, at ten o'clock a chapatti and a spoonful of dal. In twenty-four hours five cigarettes. In the evening the chapattis are half baked and there is no meat. No sick man gets well fed. The Indians have given their lives for eleven rupees. Any man who comes here wounded is returned thrice and four times to the trenches. Only that man goes to India who has lost an arm or a leg or an eye.'[18]

Others wrote letters to family urging them not to enlist: 'For God's sake don't come, don't come, don't come to this war in Europe…tell my brother Muhammad Yakub Khan for God's sake not to enlist.'

Lying within the walls of the Kitchener Hospital, some soldiers grew depressed: 'As tired bullocks and bull buffaloes lie down in the month of Bhadon [August–September] so lies the weary world,' wrote a soldier. 'Our hearts are breaking, for a year has passed while we stood to arms without a rest…we have bound ourselves under her flag and we must give our bodies.' The charms of going to *Vilayat* had worn out for many of them. They did not want to spend any more time in this war.

Desperate not to return to the trenches, some of the wounded Indians resorted to malingering. In letters home they asked for herbs and potions that would bring out symptoms of rash or high fever, so they would not clear the medical tests required of them.

'Please get an amulet for me from Badruddin, which will have the effect of making me ill, so that I shall be sent back to India,' a Deccani Muslim from the Indian convalescent home in New Milton, wrote to his friend in Madras. 'The amulet should be of such a nature as to cause slight fever and general debility, so that, when I appear before the medical board, the doctors will find me suffering from fever and general debility with all the outward signs of illness… If you will be so good as to do this for me I shall never forget it until the day of judgment.'[19]

Families back in India obliged the soldiers. The wounded received many letters advising them about how they could make themselves ill.

These ranged from instructions on cutting one's foot with a knife and sticking a piece of copper in the wound to allowing the smoke of the *bhalwa* plant to cover a part of the body to cause an inflammation.

However, despite the plea to their families to supply the drugs, the actual number of Indians found to malinger was low. Col. Seton, driven by the rumours and the discontent at Kitchener Hospital, decided to conduct a detailed investigation into 1000 wounds and establish how many could have been self-inflicted.

Like a veritable detective, Seton analysed and eliminated all those with trench, gas and artillery wounds and narrowed the focus to injuries on the left hand or legs alone (as soldiers would not want to hurt themselves in the right hand). His investigation revealed that only six cases could have been self-inflicted. He grandly declared that there was 'no evidence of self-infliction of wounds which could be supported by statistical examinations.'[20]

In December 1914 many cases of self-inflicted wounds were noticed, in the feet and calf, as the soldiers desperately tried to prevent being sent back to the firing line. It was also around this time that Walter Lawrence noted the return of the coded term 'black pepper'in the soldiers' letters home. He was concerned that the Indian soldiers felt that the British government was deliberately keeping the Indian Army in France until it was completely destroyed.

'In the sepoy's letters there is constant mention of the fact that the "black pepper"is being used up and the "red pepper" is being saved,' Lawrence reported to Kitchener. 'In other words that the Indian troops are being deliberately sacrificed and the British troops preserved.' Lawrence felt that the Indians in hospitals seeing only other wounded Indians did not know the extent of losses on the British side which he felt needed to be conveyed to them.

Many Indians who had been brought to the front as clerks submitted a petition to the Viceroy asking to be re-called to India. 'We have all submitted a memorial to His Excellency the Viceroy, praying that we may be sent back to India, as we have been separated from our wives and families for such a long time. We have been serving in unaccustomed conditions in a cold country with no leave, and the circumstances of our families are such that is impossible for us Indians to stay away from our homes for a long time. We have therefore asked that clerks may be sent from India to fill our places, and that we may be allowed to go back and see to the urgent private affairs that have arisen in our absence.'[21]

By November 1915, over one year into the war and into the second winter, the morale was incredibly low. In York Place Hospital a Gurkha committed suicide. He was from Darjeeling, the picturesque hill station in North Bengal in the Eastern Himalayas. The mud and bog of Flanders had taken its toll. Lawrence found that there were two other Gurkhas in the hospital who were also very depressed. 'All castes regard this long absence from India as painful exile,' he wrote. 'Amongst all there has been a longing to get back to India, and I have reason to believe that some of the desertions were not due to disloyalty or a desire to join the enemy, but were as a short cut to India and home.'

A soldier captured the pain of leaving behind his loved ones in verse:

> I know not that one day I should leave my country thus
> As the bulbul leaves his garden of pleasure
> Where are now those days of joy when I roamed my native land?
> Where are the pleasant companions I am now leaving behind?
> Where is my loved one? Where are my children? Where the sweet society of my friends?
> Where are they all? I am leaving India behind.[22]

The war was taking its toll and no amount of bright lights in Brighton and London could entice the soldiers to stay on.

11

Funerals

The Friday prayers had just finished at the Shah Jehan Mosque in Woking. It was a balmy August day and the small gathering of Muslims seemed to have come from all over the world: India, Arabia, Nigeria, Egypt and Tunisia. There were also some white converts. It was a year into the war and many of the people present knew someone serving in the trenches or who had died. Maulvi Sadr-ud-Din had said a prayer for everyone. But he was troubled. As the head of the only purpose-built mosque in Britain, the war had brought additional responsibilities.

Built in 1889, the Shah Jehan Mosque had been funded by the Begum of Bhopal and built by the Orientalist Dr Gottlieb Wilhelm Leitner, a professor of Arabic and Islamic law, who had lived for several years in Istanbul, London and India. It was an inclusive mosque functioning within the remit of the West and attracted mostly middle class educated Muslims. The mosque, with its green dome and pillars, looked somewhat like the Brighton Pavilion, and was where Muslims around Britain gathered on Fridays and during the Eid festival. Visiting Muslim dignitaries made it a point to see the mosque when in Britain. Queen Victoria's munshi, Abdul Karim, used to worship there, as did the first Prime Minister of Pakistan, Muhammad Ali Jinnah.

The mosque had fallen into disuse after Leitner's death in 1899, but was revived in 1912 when the Indian lawyer Khwaja Kamuluddin established the Woking Muslim Mission there and the Ahmadiya Muslims took over the running of the mosque. In 1913 Kamaluddin returned to Lahore and Sadr-ud-Din was sent to take charge as the head Maulavi. A highly articulate and scholarly man, Sadr-ud-Din was responsible for the first German translation of the Quran. On that August day, however, he was angry and upset. He had been forced to write a letter to the authorities criticising them for not doing enough for the Muslim soldiers who had died.

Sadr-ud-Din had been requested by the government to bury the Muslim soldiers who died in the hospitals in England. When he consented to do this, the letter was sent to the Viceroy and much publicity given in India to the fact that Muslims would be buried with full religious rites by the Imam of the mosque. Initially the burial ground at Netley Hospital was offered to him, but the Maulvi felt that it was not right for Muslims to be buried in a Christian cemetery. It would also be inconvenient for visitors as they would need the permission of the War Office to visit the burial grounds. Furthermore, as there were six hospitals in the area, it would not be possible for him to go from Woking to the various hospitals to carry out the burials. He had therefore requested that the Muslim soldiers be buried in grounds near the mosque at Woking.

It caused a great controversy but ultimately a plot of land was procured. However, the Maulvi, was not satisfied:

> I then asked the government whether they would not (1) rail in the cemetery (2) make paths in the ground (3) provide a gravedigger (4) provide a caretaker (5) provide some place where the bodies should be left for the night (6) provide a decent waiting room (7) erect a gateway in Eastern style – however inexpensive – as a Memorial to the fallen Indian soldiers.
>
> At first the government blankly refused to do anything, and many months went past. I could not bury the dead soldiers in the marshy piece of unfenced ground over which people and dogs could stray. Therefore I buried twenty-five of them in the Mahomedan burial ground at Brookwook at my own expense. This is now full, and I have already buried three in the new burial place, but though it is fenced in, it is in such a disgraceful state that it would not be policy to allow the Indian soldiers to go and see the burial place of their comrades. They have frequently asked, but I have had to put them off because – being a loyal subject of His Majesty – I did not desire to raise the resentment which

must inevitably be felt when the truth becomes known of the manner in which the British government have treated their dead heroes.

I have had bodies sent to me bearing the wrong names, bodies sent without any flowers; bodies sent to me at any hour of the day or night without any previous notice, and no respect shown for them whatever – not even any military demonstration at their graves.

I desire to point out to the government the very grave danger of allowing the impression to gain ground in India that England is not showing sufficient respect to the memories of her Indian heroes.

I need not enlarge upon the very serious effect which an exposure of this kind would make, both among the soldiers at the front, and the entire population throughout India.[1]

The Maulvi's scathing letter was not received well by Walter Lawrence, who was in charge of the welfare of Indian soldiers. Lawrence blamed Sadr-ud-Din for the problems. In his report to Lord Kitchener he said that the burial ground had been waterlogged because the Maulavi had been in a hurry and not waited for the trial pits to be sunk into the ground first. 'His object is to make mischief,' wrote Lawrence. The matter, he said, was in the hands of the India Office and the War Office had no responsibility. 'In France, where the burials and cremation are under the military authorities, and in England where cremation has been carried out by the same agency, the greatest pains have been taken and everything has been done to the complete satisfaction of the Hindus and Mahomedans,' Lawrence said.

The Maulvi's letter nevertheless had the desired effect. Efforts were made to ensure that the bodies of the Muslim soldiers were taken to Woking from hospitals in Brighton, Bournemouth and Netley in a convoy, with the body in a hearse and forty to fifty mourners in lorries. The Assistant Quarter Master of the Muslim priest at Woking Mosque, D.R. Thaper, wrote that each death meant a whole day's travel to London and back. Though Thaper was not a Muslim, he soon became proficient as an undertaker and the chief mourner. To make the Muslims feel that they had not been neglected, the souvenir on the Brighton Pavilion mentioned the fact that the Muslims were taken to Woking accompanied by a Muslim doctor and that the burial was conducted with full military honours including a firing party. This was circulated in India for the satisfaction of those Muslims who may have been critical of the British government for fighting the Turks.

A letter written from Brighton in January 1916 described the funeral of a fellow Muslim soldier: 'A fine coffin was provided on which his name and age were engraved. The inside was lined with silk cloth and cushions of silk. In our country doubtless only the greatest in the land are furnished with coffins of this sort. He was buried in a Muslim cemetery near London with great honour and dignity.'[2]

It was decided that the Hindu soldiers who died in the hospitals would be cremated on the South Downs in Patcham near Brighton. The 'burning ghats of Patcham' consisted of three cement platforms built on the Downs on which the funeral pyres were lit. A corrugated tin roof provided shelter from the elements and a Brahmin priest performed the last rites. The tranquil spot with its sweeping views over the Downs made it the perfect place for the last rites of the Hindu and Sikh soldiers. The reporter for *The Times* newspaper witnessing a funeral in October 1915 reported: 'but a short time ago to find its parallel, one must have journeyed thousands of miles. For this was the burning ghat of our Hindu troops.'

Fifty-three Indian soldiers were cremated on the Downs and their ashes scattered in the sea near Brighton. Subedar Manta Singh was one of them. He had been brought to the Kitchener General Hospital after he was injured in the Battle of Neuve Chapelle. The Chief Resident Officer recorded his wounds: 'one, gunshot wound, left leg, two, gangrene of leg and toxaemia.' The gangrene had spread across his leg and the doctors told him they would have to amputate it. 'What use would a cripple be to his family,' moaned Manta Singh.[3] The young Sikh despaired about his wife and son in Punjab. Despite the amputation, there was no hope for Manta Singh. The infection spread in his body and he died in the hospital a few weeks later. Lying on a hospital bed, his friend, Captain Henderson, heard the news of the death of the man who had saved his life.

In August 1915 Lieutenant Das Gupta of the Indian Medical Service, approached the Mayor of Brighton, John Otter, for permission to erect a memorial on the site where the cremations took place. Otter was immediately enthusiastic, taking on the role as Chair of the Indian Memorial Committee of Brighton. He proposed a memorial at the site of the crematorium and another on the walls of the Brighton Pavilion to mark the link the town had with the Indians. Otter was later knighted for his services.

In December that year, Sir Walter Lawrence also proposed to the India Office 'on political and historical grounds' to do something to preserve the memory of the Indian soldiers who had died in England and France. In response to his note, a War Office staffer suggested that the Army Council make arrangements for the erection of 'adequate memorials' starting with the cemeteries at Netley and Brockenhurst. The notes eventually reached the Secretary of State for India, Austen Chamberlain, who had visited the Indians in hospital, and on 16 February 1916 he recommended that 'where cremation has been resorted to, a simple monument of an oriental character should be erected on the site of the crematorium'.[4]

Brighton Council agreed to bear half the costs along with the India Office. The architect Sir Swinton Jacob was consulted who proposed a structure in an Indian chhatri-style built with granite, sandstone and marble. The umbrella design symbolising the protection offered to the memory of the dead was completed by E.C. Henriques. The dome and eight pillars would be of Sicilian marble in keeping with Indian traditions and three large granite slabs would be laid over the original platform of the crematorium. The marble from Sicily, however, could only arrive after the war and construction began in 1920. The memorial was inaugurated on 21 February 1921 by the Prince of Wales, later Edward VIII. Inscribed in Hindi and English were the words: 'To the memory of all the Indian soldiers who gave their lives for their King-Emperor in the Great War, this monument, erected on the site of the funeral pyre where the Hindus and Sikhs who died in hospital at Brighton, passed through the fire, is in grateful admiration and brotherly affection dedicated.'

In the peaceful calm of the surroundings of Brockenhurst in the New Forest, Sukha the sweeper lay ill in the Lady Hardinge Hospital. He had journeyed a long way from his village in Uttar Pradesh to come to this war. It had seemed like a good idea to volunteer for service. The pay was good, better than back home. At least it was regular. He had been promised food and clothes and a chance to serve the King Emperor. He had nothing to lose. Or so it seemed at the time.

Sukha watched the nurses as they walked between the beds in his ward in their starched aprons talking to the orderlies and wounded soldiers. All of them spoke Hindustani and some had lived in India. Occasionally one of them would walk by Sukha's bed and ask him how he felt. He was too sick to reply, and would just nod to them weakly. His lung was infected and he had been suffering from pneumonia for weeks. He wanted to go back home, where he could feel the hot summer sun burn his back as he worked in his Sahib's house. He had not seen the sun for months. He pulled the warm turkey twill quilt over himself and fought back the tears that were threatening to overcome him.

The series of huts that made up the Lady Hardinge Hospital had been Sukha's home for the past month. The locals called it 'Tin Town'. There were 500 beds in the hospital but as there were more injured soldiers than beds there were men lying on mattresses and makeshift beds.Those who managed to walk limped around the room or through the corridor which connected the huts, The Matron, Edith McCall Anderson, was a kindly lady whom Sukha saw occasionally. She was assisted by nineteen nursing staff including two senior nurses. There were twenty wards in the hospital with twenty-four beds in each room and the nurses looked after fifty beds each. Their job was supervisory. They did not tend to the wounded soldiers or change their dressing. Nursing work was done by the orderlies. The Indians worked as cleaners and cooks. Some Indian students worked as volunteers. The Indian officers had a separate room. They had been sent presents of dressing gowns by Lady Rothschild and they looked smart and warm in their dark blue dressing gowns with red facings. Sukha wished he had a dressing gown. He had been given a muffler. English ladies were knitting mufflers all around the country and sending them to the hospitals. There were some Indian soldiers who wore the mufflers as turbans. Sukha had wrapped his around his neck.

It seemed like an age since he had boarded the ship in Bombay and left for the front all set to have the adventure of his life. He, Sukha Kalloo, had been recruited as a sweeper, Service Number 16, in the Supply and Transport Corp.[5] Kalloo wasn't really his last name. He was called Kalloo ('Blackie') as he was dark skinned. Sukha did not have a last name. He had been given a uniform and a bronze metal badge number which rattled on his lanky chest. He was an 'untouchable', and the high caste soldiers had nothing to do with him. His only job was to clean. Sukha had prepared the ship in Bombay before the soldiers embarked in their smart khaki uniforms with their rolls of luggage. He had swept and cleared the mess made by the mules and horses. He had kept the ship clean on the five-week journey. He had marched in the crisp October air in France behind the soldiers listening to the roar of the French crowds shouting 'Indienne', 'Indienne' and welcoming him like he had never been greeted before. He had marvelled at the beauty of the women and the rosy-cheeked children who had mischievously pulled at his hand.

Sukha had swept and cleaned in the camps and even been sent to the trenches to clean up. He had seen things he had never seen before and never wanted to see again. Bodies piled on bodies, some of them men who had been laughing and joking a few days before. He had heard the moans of the injured, seen the vacant look on those about to die. He had seen mud and blood and incessant rain that had been nothing like the monsoons in his country. But he had battled on, cleaning the sewage and garbage left behind, preparing the trenches for the next set of soldiers who would spend up to forty-eight hours standing in them. The damp and rain had seeped through his bones, but he had not complained.

The number of injured had gone up and there were no Indian sweepers in the hospitals in England. Strict caste and religious regulations meant that they needed Indian sweepers. The Bandobust Sahib, Walter Lawrence, had urgently appealed for sweepers. The Empire depended on Sukha and his broom. When Sukha was ordered to go to the motherland, he was relieved to get away from the guns. He didn't feel too well himself, but he consoled himself looking at the wounded soldiers. Some were missing limbs, others had lost their fingers and toes from frostbite. Some had damaged their backs as whole trenches had collapsed and fallen on them during the heavy bombing. Yet they were men who had once had a past and a home. Sukha had seen them on the ships sailing to Marseilles, bright and enthusiastic, raring to play their part in the war. They had not noticed him, but he had heard them sing and had listened to their chatter. Now they looked like ghosts as he travelled with them on the hospital ship to England. The soldiers' chatter had been replaced with deathly moans.

He looked after them, sweeping their mess and cleaning the ship. They still did not notice him but he did not mind. Sukha wished he too could lie down for a while. He was suffering from a cold but he had a job to do.

Ambulances had taken them from the Port of Southampton to the hospital in Brockenhurst. Sukha got a fleeting view of green countryside and wild ponies. The hospital was set on a rising ground and was clearly a newly constructed one made of temporary huts. Sukha was explained his duties by an Indian orderly. His job was to keep the wards and lavatories clean. He would have to scrub the wooden floors which got messy quickly as the doors opened straight into the surrounding grounds which were often muddy in the rain.

Sukha marvelled at the way the hospital was run. They had built Indian-style toilets for the soldiers and there were two kitchens for Hindus and Muslims. The neat wards had lockers with each bed, on which *lotas* were placed, aluminium for the Muslims and brass for the Hindus. The plates, mugs and other crockery were also labelled to distinguish between the two religions: the crockery enamelled dark blue outside and white inside was for the Muslims and that of the Hindus was white with a blue border. Over the beds hung different coloured discs, marking the different diets of which there were six. It made the job easier for the two cooks who served the food – chicken mutton and dal soups, milk, sugar, rice and chapatis in various combinations. Sukha himself had no diet restrictions and was happy to eat anything except, that of late, he had lost his appetite.

The part of the hospital he liked best were the wide corridors connecting the various blocks. They were warm and furnished with divans covered with thick rugs and scattered with fat bolster cushions with blue, red and green velvet covers on which the soldiers sat around and chatted. The atmosphere reminded him of the houses back in India. The cold that had been troubling Sukha for some time felt instantly better when he worked in these bright warm areas of the hospital. There was also a recreation room similarly furnished with a comfortable carpet, bright cushions and low tables on which the men could play cards or chess and other board games. This was the room in which they smoked cigarettes or makeshift water pipes. Often the soldiers would put on a song on the gramophone and Sukha enjoyed the music as he swept. When they were ghazals about love and longing the soldiers would applaud as they listened. Sometimes there were folk songs or devotional music. The banter of the soldiers also kept him amused. They mostly described their experiences in the trenches or in the French and Belgian countryside. They despaired that the war showed no signs of ending and spoke of the loved ones they had left behind. Hindus and Muslims sat together and shared news of their villages, some read out letters from home, others dictated them to a volunteer who would write the letters for them.

'Like nightingales we've left the woods we know/May God keep others from the way we go,'[6] a soldier wrote from the Lady Hardinge Hospital. Sukha heard the lines of the verse recited as it was being written.

But it was to end all too soon for Sukha. His cold and congestion got worse. One day as he swept the wards, he felt dizzy and fell to the floor clutching his broom. One of the doctors examining Sukha told him he had to rest. Sukha had pneumonia. His body had finally yielded to the relentless cold of the West. Soon he was lying in one of the hospital wards that until recently he had been sweeping. Sukha Kalloo died on 12 January 1915, a few months after he had arrived to serve King and another country.

But even in death, there was no peace. When it was suggested that Sukha be cremated in the 'burning ghats' at Patcham, the Hindus objected saying he was from a low caste and could not be cremated at their site. An appeal was then made to Maulvi Sadr-ud-Din in Woking. However, the response from the mosque was negative as well. Sukha was clearly not a Muslim, said the Maulvi, and he could not be buried there. Sukha the sweeper was in no man's land, this time because of the caste and religious prejudices of his own countrymen.

It was then that the vicar of St Nicholas Church in Brockenhurst stepped forward saying that Sukha had died for England and that he would be buried in the church graveyard. And so it happened that Sukha Kalloo found his final resting place in the quiet graveyard of a church in the heart of the scenic New Forest.

The story of Sukha's funeral caught the imagination of Sir George Fletcher MacMunn, an old India-hand who was fascinated by the

Indian Army and the caste system in particular. MacMunn wrote a short story called 'The Prince' which was circulated among army personnel. The story focussed upon the curse of untouchability and centred on a sweeper who was finally given the last rites by an Englishman. Sukha was transformed into the fictional 'Buldoo' and his story had all the embellishments of a Raj writer.

In MacMunn's three-and-a-half page story, 'Buldoo was a fine specimen of his kind and ranked among the princes as something of a swaggerer, for he had grown a fine beard and curled it somewhat as the warrior castes might...' For the author it was as much a commentary on India's caste system as a glorification of the British Raj that gave Buldoo equal status by burying him in the fictional church of 'St Mary Within' in the 'Christian ground in old England.'

The story was widely circulated, inspiring the author to use the story of 'Buldoo' in another book.[7] In this version, 'The War Story of an Outcaste Sweeper', MacMunn's Buldoo, the 'Prince of the Broom' wore his waistcoat and *pagri* with pride. He befriended an English sweeper from Stepney and even had a girlfriend in the bazaar before journeying to Mesopotamia, partaking in florid adventures and finally dying a hero on the battlefield with a bullet through his head.

On a cold wintry morning in January, a small crowd gathered in St Nicholas Church in Brockenhurst to bid Sukha his last farewell. The vicar said a few words and blessed the sweeper from India who had travelled thousands of miles to play his role in the war. A few parishioners, a nurse from the hospital and a follower watched as Sukha's mortal remains were buried in the stretch of green just behind the church building. The parishioners had raised money to erect a headstone in his honour. His grave, which is now looked after by the Commonwealth War Graves Association, lies amongst those of soldiers from New Zealand, many of whom were from the Maori regiment. Two other Indian Christian soldiers are buried next to him. Sukha's large headstone is distinct from the other graves. On it are the words:

This stone
was erected by
Parishioners of Brockenhurst
To mark the spot where is laid
the Earthly body of
SUKHA
A resident of Mohulla Gungapur,
City Bareilly, United Provinces of India
He left country, home & friends to serve our
King & Empire in the Great European War.
As a humble servant in the Lady Hardinge
Hospital for wounded Indian soldiers
in this Parish.
He departed this life on January 12th 1915
Aged 30 years
By creed, he was not Christian
But his earthly life was sacrificed in the
interests of others
"There is one God and father of all: who is
Over all and through all and in all"
EPHESIANS.IV.6

By the autumn of 1915 the Indians Corps had begun their withdrawal from the Western Front. It was decided that they should not have to spend another winter in the trenches as their numbers were greatly depleted. The soldiers would go to Africa and West Asia and join the Indian Expeditionary Force there. Their new destinations were Turkey, Persia, Basra, Salonica, Gallipoli, and Egypt. Ships leaving the port of Marseille saw the French line up once again, this time to bid goodbye to the 'Hindoues' who had come from thousands of miles away to fight their war. The hospitals in Brockenhurst and Brighton slowly emptied out, the turbaned men so much a part of the city landscape for over a year, boarding the trains and returning to the port of Southampton. Those too injured to return to the front, went back to India. Entire villages in the

Punjab, North West Frontier and the Garhwal would have men limping back, a shadow of their former selves, a part of them left behind in the fields of France and Flanders.

A Sikh soldier mourned that only the injured would return home:

> And so the war is raging by sky and land and sea
> And underneath the water, five kings are fighting three.
> The cannon roar like thunder, the bullets fall like rain,
> And only the hurt, the maimed and blind will ever see home again.[8]

12

The Maharaja and the War Cabinet

Maharaja Ganga Singh of Bikaner was dressed in a morning suit. His flamboyant turban and British military uniform were packed up in his suitcase. Frustrated at being kept away from the trenches on the Western Front, and because his daughter Chand Kumar was ill, he had returned to Bikaner in 1915 stopping in Egypt on his way back. It was in the desert that the Maharaja finally managed to see some action. His Ganga Risala or Bikaner Camel Corp was guarding the Suez Canal. They were the only Camel Corps available to the Allies. When the Turks under the command of Djemel Pasha attacked the Suez Canal in February 1915, it was left to the Ganga Risala to block them. At Katib al Khail, the Corps led by the Maharaja fired at the Turks, defeating them and driving them back. Charged up, the Ganga Risala pursued the retreating Turks, the Maharaja thoroughly enjoying his first real battle.

For the rest of the war, the Maharaja did not return to the firing line. His presence, however, was now requested in London for the Imperial War Cabinet, to discuss financing and recruitment from the colonies and the issue of peace once the war was over. There was also the troubled matter of dominion status, enjoyed by Canada, Australia, New Zealand and South Africa, but denied to India. Before embarking on his ship for London, the Maharaja had been honoured at a banquet in Bombay hosted by his fellow princes. At the dinner he called for reform in the administration of both princely India and British India saying: 'I sincerely believe that British statesmanship and sense of justice will accord to our country that place to which her position in the Empire entitles her.' It was a departure from the usual grovelling loyalty shown towards the British by the Princely states. In the long run, the Maharaja wanted to see India get dominion status. For now he was happy to bargain for India's rights at the Imperial War Cabinet.

The Maharaja would attend the meeting with his fellow national, Sir Satyendra Prasanno Sinha, the only other Indian on the Cabinet. While Bikaner – as he was fondly called – would represent the Princely states, Sinha would represent the Executive Council of the Governor of Bengal. Sinha was a sharp Bengali barrister from a privileged land-holding family. Like many intellectuals of his time, he had been called to the bar at Lincoln's Inn, had returned to India with a keen interest in politics and joined the Indian National Congress. He was the first Indian to be appointed Advocate General of West Bengal, and in 1909 became the first Indian member of the Governor General's Executive Council. Sinha, soon to be given the job of Undersecretary of State for India, would go on to make history as the first Indian to be appointed a peer.

Both Indians had contrasting styles. While the grey-haired, small-built Sinha was low-key, the six-foot turbaned Bikaner was flamboyant, fluent in both English and French. Sinha represented the intellectual elite of India, which was given to questioning British rule within the parameters of democratic debate, while Bikaner spoke for the Princely states loyal to the Crown. Though India was not a self-governing dominion, she was invited to the conference on account of her large contribution to the war effort. Prime Minister David Lloyd George had personally insisted that India be represented at the table. There had been a change of guard in India during the war years. Lord Hardinge had ended his tenure as Viceroy, left his grand vice-regal houses and returned to England in 1916 after a series of farewell luncheons, dinners and town hall meetings. Lord Chelmsford had taken over as the new Viceroy. It was he who recommended the names of Bikaner and Sinha.

The Maharaja was proud to be chosen to represent the Princely states of India. He left with his entourage, arrived in a wintry London at the end of February 1917 and checked into his suite at the Ritz Hotel. Sinha preferred to stay at the Hampstead residence of his friend, the civil servant, MP and one of the founders of the Indian National Congress, Sir William Wedderburn. The high-power delegation attending the Imperial

War Cabinet included Lord Curzon of Kedleston, former Viceroy of India, Austen Chamberlain, the Secretary of State for India, Bonar Law, the Chancellor of the Exchequer, A.T. Balfour, Secretary of State for Foreign Affairs and W.H. Long, the Secretary of State for the Colonies. Prime Minister Lloyd George was Chair. Representing the Dominions were the Prime Minister of Canada, Robert Borden, the Prime Minister of New Zealand, William Ferguson Massey, who was known as Bill Massey or 'Farmer Bill', and the Minister of Defence of South Africa, Lt Gen J.C. Smuts.

The first meeting was held at 10 Downing Street on March 20 with opening remarks by the Prime Minister who welcomed all members to the 'first Imperial Cabinet ever held in the British Empire'.[1] The atmosphere was particularly cordial. Lord Curzon already knew the Maharaja of Bikaner and Lord Sinha from his days as Viceroy. The Prime Minister of New Zealand told the Cabinet how pleased he was to see the representatives of India, who had taken part as soldiers and citizens in the great struggle, because it was 'undoubtedly a recognition of their right to take part in the consideration of questions specially affecting the great country to which they belong'. In 1907, India had not been allowed to participate in the Imperial War Cabinet because it was not a self-governing country. Therefore, their inclusion this time was significant. To show the support of the ruling princes, the Maharaja of Bikaner proceeded to read a message from the Maharaja of Patiala, who described the war as a '"Dharma Yudha"– a fight for righteousness',[2] in which India was proud to participate.

Thrice a week the delegates would drive to Downing Street for the Cabinet meeting. Londoners lined the streets to get a glimpse of the world leaders who were making crucial decisions in the war. Massey was the most popular and women carried placards with his picture on it. The Maharaja of Bikaner added a touch of glamour. He threw lavish parties at the Ritz and was invited to address Indian gatherings. He told a group of Indian students that they must never forget that they represented India when they came abroad and that they had to make their country proud. Sinha, on the other hand, remained in the background sticking to the company of his Hampstead friends.

The Cabinet discussed the need to recruit further troops from India. Casualties in Mesopotamia, Egypt and Gallipoli had been high and reinforcements were urgently needed. The Secretary of State for India had earlier requested the Viceroy to raise no less than an additional 100,000 troops by the spring of 1918 to fight the Turks. Those troops not suitable for the East could be used in France.[3]

Propaganda leaflets and posters were distributed around India encouraging young men to sign up for King and country. Unlike Britain, where they had to resort to conscription, in India recruitment was voluntary. Yet there was more than a subtle pressure on headmen of villages to bring out recruits. Financial incentives and rewards were also handed to those who could run successful recruitment drives. Short stories glorifying Indian soldiers and the awards they had won were printed in magazines and circulated among cantonment towns. These included the stories 'How Gul Mahomed joined the King's Army' and 'Teja Singh Khalsa Joins the Army' which saw peasant farmers finding their calling when they signed up for the army and went abroad to fight for Britain, winning honours and awards, making their village proud. Over 20,000 copies of the booklet about Brighton Pavilion hospital were distributed in India, showing relaxed, happy soldiers playing cards, and efforts made to emphasize how the soldiers were allowed to observe their religious duties. While hundreds of thousands in Britain flocked to see the footage of the Battle of the Somme, in India they watched footage of King George V and Queen Mary chatting casually with Indian soldiers.

The Cabinet discussed the difficulty of securing Indian officers for such a large increase in the army. It had always been a prickly issue that Indians were not allowed to graduate from Sandhurst as commissioned officers. The Secretary of State assured the cabinet that the question of giving commissions to Indian officers was being discussed with the government of India and it was hoped that definite proposals for the same would soon be laid before the War Cabinet.

As the sessions progressed into the early summer, Bikaner and Smuts inspected a guard of honour in London near Horse Guards Parade, Bikaner wearing his characteristic turban with his regimental uniform. Meanwhile, in the Imperial War Cabinet, the Indians were getting more demanding. Sinha expressed his wish to see India represented in the future by someone from India rather than the Secretary of State. The mild-mannered barrister surprised the Cabinet by going so far as to say that he 'looked forward to the time when the government of India would have an Indian Prime Minister'[4] but hastened to add that until that day he was quite content that India should be represented in such a manner as the government of India thought best. The first session of the Imperial War Cabinet concluded in May. The next was scheduled from 11 June 1918. All the members earnestly hoped it would be the last session in wartime.

Four summers had passed bringing only news of the dead. The Imperial War Cabinet was preparing to begin its second session in the summer of 1918. The weather had not been very good the last few days with cloudy afternoons and a slightly chilly breeze. On 11 June, a line of official cars could be seen driving up to the gates of 10 Downing Street and the familiar leaders from Britain and the Dominions emerged once again. The war had taken its toll. The light had gone out from many homes in India. Laddie Roy had died in the skies over France months before his twentieth birthday. His brother, Poresh, had been transferred from the Honorary Artillery Company to the Royal Air Force as a cadet. His mother prayed that he would not meet the same fate as his brother. In the hills of Garhwal, Gabar Singh Negi's family mourned his death. In Punjab the women sang songs about the soldiers who had gone away and would never return. Manta Singh's wife wept for her husband and wondered how she would bring up their little boy, Assa Singh. Only the old and infirm were left in the village of Dulmial in Chakwal. The total number of Indian dead was almost 70,000.

The delegates from India were in a more aggressive mood. The Maharaja of Patiala, Sir Bhupinder Singh Mahinder took the place of Bikaner who was unable to attend. Sinha had been made a peer, becoming the first Indian to be offered a seat in the House of Lords. There were also changes in office. Lord Edwin Samuel Montagu was the new Secretary of State for India, and Chamberlain was now only an M.P. Welcoming the delegates,

Prime Minister Lloyd George had a special word for the Indians: 'At this point I think I ought to say how much we owe to India. Had it not been for India, which made special efforts to increase and strengthen our forces in Mesopotamia and Egypt, it would have been impossible to withdraw divisions as we did in Egypt in order to strengthen our forces in France.'[5]

The Indians felt a sense of entitlement for the losses they had suffered. Sinha told the Cabinet that India's currency was almost depleted because she was contributing towards the War Effort and procuring goods for Britain and America without being paid on time. The skilled barrister did not mince his words and said India had already spent Rupees 130 million that year with serious consequences for the economy:[6]

'We shall no doubt be paid eventually, but the result of it is that the bullion and coin are depleted and we are faced with the gravest currency crisis… If that situation actually does arise the result will be disastrous; our credit will be gone; and it will be generally believed in the bazaars that the British Empire is bankrupt,'[7] said Sinha.

Apart from the economic consequences, there was the prickly issue of the post-war equation of the Dominions and India and their say in the Common Imperial Policy. The Dominions wanted to play an equal role in all decisions in exchange for their support of the war. Montagu pointed out that if the Dominions gained something which was not granted to India, it might have an unfavourable effect there. Sir Robert Borden, Prime Minister of Canada, said that if the Empire was to be kept together, it was a matter that needed to be discussed at a special conference after the war. 'Meanwhile the war is still going on,' said the Canadian Prime Minister, 'but the terms of the peace are being made every day.'[8] As the Dominions staked their claim in the process of Imperial Governance, the British cabinet tried to do a fine balancing act with India.

On 5 November the war with Turkey was over. Six days later, on the eleventh hour of the eleventh day of the eleventh month of 1918, the guns fell silent on the Western Front.

As the church bells rang out in Shrewsbury on the Welsh border to mark the armistice, Susan and Tom Owen received a letter that was to change their lives forever. It was the news of the death of their poet son, Wilfred, just seven days ago. While people poured on to the streets and squares to celebrate, hugging complete strangers, the Owens sat silently in their house in Monkmoor Road. No one noticed their absence. Too many had died in the war. The death of another young man was merely a statistic.

Wilfred had volunteered for the war so he could record the suffering of the soldiers and write about it later. He had gone to the front in January 1917 as a second lieutenant and platoon leader in the Manchester Regiment. Almost immediately he was in the heart of the action, entering the trenches and holding a position for fifty hours waist deep in water with shells raining down on him. The horror of the trenches would find its way into his poetry. 'The Sentry' was written after he saw a soldier blinded by the shelling. The poet proved to be a good shot and took part in the fierce fighting in St Quentin. However, in May he was hit by a shell explosion at Savy Bank and spent several days holed up in a railway embankment. His best friend was killed in the same shelling. The experience would change Owen forever. When he was brought out of the embankment, he was found to be disoriented and suffering from shell shock. He was sent to the Craiglockhart War Hospital near Edinburgh where the doctor asked him to write down his experiences. Here he met the poet, Siegfried Sassoon, who was to become a major influence on him. It was in Edinburgh that Owen wrote his poems describing the horror of the trenches and denouncing the jingoism that fired many of the soldiers and officers. It was also here in hospital that he read the poetry of Rabindranath Tagore, who had won the Nobel Prize in 1913.

Seven days before the end of the war, Owen was killed in action leading his men across the Sambre-Oise Canal in France. His unit had been ordered to cross the canal and engage the enemy on 4 November. He had been told that there should be 'no retirement under any circumstances.' The Germans had dug in with machine guns and as Owen and his men tried to cross on cork pontoons, they were simply cut to pieces. No territory was gained on either side. Owen was buried with his other fallen comrades in Ors communal cemetery. At the time of his death he had published only five poems. Owen's poetry would be recognised later, capturing the futility of the war: 'No mockeries now for them; no prayers nor bells... And bugles calling for them from sad shires.'[9]

Far away in India, a troubled Tagore would also write about the war: 'The wind is weary, the light is dead... The trumpet lies in the dust waiting for us.'[10]

On 4 December 1918, the British Prime Minister David Lloyd George told the War Cabinet that he wished to add India to the other Dominions for the peace talks. India, he said, had raised a million men for the War, and deserved to be represented. His proposal was accepted. The long process of peace was yet to begin.

13

The Peace

On 3 August 1914, the day before Britain had declared war against Germany, the British Foreign Secretary Sir Edward Grey had looked out of his office window at Whitehall to see the man lighting the lamps in St James's Park outside. 'The lamps are going out all over Europe,' he had remarked. 'We shall not see them lit again in our lifetime.' Four and a half years later the lights were on again, but the world was to change for ever. For six months in 1919, Paris was to host the biggest party of the century. Guests came from powerful countries and smaller nation states, from aspiring countries and hard-nosed republics. There were those who did not have a country, those who wanted independence and those who simply wanted to be heard. The leaders of the world argued and bartered and defined the terms of a peace that would change the boundaries of nation states, see the fall of empires and the ambitions of dominions and colonies. They would see boycott, anger and bitterness. They would see triumph and tears. Politicians, actors, economists, writers, businessmen, journalists and adventurers all flocked to the city to petition, protest or celebrate. There were wives and mistresses and dangerous liaisons. The glittering lights of Paris, its cafés and night clubs emerged out of the fog of war to sparkle before the new dawn.

The Big Four – USA, Britain, France and Italy – represented by President Woodrow Wilson of America, Britain's Lloyd George, George Clemenceau, Prime Minister of France and the Prime Minister of Italy Vittoria Orlando, would be the main architects of the peace. Attending the negotiations would be a range of countries including Japan, Canada,

Australia, New Zealand, South Africa, Brazil, Nicaragua, Portugal, Germany and India. A German journalist remarked about the crowd present at one of the meetings: 'Only Indians [American Indians] and Australian aborigines were absent among the races of the Earth,' he wrote. 'Every shade of skin apart from these: the palest ivory yellow, coffee-coloured brown, deep black.'[1]

The Maharaja of Bikaner had been summoned to London well in advance of the Peace Conference on the special request of the British Prime Minister. The Viceroy had sent him a telegram as early as October 1918 asking him to immediately secure accommodation on the *Chindwara* which was sailing from Bombay on 23 October. 'YH will be gratified to learn that the Prime Minister himself expressed a wish that you should go to London now. Precise methods in which YH's services will be asked has not yet been defined but I know that YH will understand the impossibility of getting matters clearly cut at the present juncture in the present stress.'

Bikaner was accompanied by Sinha, his companion in the talks the previous year at the Imperial War Cabinet sessions in London. Both were considered safe bets. It suited Britain to have a handsome and flamboyant Maharaja on their team. Lloyd George described him as a 'magnificent specimen of manhood'. Lloyd George's secretary and mistress, Frances Stevenson was almost poetic: 'He is a figure out of the Arabian Nights with jewel studded turban, an exceedingly handsome countenance and upright bearing.'[2] Sinha had taken his seat in the House of Lords on 10 January as Lord Sinha of Raipur a few days before the Peace Conference. The inclusion of the two Indians meant that the Secretary of State for India, Edwin Montagu, had been left out. A miffed Montagu complained to the Viceroy: 'An attempt is made to invite only your nominees, but I claim they cannot represent you without me.' He also made his displeasure known to the Prime Minister, who gave in, and India ended up with a team of three. The wording was changed: 'India was represented by her parliamentary spokesman, the Secretary of State for India and Lord Sinha with the cooperation of the Maharaja of Bikaner.' While all three shared the vision of India eventually governing itself, there was no doubt that they saw this autonomy as being within the British Empire. Lord Sinha, who had fought India's cause at the Imperial War Cabinet sessions in

London, kept a low profile at the Peace Conference, even saying that he could not think of a day when 'Britain would not be the paramount power in India.' It was just the sort of statement that Britain in the aftermath of a war which had drained India's resources wanted to hear from its colonies.

The delegation of the British Empire consisted of over four hundred officials, clerical staff and administrators who occupied five hotels near the Arc de Triomphe, the plush Majestic being the nerve centre. Strict rules of the house were laid out at the Majestic: mealtimes were specified and drinks had to be paid for by the delegates (unless they were from the Dominions or India, in which case the British government footed the bill). They were also bound to secrecy, and security was tight. The Prime Ministers of the Dominions – Robert Borden of Canada, William Massey of New Zealand and Billy Hughes of Australia – were all familiar with each other as they had attended the Imperial War Conference in London. Hughes lived on tea and toast, and was very influenced by the articles filed by a young reporter called Keith Murdoch, father of Rupert Murdoch, who was critical of the British handling of the Gallipoli landings. South Africa had its prime minister, the overweight and ailing Louis Botha and General Jan Smuts, who was highly respected by the British. All of them would fight Britain's case in the peace talks, but when it came to an issue where the Dominions had something at stake, they pressed their claims. Though the British delegation, particularly the Maharaja with his turban, attracted attention, it was the American president, Woodrow Wilson, whom the media and the public wanted to see.

Wilson had struck a chord with the people of France. His 'Fourteen Points' announced on 8 January 1918 had been welcomed by the Europeans who flocked to see the man many thought had been responsible for bringing the war to an end. Wilson was the first American President to visit Europe while in office. When he alighted from the *George Washington* at the French port of Brest on 13 December 1918, a month after the end of the war, thousands lined the street to greet him. However Clemenceau, Lloyd George and Orlando did not agree with the principles of the Fourteen Points. The Allies wanted their pound of flesh.

Britain did not want freedom of the seas and the French wanted compensation for the damage inflicted on them by Germany. The French were determined not to have a plebiscite in Alsace-Lorraine (as suggested by Wilson) as they felt the Germans had filled the area with German-speaking people. Wilson's dream was to create a League of Nations that would provide collective security and intervene in cases of disputes between nations. By the second week of January, Wilson moved into the Hotel Murat, an exclusive private house provided by the French government. The rest of the American delegation stayed at the Hotel Crillon where they organised hearty American breakfasts as opposed to the French coffee and croissant *petit déjeuner* that was commonly served. Paris still bore the scars of war – bombed buildings and boarded windows, but the city had dressed up for the Peace Conference. The cafes buzzed with journalists, academics and artistes, the weather was mild and couples returned to the nightclubs dancing the night away to celebrate the peace.

The preliminary meetings began on 12 January. The Big Four arrived at the Quai d'Orsay with their foreign secretaries, a bevy of advisers and clerical staff. The high decorated ceilings, the elaborate chandeliers, the green velvet curtains, all provided the backdrop for the meetings of the Supreme Council. Clemenceau was unanimously voted the President of the Peace Conference. Eventually twenty-seven nations would be part of the Conference assigned to fifty-two commissions holding 1,646 sessions. Hundreds of requests and petitions were sent to the Conference, from country heads, delegations and even individuals. The Japanese pressed for a 'racial equality' clause. A young kitchen assistant from Vietnam working at the Ritz Hotel sent a petition asking for his country's independence from France. His name was Ho Chi Minh. It was considered such an insignificant request that it did not even merit a reply. The end of the war meant everyone had a wish list. For six months the nations would bring theirs to the Peace Conference.

The war had changed India. The crops had failed, prices were high and a spirit of unrest was growing in the country. A famine had been declared in Bundelkhand in Central India. In Champaran in Bihar, farmers had been forced to grow indigo by British planters, leading to a food shortage as food crops were replaced by cash crops. Moreover they had been forced to sell their indigo at low prices to the British. The greatest unrest was felt in the cities and towns of the Punjab. The steep rise of income tax, sometimes up to 200 per cent, had caused severe hardship in cities like Lahore, Amritsar, Gujranwala, Wazirabad, Hafizabad, Khem Karan and others. The traders also deeply resented the seizure of wheat stocks under the Defence of India Act. The restriction on traffic affected the Punjab as producers exported large quantities of foodstuff from the region. War-weariness was also higher in the Punjab than in other places, as it was the region that had sent out most combatants to the frontline. Entire villages were still mourning the dead from the war and looking after the injured.

To add to the misery came political restrictions. The Rowlatt Act[3] passed by the Imperial Legislative Council in London on 17 March 1919 and approved by the Viceroy shortly after, led to immediate protests. The Rowlatt Act authorised the government to imprison a person for up to two years without trial if he was suspected of revolutionary activities against the British Raj. Those arrested faced *in camera* trials without a jury, often not knowing who had brought a charge or what evidence was held against them. Public meetings were banned and the press was muzzled. Rumours spread that the Act authorised the police to arrest any three Indians engaged in conversation and to search their premises without a warrant, leading to further dissent.

India's liberal-educated leaders were outraged. They felt that, having stood steadfastly by the Empire during the War, the country now deserved to be treated as an equal member of the Empire. Mohandas Karamchand Gandhi – still finding his feet in Indian politics – led the agitation against the Act. He argued that not everyone should face punishment for isolated political crimes and called for a series of *hartals* or general strikes. Shopkeepers across the Punjab shut their establishments in protest and Hindus and Muslims demonstrated their unity against the British, by pointedly drinking from the same cup and shouting, '*Hindu-Mussalman ki jai* (Victory to Hindus and Muslims)'. The two communities had fought together in the fields of Flanders and France and were once again united in demanding their rights. On 6 April, Gandhi called for a Satyagraha, the tried-and-tested method of political agitation that he had honed from his days in South Africa. The day was set aside as a day of 'humiliation and prayer'. There was little disturbance on that day, but tension against the Act continued to build and riots broke out in the cities of Amritsar, Bombay and Ahmedabad.

On 9 April two Congress leaders, Dr Satyapal and Dr Saifuddin Kitchlu, who had been prominent in the *hartal*, were issued with deportation orders by the Punjab government. They were ordered to report next day to the Deputy Commissioner. At 10.00 a.m. Kitchlu and Satyapal arrived at the house of the Deputy Commissioner with some friends. Within half an hour they were arrested and whisked off to Dharamsala by car, leading to a huge outcry. As news of the deportation spread, crowds started gathering near Hall Gate. An angry mob stormed the National Bank beating to death the Manager and Assistant Manager, Stewart and Scott, throwing the office furniture on them and burning their bodies in the middle of the bank. The bank was then looted and set on fire. The Alliance Bank was next. The Manager, G.M. Thomson, who attempted to defend himself with a revolver, was killed and his body thrown from the balcony on the street. His body was also burnt under a pile of bank furniture drenched in kerosene oil. At the Chartered Bank, glass and property were smashed but the local police managed to disperse the crowds. By evening the Town Hall and the sub post office were in flames, the Telegraph Office had been attacked and the Telephone Exchange destroyed. The Guard of the North-Western Railway, Rowlands, was chased and brutally beaten to death. A lady missionary, Marcella Sherwood, was chased by a mob as she cycled to one of her schools. She was thrown to the ground, beaten and left for dead but was picked up by a Hindu family who looked after her and helped her get medical treatment. The mob also went in search of Isabel Easdon, the lady doctor in charge of the Zenana Hospital, but she managed to hide and was eventually saved by her orderly. The crowd was clearly searching for Europeans, men or women.[4]

Troops were called in to restore order and they fired on protesting crowds killing ten civilians and wounding many more. On 11 April, Brigadier General Reginald E Dyer arrived from Jalandhar Cantonment and occupied Amritsar, determined to control the dissent. A curfew was imposed in the city and a proclamation issued that all meetings and gatherings were prohibited and would be 'dispersed at once under Military Law.'[5] The proclamation was read out – accompanied by the sound of a drum – at various places in the city on the morning of 13

April, the day of the festival of Baisakhi, the Sikh New Year. Most remained unaware of the order as no effort was made to see that it reached every corner of the city.

From dawn of 13 April, people from neighbouring villages started arriving at the Golden Temple, the holiest shrine of the Sikhs, women, children and families celebrating the New Year. Shops around the Temple were busy selling sticky jalebis, lassi and other food items. Women were buying bangles and dupattas and children were enjoying the spring sunshine. Most were dressed in yellow and orange, the colours of Baisakhi, symbolising the spring harvest. The sound of the Gurbani could be heard from the Temple complex.

Next to the Golden Temple was a park called Jallianwala Bagh. Local activists had organised a rally there at 4.30 p.m. to discuss the Rowlatt Act and the recent police firing. The main entrance to the Bagh was through a narrow lane next to the Temple through a gap between houses. The Bagh itself was an enclosed area surrounded by the walls of adjacent buildings. Four small gates at different points provided restricted access. In the middle of the park was a well. The main entrance had a raised area on either side.

Thousands had gathered in the park to listen. At one end – about 100 yards away from the main entrance – a man on a small platform was addressing the crowd, most of who were peacefully squatting on the ground before him. Children were playing near their parents and the atmosphere remained festive. At 5.15 p.m. the speeches were drowned by the noise of military boots running in formation. Dyer had arrived with two armoured cars and armed soldiers. The armoured cars could not enter the narrow lane and Dyer left them outside blocking the entrance. He took fifty soldiers inside – twenty-five Gurkha Riflemen and twenty-five Baluchis – and lined them up on the high ground on either side of the entrance. Outside were forty Gurkhas armed with *khukris*. The terrified crowds watched in confusion and horror. Without giving any warning to disperse, Dyer ordererd his soldiers to open fire.

There was nowhere for the crowds to go. When the soldiers fired in the air, he ordered them to aim at the crowds. As the men, women and children started running to the gates, he ordered the soldiers to fire near the exits. He even fired on the people lying down on the ground. As the screams of the terrified and the dying filled the air, Dyer continued firing for ten minutes till the last bullet was exhausted. 1,650 rounds were fired on the trapped and unarmed crowds. In desperation, women and children jumped into the well to escape the firing. Others were trampled to death. Thousands of bodies, dressed in their finest, lay strewn in the park. Once the last bullet was spent, Dyer simply marched his troops back to the Ram Bagh outside the city, leaving the wounded to die. The cries of the dying and the mourners could be heard across the city. While official British figures put the death toll at 379 with approximately 1,200 wounded, the Congress Party claimed that nearly 1,000 had died and more than 1,500 were wounded. The crowd in the park was estimated to be between 15–20,000.[6]

The Jallianwala Bagh massacre shocked and enraged the country. The Nobel Laureate Tagore returned his knighthood in protest, writing to the Viceroy asking to be relieved of the honour he had accepted four years earlier: 'The disproportionate severity of the punishments inflicted upon the unfortunate people and the methods of carrying them out, we are convinced, are without parallel in the history of civilized governments,' wrote the poet. 'I for my part want to stand, shorn of all special distinctions, by the side of those of my countrymen who for their so-called insignificance are liable to suffer a degradation not fit for human beings.'[7]

Barely five months after the end of the First World War – where 400,000 people from the Punjab had fought for the Empire – the killing of the innocent at Jallianwala Bagh, was seen as a cruel reward for their loyalty.

To make matters worse, Dyer was unrepentant. He reported: 'I fired and continued to fire until the crowd dispersed, and I considered this the least amount of firing which would produce the necessary moral and widespread effect it was my duty to produce, if I was to justify my action. If more troops had been at hand the casualties would have been greater in proportion. *It was no longer a question of merely dispersing the crowd*, but one of producing a sufficient moral effect from a military point of view, not only on those who were present, but more specifically throughout the Punjab. There could be no question of undue severity.'[8]

Not satisfied at the mass killing, Dyer then issued a 'Crawling Order' on the night of 19 April in Amritsar on the spot where the English missionary, Marcella Sherwood had been assaulted. The order was that no Indian be allowed to pass through the street, but, if they wanted to, would have to crawl on all fours. Pickets were set up to enforce the order from 6.00 a.m. to 8.00 p.m. The assailants of Sherwood were not residents of the street, so the order punished and humiliated the innocent. General Dyer's instructions effectively closed the street as the inhabitants could not walk out of their front door. None of the houses had back entrances. At the Hunter Committee enquiry, Dyer remained indifferent to the problem he had caused the residents and said they could have gone over the roofs of their houses instead.[9] He did not care either that if anyone on the street was ill no doctor could enter unless they were prepared to crawl. The 'Crawling Order' was imposed from 19 April to 25 April 1919.

Hardit Singh Malik was devastated to hear about the killings in Amritsar. Bur worse was to come. Following the disturbances in Punjab, aerial bombardment was ordered on Amritsar and Gujranwala. Sopwith Camel aircraft, the most advanced fighter of the Royal Air Force[10], flew low on rural areas, indiscriminately dropping bombs on the villages. Twelve civilians were killed and scores injured. Malik, who had so proudly flown his Sopwith Camel aircraft over Belgium and France, risking his life for the Allies, watched in horror as his colleagues from the Royal Air Force pounded his homeland with bombs killing innocent civilians.

Malik had married his fiancé, Prakash, on the fateful Baisakhi day of 13 April 1919, when festivities had turned into mourning on account of the massacre. The date had been fixed by his family as it was an auspicious day for weddings in the Sikh calendar. Three hundred years earlier Guru Gobind Singh, the tenth Guru of the Sikhs, had formed the Khalsa on that day. Malik had fallen in love with Prakash when he had visited Rawalpindi after the war and the couple had decided to get married before he returned to England. 'Little did we know then that this day would go down in history as one of the most tragic, bloodiest days,' Malik recalled.[11] On 15 April, martial law was extended to Lahore, Gujranwala, Gujrat and Lyallpur in Punjab. Hindus, Sikhs and Muslims who had returned from the war watched in horror as the British turned their fire on them.

Though Dyer was recalled to Britain and the Hunter Commission set up to enquire into the Amritsar Massacre, the General remained defiant. He confirmed that he had deliberately gone to Jallianwala Bagh with the aim of firing at the crowds. 'I had made up my mind that I would do all men to death if they were going to continue the meeting,' he said.

Asked whether he had from time to time changed his firing and directed it to places where the crowds were thickest, Dyer replied: 'That is so.'

On whether he would have taken in the armoured cars if the passage had been wide enough and opened fire with the machine guns, Dyer replied in the affirmative: 'I think, probably yes.'

'In that case the casualties would have been very much higher?' questioned the committee. 'Yes,' said the unrepentant General.[12]

Dyer's actions found backing in British circles. The right-wing *Morning Post* set up a fund for Dyer and raised the large sum of £26,000. Kipling described him as the 'man who saved India' and contributed £50 to the fund himself. A Thirteen Women Committee was constituted to present 'the Saviour of the Punjab with the sword of honour and a purse'. Large contributions to the fund were made by civil servants and retired British and Indian Army officers.

The wounds of Jallianwala Bagh would continue to fester. Gandhi, who had supported the British War Effort, was disillusioned with British rule. A ten-year-old Sikh boy, Udham Singh, was so affected by the incident at Jallianwala Bagh that he swore to take revenge. Fifteen years later he bathed in the holy water of the Golden Temple and vowed to restore honour to his humiliated nation. Singh's target was the former governor of Punjab, Michael O'Dwyer who had given a clean chit to Dyer for the massacre and subsequently ordered the aerial bombings of Amritsar and Gujranwala. Singh travelled to London and waited for his chance.

Though a Sikh, Udham Singh cut his hair and donned Western clothes. He visited the gurdwaras in London, helped in the langar (communal kitchen), and blended in with the Indian workers. On 13 March 1940, he got his opportunity. At a joint meeting of the East India Association and the Central Asian Society in Caxton Hall in Westminster, Singh concealed a revolver in a book and walked in. He was wearing a hat and a dark suit and looked like any ordinary Indian. Michael O'Dwyer was one of the speakers. At the end of the meeting, when O'Dwyer moved to speak to the Secretary of State for India, Lord Zetland, Singh pulled out his revolver and fired twice at him. O'Dwyer died instantly. He then fired at Zetland, injuring him along with two others. Singh made no move to escape and stood there waiting to be arrested. He was handcuffed and led out of Caxton Hall. After almost twenty-one years, Udham Singh avenged the Jallianwala Bagh killings with the assassination of Michael O'Dwyer.

On 1 April 1940 Udham Singh was taken to Brixton prison and formally charged with the murder of Michael O' Dwyer. While awaiting trial, he went on a forty-two-day hunger strike and had to be force fed. The trial began two months later, on 4 June, at the Old Bailey under Justice Atkinson. When asked for his name, Udham Singh replied: 'Ram Mohammad Singh Azad', combining Hindu, Muslim and Sikh names to symbolize the unity of India. Azad meant 'freedom'. Udham Singh was hanged in Pentonville Prison on 31 July 1940. At his trial he said: 'I did it because I had a grudge against him. He deserved it.'

The Jallianwala Bagh massacre was barely mentioned at the War Cabinet 'British Empire and Africa report' for the week ending 15 April 1919. The report mentioned 'trouble' in Amritsar and that 'troops were called in to restore order'. It made no mention of the killing.[13] Neither was the major incident brought up at the Peace Conference in Paris. The mass tragedy in India mattered little to the Big Four.

Exactly five years after the assassination of Archduke Franz Ferdinand, 28 June 1919, was chosen as the date for the signing of the Peace. The treaty was to be signed amidst the ostentatious surroundings of the Hall of Mirrors at Versailles Palace, built by Louis XIV at vast expense as a reflection of his political power. Every attention had been paid to the details of the ceremony.

The Hall of Mirrors was a long and narrow room, more like a corridor. The delegates had to walk up the grand marble staircase, pass through the state apartments of Marie Antionette and the Hall of Peace. A long horseshoe shaped table ran along the mirrored side of the hall. Clemenceau sat in the centre. To his left were the delegates from Britain, the Dominions and India. The world press occupied chairs on the side of the Hall of War. In the middle of the horseshoe was a table on which lay the Treaty of Versailles.

Hours before the formal signing, the room was packed with officials, guests and reporters. Patrolling guards ensured that booty hunters did not make off with the inkwells and pens. At 2.30 p.m. Clemenceau entered the room, looked around and went up to some wounded soldiers wearing medals seated near the window and engaged them in conversation. At 2.45 he moved to the middle table and took the seat of the presiding officer. Wilson entered immediately after Clemenceau and was greeted with discreet applause. Soon the rest of the delegates filed in, the audience craning their necks to spot the leaders. The German delegation consisted of Foreign Minister Hermann Mueller and the colonial minister, Dr Johannes Bell.

At 3.15 p.m. Clemenceau rose and announced that the session had opened. 'An agreement has been reached upon the conditions of the treaty of peace between the allied and associated powers and the German Empire,' he said. He then invited the German plenipotentiaries to sign the treaty. As the interpreter translated Clemenceau's speech from French to German, he stopped briefly when it came to using the words 'German Empire' as used by the French President: '*l'empire allemand*'. He translated it as 'The German Republic'. Clemenceau promptly whispered, 'Say German Reich'. Getting past the minor incident, Mueller and Bell proceeded to the table and signed their names. The delegation from the US followed the Germans. As Wilson walked to the table, the other delegates shook his hand and congratulated him. He gave a broad smile and signed his name on the historic treaty. Lloyd George followed. After him came the Prime Ministers of the Dominions, and, finally India.

The British authorities had been at pains to decide which of the two Indians at the Conference should sign the Treaty of Versailles. Should it be Bikaner, the Maharaja and soldier, or the Bengali politician, Lord Sinha? George V was consulted and he told Montagu that Bikaner 'should come first'. An old friend of the King's, Bikaner had been his ADC when he was Prince of Wales and visited India for the coronation of Edward VII. They were shooting partners and went to parties and meetings together, the Maharaja giving the King much gossip from the Princely States and the King indulging him with the same from England. The King was apparently surprised to learn that Bikaner was not a British subject. And so the Maharaja, wearing the British military uniform and his golden turban, put pen to paper and signed the Treaty on behalf of India. He was followed by Edwin Montagu. Sinha did not sign. He preferred to remain on the sidelines and described himself as 'just a foot-soldier of reform'.[14]

The scene is captured on canvas in the painting, *The Signing of Peace in the Hall of Mirrors, Versailles, 28th June 1919* by Sir William Orpen. It highlights the grandeur of the hall, the famous mirrors dazzling in the light and reflecting the large front windows. The German representative Johannes Bell is seen from the back signing the Treaty while his colleague Hermann Mueller stands next to him. Clemenceau sits opposite. The politicians sit or stand around the table, a sea of black suits. However, it is the Maharaja of Bikaner that the eye is drawn to. He is positioned at the centre of the canvas flanked by two grand pillars. His proud figure stands directly behind Lloyd George. He looks straight ahead, his arms in his pocket. His imposing presence reflects the role that India played in the Great War and the reason they came to sign the peace.

In six months the powers had decided the fate of nations. The spoils of war had been carved up. Wilson's Fourteen Points had been extensively modified. The French had had their way and the Germans had been made to pay. The Treaty made Germany and her allies accept responsibility 'for causing all the loss and damage' during the war. Germany was forced to disarm and pay expensive reparations. The French achieved the demilitarisation of the Rhineland. In 1921 the total cost of German reparations was assessed at 132 billion Marks or $31.4 billion. Their protests were ignored.

Wilson's dream of establishing the League of Nations, however, became a reality and the first session took place in Paris on 16 January 1920, six months after the Treaty of Versailles came into force. India had taken its place in the League of Nations, but not without a struggle. It was the Maharaja of Bikaner who had spoken out strongly stating

India's case. 'Where it is a question of securing the peace of the world, the important fact must be borne in mind that India represents one fifth of the entire human race,' said the Maharaja. His argument was immediately accepted. It was a symbolic victory for a country that was aspiring towards nationhood.

Despite Wilson's efforts, the Treaty was not popular in the United States. The Senate was cold to the Treaty and, on 19 March, finally rejected it. 'The Devil is a busy man,' a broken Wilson told his doctor that day. Despite all the President's efforts, for which he was given the Nobel Peace Prize, the Senate did not ratify any of the peace treaties and the U.S. never joined the League of Nations. It later signed separate treaties with Germany, Austria and Hungary. It was a fragile peace. Nineteen years later the world would be at war once again.

Four and a half years after the summer of 1914, the ships were returning to the ports of Bombay and Karachi. The crowds stood in the docks again waiting to receive the men who had left as boys and come back changed forever. Darwan Singh Negi's eyes filled with tears as he saw the familiar coastline of his homeland. Less than sixty men of the Garhwal regiment had survived the war. All their officers were dead. George Henderson remembered his friend Manta Singh, who had saved his life. The cantonment would not be the same without him. Mir Dast still had headaches from the gas and wondered if he would ever be well again. He also thought about his brother and whether he had indeed survived the war and returned to Tirah. He had heard rumours of the same, but couldn't be sure. He wondered if the village had forgiven Mir Mast for deserting. At least he had given them something to be proud of. He would hold his head high and wear his Victoria Cross. Khudadad Khan longed to return to his beloved mountains. He was impatient to be reunited with his sisters and show them his Victoria Cross. The village of Dulmial waited for over four hundred of their sons to return.

The soldiers walked off the ship, some on crutches, supporting each other, clutching their gallantry medals. A band was playing on the docks and there were marigold flowers, but there was an aching feeling of emptiness. How different was this day from the one four years ago when they had arrived at the port of Marseilles and been greeted by the cheers of the French people. Too many of their comrades had died. Many were blind and would never be able to see their loved ones. Others were shell-shocked and would live the life of the dead, tormented by nightmares, alone and untreated. A hospital for the limbless soldiers was set up in Bombay, but few of the injured from the remote villages in the Himalayas or the North West Frontier Provinces could travel the distance for treatment and artificial limbs. They remained in their villages, unable to work the land they had tended before, a shadow of their former selves.

They had done their duty and served their *Sarkar*, but the soldiers found they had returned to a changed land. They had expected to be hailed as heroes, but no one really cared any more. The crops had failed, unrest was rife and the mood had completely changed. The intellectual elite of India had backed the War Effort thinking it would help secure concessions from the British government. But they were disappointed. The Government of India Act of 1919, which gave some authority to Central and Provincial Legislative Councils, did not go far enough. Post Jallianwala, a wave of nationalism swept over the country. The soldiers and the war were already in the past.

India now had its new heroes. They were the ones who were fighting for Independence and kissing the hangman's noose like Bhagat Singh, Raj Guru, Sukhdev and Udham Singh. Soon the story of the soldiers would be completely forgotten except in regimental headquarters and remote villages. The extensive British accounts of the Battles of Neuve Chapelle, Ypres and the Somme would rarely mention the presence of the Indians. Over the years the visits to the memorials would thin out and gradually there would be nobody to visit the graves dotting the countryside of France and Belgium. Few would remember that one and a half million of them crossed the *Kala Pani* for the first time in the autumn of 1914 to fight and die in the 'war that was to end all wars'. Their names – carved in a corner of a foreign field – would be all that was left to tell their tale.

Epilogue

Darwan Singh Negi returned to his village of Kerfarteer after the War. He had learnt many lessons in the West. He knew that the illiterate peasants of Garhwal would never make progress unless they received an education. In France, during the presentation of his Victoria Cross, he had made a special request to the King that he start a school in Karnaprayag in the Garhwal hills which would be called the War Memorial School. The King had granted his request and the school was built, drawing in children from the neighbouring villages, but the campaigning Negi had another wish. He met the Viceroy of India, Lord Chelmsford and asked for a train to be built from Dehradun to Kefarteer so that the people of his village could benefit economically. The Viceroy agreed to the request, but the Garhwali soldier would not see it happen. Cash-strapped between the wars, Britain had no interest or financial motive in developing the rail line in Garhwal. Post-independence, the plan was shelved. Darwan Singh's village still remains a three hour trek from the nearest motorable road. He was promoted to the rank of Subedar and continued to work in the Army till his retirement. He died in 1951 leaving behind five children. The Yudh Smarak Uttarkhand Madhyamik Vidyalaya that he built still stands today, having now grown into a secondary school.

Gabar Singh's widow, Satoori Devi, spent her life keeping the memory of her husband alive. When she received the Victoria Cross awarded to her husband, she could not read his name inscribed on the back of the gunmetal cross on its crimson ribbon, but she knew it was special. The fourteen-year-old pinned the medal to her sari and would not be separated from it. She would wear Gabar Singh's medal when she went to the forest to gather wood and crouched over the coal stove cooking the family meals. People would salute her in the street as she walked past them wearing the medal. Until an artist in Lansdowne painted a portrait of Gabar Singh, she did not even have a photo of her husband to remember him by. When the Memorial to Gabar Singh was built in the square in Chamba in 1925, she organised the annual Chamba Mela on his birth anniversary. Till her death in 1981, Satoori Devi wore the Victoria Cross and took the salute at the Memorial. A tiny figure, her once pretty face now lined and wrinkled, she would stand proudly receiving the salute on behalf of her husband. After her death, Gabar Singh's Victoria Cross was handed over to the Garhwal Rifles Regiment for safekeeping and is now with the Quarter Guard at Lansdowne with a replica on display at the Centre Museum. The annual Chamba Mela in April is held even today. Gabar Singh's grandnephew, Kamal Singh Negi, supervises the arrangements. The sound of conch shells mixes with the tunes of bagpipes in the religious and military ceremony to remember the war hero. The story of his bravery in Neuve Chapelle is narrated over loudspeakers in the remote hill town. Kamal Singh Negi fears that his generation will be the last to remember Gabar Singh's courage and sacrifice.

Khudadad Khan remained with the army after the First World War, being promoted to Subedar in December 1929. He received a gift of 50 acres of land and ensured that his extended family could live with him. He had two sons and a daughter. Aware of the water problem in the area, he funded the construction of a reservoir in his village and spent time in charitable activities. He boosted the morale of young soldiers from the area and made several visits to Britain in connection with the Victoria Cross. On 26 June 1956, Khan proudly participated in the Victoria Cross centenary review parade in Hyde Park, London. He died on 8 March 1971 in Pakistan and was buried in his village in Chakwal. A life-size statue of Khudadad Khan stands in the grounds of the Army Museum in Rawalpindi. His grandsons are calling for a university in his name in Chakwal.

Mir Dast returned to the North West Frontier after the war, but never recovered from the effect of the gassing in the trenches and had to retire early from the army in 1917. He died on 19 January 1945 at Shagi Landi Kyan Village and is buried at Warsak Road Cemetery in Peshawar, Pakistan.

Manta Singh's son, Assa Singh Johal, was looked after by Captain George Henderson. Assa joined the same regiment as his father, and fought in the Second World War alongside Robert, George Henderson's son. Robert's son, Ian, became a good friend of Assa's son, Jaimal Singh Johal. In the 1980s, when Assa Singh suffered a stroke and needed to go to Britain to join his son Jaimal, the British government delayed his entry. Robert Henderson went with him to the Home Office, and said that he had served with Assa Singh in the war and that if he, Robert (who had been born and raised in India), could be allowed to enter the country, so should Assa. The immigration officials immediately stamped Assa Singh's forms. Assa Singh went on to start the Undivided Servicemen's Association in Britain, brought together many of the Indian veterans who had served in the First and Second World Wars, attended the annual veterans' dinner at Sandhurst, met the Queen and Prince Charles on several occasions and always attended the annual service for Indian servicemen at the Chhatri Memorial in Patcham Downs, where his father Manta Singh was cremated. The story of the friendship of the Subedar from Punjab and the English officer remains one of the moving stories of the war.

Hardit Singh Malik returned to Rawalpindi after the War and took up a career in the Indian Civil Service taking on assignments as Trade Commissioner in London, Hamburg, Washington and Ottawa and becoming Prime Minister of Patiala State. After Indian Independence, Prime Minister Jawaharlal Nehru posted him as High Commissioner to Canada and then as Ambassador to France. He retired in 1956 and returned to his first passion, golf, which he continued to play even with the German bullet still embedded in his leg. He wrote his memoirs *A Little Work, A Little Play* at the age of 87 after being persuaded by his family. He died peacefully in November 1985 at the age of ninety-one.

Indra Lal Roy had a road named after him in Calcutta. On his hundredth birth anniversary the Indian government issued a postage stamp in his honour. A textbook in Bengali *Biman Bir Indra Lal Roy* (Hero of the Air, Indra Lal Roy) was published in the early thirties for primary school children. The Air Force Museum in Delhi has a collection of his sketches on display.

Poresh Lal Roy survived the War and returned to India to become a champion boxer. He was known as the 'Father of Indian boxing', starting a boxing academy in Calcutta and mentoring many young boxers. He joined the Indian Railways and eventually became the Director of the Railway Board. During the Second World War he returned to the frontline with the rank of Major.

General Willcocks wrote his memoirs *With the Indians in France* where he spoke fondly of the brave men who had gone to fight their first western war. In 1917 he was appointed Governor of Bermuda and he served in that post till 1922. He remained in love with India and returned to the country after his term as Governor was over. He died in Bharatpur in Rajasthan in 1926 and was given a full state funeral by the Maharaja of Bharatpur, his last rites performed in Hindu tradition. There is a memorial on the site.

Ganga Singh, the Maharaja of Bikaner, concentrated on development work in his kingdom after the War. He commissioned the building of the Ganga Dam in 1925. It was completed in 1927 and involved 89 miles of lined canal. The opening ceremony on 26 October 1927 was presided over by Lord Irwin, the then Viceroy of India. Bikaner planned and developed the city of Sri Ganganagar which became the food bowl of Rajasthan. He died in Bombay on 2 February 1943 aged sixty-two after a reign of fifty-six years.

Lord Sinha became Governor of Bihar and Orissa in 1920, the first Indian to be appointed to such a high rank in the administration. He retired in 1921 on grounds of health and became a member of the Judicial Committee of the Privy Council in 1926. He died on 4 March 1928 at Behrampore in West Bengal. His sons never took on his hereditary title and did not sit in the House of Lords.

Walter Lawrence wrote *The India We Served*, published in 1929, about the days he and his wife Lillian, spent in India. He died at the age of eighty-three on 25 May 1940 at Gorse Hill, Woking, in Surrey, survived by two sons.

Sukha's grave with its headstone can be seen in St Nicholas Parish Church in Brockenhurst alongside graves of New Zealand soldiers from the First World War. It is looked after by the Commonwealth War Graves Commission.

The 460 men of the small village of Dulmial who went to the War are largely forgotten. Nine of them never returned. In the 1920s, the British government gifted the village with a cannon which was placed on an embankment near the pond. Today the cannon has become the central point of the sleepy village, but few of the children playing near it know why it is there. The village is referred to as the 'Village of the Gun'.

The Muslim graves in Woking were sadly neglected and vandalised in the 1960s. In 1968 the bodies were transferred to the Brookwood Military Cemetery nearby. The monument was restored in the 1990s by the musician Paul Weller, a local resident of Woking. In 2012, English Heritage and Woking Council, at the request of the Horsell Common Preservation Society, offered to preserve the monument for the centenary of the war in 2014. The final phase of the project will create an Islamic style garden within the walled structure.

An Annual Memorial Service is held at the Chhatri on the second Sunday of June. It is attended by, among others, the grandsons of Manta Singh and Captain Henderson, Jaimal Singh Johal and Ian Henderson, and James Whittaker, great-grandson of General Willcocks.

Few visit the memorial to Indian soldiers at Neuve Chapelle. Only the songbirds pay tribute to the memory of the dead.

Appendix

Indian VCs of the First World War

1. Sepoy Khudadad Khan – 129th Duke of Connaught's Own Baluchis, 31 October 1914, First Battle of Ypres Hollebeke, Belgium.
2. Naik Darwan Singh Negi – 1/39th Garhwal Rifles, 24 November 1914, Festubert, France.
3. Gabar Singh Negi – 2/39th Garhwal Rifles, 10 March 1915, Neuve Chapelle, France.
4. Mir Dast – 57th Wilde's Rifles (Frontier Force) August 1915, Ypres, Belgium.
5. Rifleman Kulbir Thapa – 3rd Queen Alexandra's Own Gurkha Rifles, – 26 September 1915, Fauquissart, France.
6. Jemadar Gobind Singh – 28th Light Cavalry – 1 December 1917, East of Peizieres, Battle of Cambrai.
7. Jemadar Lala – 41st Dogras – 21 January 1916, El Orah, Mesopotamia.
8. Karna Bahadur Rana – 2nd Battalion, 3rd Gurkha Rifles, 10 April 1918, El Kefr, Egypt.
9. Shahamand Khan – 89th Punjabis– 13 April 1916, Mespotamia.
10. Sepoy Chattah Singh – 9th Bhopal Infantry – 13 January 1916, Mesopotamia.
11. Badlu Singh – 14th Murray's Jat Lancers(Scinde Horse), attached to 29th Lancers (Deccan Horse). – 23 September 1918, Kh.es Samariyeh, Jordan River, Palestine.

Notes

Introduction

1. Pictures of Madras after Emden struck, by A Srivathsan, *The Hindu*, 14 August 2013.

2. *The Last Gentleman of War: The Raider Exploits of the Cruiser Emden* by R.K. Lochner quoted in *Frontline* magazine article "The Guns of Emden", by S. Theodore Baskaran. 12 September 2009.

3. *The Times*, 22 October 1914.

4. *Rabindranath Tagore, The Myriad-Minded Man* by Krishna Dutta and Andrew Robinson, Bloomsbury, 1995, London p. 2.

5. BL/IOR/ MSS Eur 143/92 Further extracts from reports made by the censor for Indian mails in France.

6. BL/IOR/ MSS Eur 143/92 Further extracts from reports made by the censor for Indian mails in France.

7. In addition, 172,815 animals (including horses, mules and camels) were sent to the Front. (Source: The National Archives).

8. Official figures put the number at 64,459.

9. 140,000 went to the Western Front including 90,000 combatants and 50,000 non-combatants.

10. Before the War, the Indian Army was made up of 76,953 British soldiers, 193,901 Indian soldiers and 45,660 non-combatants. Source: The National Archives

11. BL/IOR/ MSS Eur 143/92 Further extracts from reports made by the censor for Indian mails in France.

1: Monsoon

1. Author interview with Kamal Singh Negi, grandnephew of Gabar Singh Negi, Chamba, India, April 2013.

2. *First World War* by Martin Gilbert, Harper Collins, London, 1995. p. 15.

3. *The Times*, June 29, 1914.

4. Ibid.

5. BL/IOR/ MSS Eur F170/8 Papers related to the Indian involvement in the First World War.

6. BL/IOR/L/MIL/17/5/2421 War Diaries World War I 1914–1921.

7. Ibid.

8. BL/IOR/ MSS Eur F170/8.

9. Quoted in *Dadabhai Naoroji, The Grand Old Man of India* by R.P.Masani, Allen and Unwin, London, 1939. pp. 527–8.

10. Ibid.

11. BL/IOR/MSS Eur F170/8.

12. *The Times*, 13 September, 1914.

13. BL/IOR/ MSS Eur F170/8.

14. *A Little Work, A Little Play, The Autobiography of Hardit Singh Malik*, Book Wise, India, 2011 p. 51.

15. Ibid. p. 56.

16. Ibid.

17. Ibid., p. 13.

18. *Chhelebela* (Boyhood), Article by Poresh Lal Roy, *Jugantar*, 1 Feb 1972.

19. A Day with a Pugilist, Interview with Poresh Lal Roy by Sunit K. Mukherjee, *Patrika* newspaper, Calcutta. 3 July 1978.

20. *Victoria & Abdul* by Shrabani Basu, The History Press, Stroud, 2010.

21. BL/IOR/V/27/230/14 Hardinge Papers 1913–16.

22. Rabindranath Tagore and World Peace by Kalyan Kundu, Asiatic, Vol 4, 1 June 2010.

23. *English Writings of Rabindranath Tagore, A Miscellany, Vol Two.* Sisir Kumar Das (Ed), Sahitya Akademi, Delhi, 1996.

24. TNA/WO 95/3926/1, National Archives, Kew, War diaries of Jullunder Brigade, 3rd Lahore Division.

25. Author interview with Jaimal Singh Johal, grandson of Manta Singh, Buckinghamshire, May 2013.

2: Arrival

1. TNA/WO 95/3926/1 Regimental diaries of Jullunder Brigade.

2. Ibid.

3. TNA/ WO/95/3923/5 Regimental diaries of 57th Wilde's Rifles.

4. Author interview with Ghulam Rabbani, grandson of Khudadad Khan, February 2015.

5. TNA/WO 95/3926/1, entry by Major Harry Hill.

6. *Forty-one Years in India, From Subaltern to Commander-in-Chief*, F.S. Roberts, Richard Bentley & Sons, London 1898 .

7. Ibid.

8. Ibid.

9. TNA/WO 95/3920/1 War Diary Indian Field Ambulance and British Field Ambulance.

10. Ibid.

11. BL/IOR/ Mss Eur F143/92 Further extracts from reports made by the censor for Indian mails in France.

12. TNA/WO 95/3920/1.

13. TNA/WO 95/3926/1 War Diary Jullundur Brigade.

14. Ibid.

15. TNA/WO 95/3926/1.

16. *The Indian Corps in France*, Lt Col Merewether and Sir Frederick Smith, p. xvii.

17. TNA/WO 95/3926/1.

18. *The Manchester Guardian* 12 November 1914.

19. *Indian Cavalry Officer, 1914–15, Captain Roly Grimshaw*, Col J Wakefield and Lt Col J.M.Weippert (ed). Costello 1986 p. 105.

20. TNA/WO 95/3926/1.

21. TNA/ WO 95/3923/5.

22. BL/IOR/Mss Eur F143 92–97, Extracts from reports made by the censor for Indian mails in France.

23. Ibid.

24. *Sepoys in the Trenches, The Indian Corps on the Western Front 1914–15*, Gordon Corrigan, p. 45.

25. *With the Indians in France*, James Willcocks, Constable and Company, London, 1920.

3: Comfort Kameti

1. BL/IOR/Mss Eur F 120/6 Report of the first six months of the Indian Soldiers' Fund.

2. *Oxford Dictionary of National Biography* (entry on John Hewett by Katherine Prior).

3. BL/IOR/Mss Eur F120/6.

4. Ibid.

5. Ibid.

6. Oral recording from LGOG volunteer at the London Transport Museum.

7. *With the Indians in France*, General Sir James Willcocks,Constable and Company Ltd, London, 1920.

8. Ibid., p. 28.

9. BL/IOR/L/MIL/17347 Censorship of correspondence to and from Indian Expeditionary Force in France 1914–1918.

10. Ibid.

11. Ibid.

12. ibid

13. Ibid.

14. Ibid.

15. Ibid.

4: First Blood

1. *The Indian Corps in France*, Merewether and Smith, John Murray, London, 1918, reprint edition, Naval and Military Press.

2. A portion of land that is surrounded on three sides by enemy territory.

3. *With the Indians in France*, James Willcocks, Constable and Company, London. p. 35.

4. *The Indian Corps in France*, Merewether and Smith, John Murray, London, 1918, reprint edition, Naval and Military Press, p. 38.

5. Ibid., p. 44.

6. *English Writings of Rabindranath Tagore*, Vol Two. Sisir Kumar Das (ed). Sahitya Akademi, Delhi, 1996. pp. 231–232.

7. BL/IOR/L/PO/476.

8. BL/IOR/Mss Eur F120/17.

9. TNA/WO 95/3948 War Diary Bareilly Brigade, Meerut Division.

10. *With the Indians in France*, James Willcocks, p. 47.

11. Ibid., p. 69.

12. *The Indian Army And the King's Enemies 1900–1947* by Charles Chenevix Trench, Thames and Hudson, London, p. 44.

13. BL/IOR/L/PO/476.

14. *With the Indians in France,* James Willcocks, p. 70.

15. BL/IOR/L/PO/476.

16. Ibid.

17. *A Brief History of the First World War, Eyewitness Accounts of the War to End all Wars, 1914–18.* Jon E Lewis (ed), Constable & Robinson, London, revised edition 2014, p 67.

18. Historical Record of the 39th Royal Garhwal Rifles Vol 1 1887–1922. Comment by Captain D.H. Acworth. Compiled by Brig Gen J Evatt, Gale and Polden Ltd, Aldershot.

19. TNA/ WO 95/3923/5 War diary 57th Wilde's.

20. Author interview with Balbir Singh Negi, son of Darwan Singh Negi, Lucknow, India, April 2013.

5: The Trenches

1. BL/IOR/L/PO/476 Benson to Viceroy.

2. TNA/ WO 95/3923/5 War diary 57th Wilde's.

3. BL/IOR Mss Eur 143/92 Further extracts from reports made by the censor for Indian mails in France.

4. Ibid.

5. BL/IOR/L/PO/10/27.

6. BL/IOR/Mss Eur F143/92 Further extracts from reports made by the censor for Indian mails in France.

7. BL/IOR/L/PO/476 Willingdon to Viceroy.

8. BL/IOR/L/PO/476.

9. BL/IOR/L/PO/476 Willingdon to Viceroy.

10. BL/IOR/L/PO/476 Duff to Viceroy.

11. *Diary of an Indian Cavalry Officer, Captain Roly Grimshaw,*. Wakefield, J., and Weippert, J.M. (ed.) Costello, 1986, p. 38.

12. Ibid p. 29.

13. Ibid. p. 39.

14. Ibid. p. 44.

15. BL/IOR/L/PO/476 Willcocks to Viceroy.

16. Ibid. Secretary of state to Viceroy 26 November.

17. BL/IOR/Mss/Eur/F143/93 Further extracts of reports by the censor for Indian mails in France.

18. Grimshaw wrote 'The experiences of Ram Singh, Dafadar of Horse', a semi-fictional account of the experience of an Indian cavalry soldier. It was published in serial form in the *Assam Journal* in 1930. Extracts from Grimshaw's diary were published in 1931 in the Regimental History of the Poona Horse.

19. Historical Record of the 39th Royal Garhwal Rifles.

20. *The Indian Army and the King's Enemies 1900–1947* p. 39.

21. *The English Writings of Rabindranath Tagore,* Sisir Kumar Das (Ed), Sahitya Akademi, Delhi, 1996, p. 610.

6: Winter

1. BL/IOR/L/PO/476 Benson to Viceroy.
2. BL/IOR/L/PO/10/27 Bikaner to Viceroy, 8 November 1914 .
3. BL/IOR/L/PO/476 Ranjit Singhji to Viceroy.
4. Ibid. Willcocks to Viceroy.
5. Ibid. Bikaner to Viceroy.
6. Ibid. Pratap Singh to Viceroy.
7. Ibid. Willcocks to Viceroy.
8. Ibid. Willcocks to Viceroy.
9. BL/IOR Mss Eur 143/92 Further extracts from reports made by the censor for Indian mails in France.
10. BL/IOR/Mss Eur F 143/78 Walter Lawrence papers.
11. BL/IOR/L/MIL/7/17347 Censorship of correspondence to and from Indian Expeditionary Force in France 1914–1918.
12. BL/IOR/Mss/Eur/143/92.
13. Ibid.
14. BL/IOR/Mss/Eur/143/92.

7: Bandobust Sahib

1. Published in 1895.
2. BL/IOR/Mss Eur F 143 Walter Lawrence papers.
3. Ibid.
4. Ibid.
5. Ibid.
6. Ibid.
7. Ibid.
8. Ibid.

9. Ibid.

10. Ibid.

11. Ibid.

12. The word 'missionary' was dropped during the war.

13. Ibid.

14. BL/IOR/L/PO/476 Willcocks to Viceroy.

15. Ibid. Viceroy to Secretary of State, 24 February 1915.

8: Neuve Chapelle

1. BL/IOR/Mss Eur D978 Indian Army Corps in Battle of Neuve Chapelle March 10–March 13 1915, Official narratives and war diaries, general staff, Indian Corps.

2. Ibid.

3. Author interview, Kamal Singh Negi, grandnephew of Gabar Singh Negi, Chamba, India, April 2013.

4. Historical Record of the 39th Royal Garhwal Rifles Vol I 1887–1922 compiled by Brigadier General J Evatt.

5. *With the Indians in France*, Willcocks, p. 232.

6. BL/IOR/L/PO/476 Willcocks to Viceroy.

7. Ibid.

8. *With the Indians in France*, Willcocks.

9. BL/IOR/Mss/Eur D 978.

10. *The World's War: Forgotten Soldiers of Empire*, David Olusoga, Head of Zeus, London, 2014.

11. BL/IOR L/MIL/17/5/2403 Report on Deserters List A.

12. *Race, Empire and First World War Writing*, Santanu Das (ed), Cambridge University Press, 2011.

13. In 2006 the British government pardoned 306 of the 346. www.ww1cemetries.com.

14. BL/IOR L/PO/476 Viceroy to Willcocks.

15. BL/IOR L/PO/476 Willcocks to Viceroy.

9: Clouds

1. *The Indian Corp in France*, Merewether and Smith, John Murray, London, 1919.

2. BL/IOR/Mss Eur/143/92.

3. *The Indian Corps in France,* Merewether and Smith, p. 335.

4. Ibid.

5. *With the Indians in France,* James Willcocks, Constable and Company, London 1920. p. 322.

6. Ibid., p. 323.

7. *The Indian Corps in France,* Merewether and Smith, p. 399.

8. BL/IOR/Mss Eur/143 Further extracts from reports from the Censor Board of letters from Indian soldiers.

9. Punjabi POW recording accessed online Amin Mughal Links. Author translation.

10. Documentary "The Halfmoon Files" Philip Scheffner (2007) and "The Making of the Halfmoon Files" exhibition.

11. BL/IOR/Eur Mss/F143/93 Further extracts of reports by the censor for Indian mails in France.

12. *A Little Work, A Little Play*, Hardit Singh Malik, Bookwise, India, p. 59.

13. Ibid., p. 67.

14. Ibid., p. 91.

15. TNA/ AIR 76/331 Service records of H.S. Malik.

16. *A Little Work, A Little Play*, Hardit Singh Malik, Bookwise, India, p. 88.

17. Ibid., p. 91.

18. Letter written by Indra Lal Roy dated June 1916 displayed in the Indian Air Force Museum, Delhi.

19. *St Paul's School and the First World War,* Carter Cortazzi, Nico Hedegaard, Oliver Hirsch, Joe Millard and Archie Foster.

20. TNA/AIR/76/438 Service record of Indra Lal Roy.

21. Displayed at Air Force Museum, New Delhi.

22. Flying High by M.S.Ray, *The Telegraph,* Calcutta, 11 October 1987.

23. *Flight* magazine, 5 September 1918.

10: Brighton

1. BL/IOR/Eur MSS F143 Excerpts from reports made by the Censor for Indian mails in France.

2. Ibid.

3. Inayat Khan's daughter, Noor Inayat Khan, would be dropped behind enemy lines in France in the Second World War, and be posthumously decorated with the George Cross for her bravery.

4. *Sovereign, Squire & Rebel, Maharaja Duleep Singh and The Heirs of a Lost Kingdom*, Peter Bance, Coronet House, London, 2009.

5. BL/IOR Mss Eur F143/60 Report on Indian Gift House, Brighton, Walter Lawrence papers.

6. BL/IOR Mss Eur F143 Arrangements made for Indian Sick and Wounded in England and France – report by Col Sir Walter Lawrence to Secretary of State for War.

7. *Akhbar e Jung Letter* 30 July 1915.

8. BL/IOR/Mss Eur F143/92 Further extracts from reports made by the censor for Indian mails in France.

9. Ibid.

10. Ibid.

11. Exhibition notes, Indian Military Hospital Gallery, Brighton Pavilion.

12. BL/IOR/Mss Eur F143/92.

13. BL/IOR/Mss Eur F143/92 Further extracts from reports made by the censor for Indian mails in France. Letter dated 20 July 1915.

14. Ibid.

15. Ibid.

16. Ibid.

17. BL/IOR/Mss Eur F/143.

18. BL/IOR/Eur MSS F143 Excerpts from reports made by the Censor for Indian mails in France.

19. Ibid.

20. BL/IOR/L/MIL/17/5/2402 An analysis of 1000 wounds and injuries received in action with special reference to the theory of the prevalence of self-infliction by Col. Sir Bruce Seton.

21. BL/IOR/Eur Mss 143/92.

22. BL/IOR/Eur Mss F/143.

11: Funerals

1. BL/IOR Mss Eur F143/80.

2 .BL/IOR/Mss Eur F/143.

3. Author interview with Jaimal Singh Johal, grandson of Manta Singh, Buckinghamshire, May 2013.

4. BL/IOR/Mss Eur F/143.

5. Commonwealth War Graves Commission records.

6. BL/IOR/MSS Eur/143 Further extracts from reports made by the censor for Indian mails in France.

7. *The Underworld of India* by Sir George MacMunn, Hutchinson & Co, London.

8. BL/IOR/MSS Eur/F 143 Further extracts from reports made by the censor for Indian mails in France.

12: The Maharaja and the War Cabinet

1. TNA/CAB 23/43 Proceedings of Imperial War Cabinet.
2. Ibid.
3. TNA/CAB 23/40.
4. Ibid.
5. TNA/CAB 23/43.
6. Ibid.
7. Ibid.
8. TNA/CAB 23/41.
9. *Anthem for Doomed Youth* by Wilfred Owen.
10. *The Trumpet* by Rabindranath Tagore.

13: The Peace

1. Quoted in *Paris 1919, Six Months that Changed the World* by Margaret Macmillan, Random House, p. 464.

2. Quoted in *Maharaja of Bikaner* by Hugo Purcell, Haus Publishing, London, 2010.

3. The Act was named after the president of the Committee, Justice Sir Sidney Rowlatt.

4. *The Amritsar Massacre 1919: General Dyer in the Punjab*. The Hunter Committee Report. The Stationary Office, London.

5. Ibid.

6. Plaque at Jallianwala Bagh.

7. *Rabindranath Tagore, The Myriad-Minded Man* by Krishna Dutta and Andrew Robinson, Bloomsbury, 1995, London.

8. Report by General Dyer on 25 August 1919 to the General Staff, 16th Division. Report of the Hunter Committee to investigate disturbances in the Punjab, 1920.

9. Report of the Hunter Committee. The Amritsar Massacre 1919. General Dyer in the Punjab, Stationery Office, London. p. 82.

10. Formerly known as the Royal Flying Corps.

11. *A Little Work, A Little Play,* Hardit Singh Malik, p. 101.

12. Report of the Hunter Committee. The Amritsar Massacre 1919. General Dyer in the Punjab, Stationery Office, London, p. 66.

13. TNA/CAB 24/153 Cabinet Papers, Report on the Amritsar Massacre.

14. Quoted in *Maharaja of Bikaner* by Hugo Purcell, Haus Publishing, London, 2010.

Bibliography

INDIA OFFICE RECORDS, BRITISH LIBRARY, LONDON

Hardinge Papers

Walter Lawrence Papers

Lord Curzon papers (1915–19)

Censorship of correspondence to and from Indian Expeditionary Force in France 1914–1918

Details of Censors of India mails with extracts form letters of Indian soldiers

Censors of Prohibited Indian newspapers addressed to soldiers in Europe

Correspondence relating to travelling and hospitals for Indian soldiers in France

Correspondence regarding the European War

Papers relating to the Indian involvement in the First World War

Indian Soldiers' Fund reports

Proceedings of Comforts Committee

Lady Hardinge Hospital Report

Reports on visit to Indian troops in France

Question of leave for Indians troops in France and Egypt

Military Reports of Battle of Neuve Chapelle

War Diaries 1914–1921

Report on Deserters

Memorandum on India's Contribution to the War in Men, Material and Money

Our Indian Empire, Pocket Book for Soldiers in India

Akhbar-e-Jang

Royal Pavilion Brighton, A Description of it as a hospital for Indian Soldiers

NATIONAL ARCHIVES, KEW (TNA)

Imperial War Cabinet papers and minutes
Indra Lal Roy – service records
Poresh Lal Roy – service records
Hardit Singh Malik – service records
Khudadad Khan – Victoria Cross records
Mir Dast – Victoria Cross records
Regimental War Diaries
Jullunder Brigade
57th Wilde's Rifles
129th Baluchis
Bareilly Brigade
Indian Field Ambulance

GARHWAL RIFLES HQ, LANSDOWNE, INDIA

Garhwal Rifles Regimental History

Newspapers and Magazines:

The Times
The Daily Mirror
The Manchester Guardian
The Graphic
Illustrated London News
The Hindu, Madras
Frontline Magazine
The Telegraph, Calcutta
Jugantar, Calcutta
Patrika, Calcutta
Ananda Bazar Patrika, Calcutta
The Dawn, Lahore

Books:

The Amritsar Massacre: General Dyer in the Punjab 1919, The Stationery Office, London (Reprint) 2000

Bangali Charita Bhidhan Vol I (Bengali Biography)

India's Imperial Partnership, Speeches of the Maharaja of Bikaner, The Times, London 1917

Bance, Peter, *Sovereign, Squire & Rebel, Maharaja Duleep Singh & The Heirs of a Lost Kingdom* Coronet House, London, 2009

______ *The Sikhs in Britain,* Coronet House, London, 2012

Basu, Shrabani, *Victoria & Abdul,* The History Press 2010, Stroud, Gloucestershire.

Brown, Malcolm (Foreword.) *On the Front Line, True World War I Stories,* Constable, London, 2009

Carter, Miranda, *George, Nicholas and Wilhelm: Three Royal Cousins and the Road to World War I,* First Vintage Books, London, 2011

Clark, Christopher, *The Sleepwalkers: How Europe Went to War in 1914,* Harper, London, 2013

Coombs, Rose E.B, *Before Endeavours Fade, A Guide to the Battlefields of the First World War,* After the Battle, Essex, 2006

Cornish, Paul, *The First World War,* Imperial War Museum, London 2014

Corrigan, Gordon. *Sepoys in the Trenches, The Indian Corps on the Western Front 1914–15,* Spellmount, Gloucestershire 2006

Das, Santanu (Ed) Race, Empire and First World War Writing, Cambridge University Press, 2011

Doyle, Arthur Conan, *The British Campaign in France & Flanders* (6 Volumes 1914–18), Hodder & Stoughton, London. (1916–19)

Dutta, Krishna and Robinson, Andrew, (eds) Selected Lettrs of Rabindranath Tagore, Cambridge University Press, 1997

_The Myriad Minded Man, St Martin's Press, 1995

Ellinwood, De Witt C. and Pradhan, S.D. (Ed) *India and World War I,* Manohar, New Delhi 1978

Evatt, J, *Historical Record of the 39th Royal Garhwal Rifles Vol I 1887–1922* Gale and Polden, Aldershot

Fowler, Will. *Battle Story: Ypres 1914–15,* Spellmount, Gloucestershire, 2011

Ganga Singh, *A Voice from India,* Empire Parliamentary Association, U.K., 1917

Gliddon, Gerald. *VC's of the First World War 1914,* The History Press, Stroud, 2011

Gilbert, Martin. *First World War,* Harper Collins, London, 1994

Giles, John, *The Western Front: Then and Now – From Mons to the Marne and Back,* After the Battle, 1992

Hastings, Max, *Catastrophe: Europe Goes to War 1914,* William Collins, London, 2014

Heathcote, T.A., *Indian Army: The Garrison of British Imperial India, 1822–1922,* David & Charles, Newton Abbot, 1974

Lewis, Jon E (ed) *A Brief History of the First World War*, Constable & Robinson, London, (reprint edition 2014)

Lucas, Charles Prestwood. *The Empire at War*, Oxford University Press, Oxford, 1926

Macmillan, Margaret. *Paris 1919, Six Months That Changed the World*, Random House, New York 2003

______ *The War that Ended Peace*, Profile Books, London, 2014

MacMunn, George. *The Underworld of India*, Hutchinson & Co, London

______ *The Armies of India*, A. & C. Black, London, 1911

______ *The Martial Races of India*, Sampson Low, Marston & Co, London, 1932

Malik Hardit Singh, *A Little Work, A Little Play, The Autobiography of H.S Malik*, Bookwise India., 2010

Mason, Philip. *A Matter of Honour: An Account of the Indian Army, Its Officers and Men*, Jonathan Cape, London, 1974

Merewether, J.W.B. and Smith, Frederick, *The Indian Corps in France*, John Murray, London 1918

Olusoga, David, *The World's War*, Head of Zeus, London, 2014

Omissi, David. *Indian Voices of the Great War, Soldier's Letters, 1914–18*, Palgrave Macmillan, London 1999

______ *The Sepoy and the Raj: The Indian Army, 1860–1940*, Palgrave Macmillan, 1998

O'Prey, Paul (ed), *First World War, Poems from the Front*, Imperial War Museum, London 2014

Purcell, Hugh. *Maharaja of Bikaner*, Makers of the Modern World series, Haus Publishing, London, 2010

Roberts, Frederick Sleigh, Lord, *Forty-one Years in India, From Subaltern to Commander-in-Chief*, Richard Bentley & Son, London 1898

Robertshaw, Andrew. *Battle Story: Somme 1916*, Spellmount, Gloucestershire, 2014

Stone, Norman *World War I, A Short History*,Penguin, London, 2008

Taylor, A.J.P. The First World War, An Illustrated History, Penguin Books, 1966

Trench, Charles Chevenix, *The Indian Army and the King's Enemies 1900–1947*, Thames & Hudson, London 1988

Wakefield, J., and Weippert, J.M. (ed) *Diary of an Indian Cavalry Officer, 1914–15, Captain Roly Grimshaw*, Costello, Tumbridge Wells, 1986

Whittaker, James. *The General's Footprint*, Progression, London, 2006

Willcocks, James. *With The Indians in France*, Constable and Company, London 1920

Acknowledgements

This book would not have been written without the generosity and encouragement of many people who went out of their way to help me.

I would like to begin by thanking the descendants of the Indian soldiers, who gave me access to the all-important family history. I would like to thank Lieut Col Balbir Singh Negi, who invited me to his home in Lucknow and told me about his father Darwan Singh Negi. I am grateful to Havildar Kamal Singh Negi who took me to the original village house of his grand-uncle Gabar Singh Negi in Chamba in the Garhwal hills and helped me to understand Gabar Singh's life and background.

My thanks to the family of Hardit Singh Malik – Nicole and Harmala Singh Malik and Vinita Tripathi – for their help.

In Pakistan, I am grateful to Ghulam Rabbani, who told me about his grandfather, Khudadad Khan.

In London, I am grateful to Jaimal Singh Johal, grandson of Manta Singh and his wife Sushil, for stories about the family and the three generations of friendship with the Hendersons. Thanks also to Ian Henderson for his inputs on his grandfather, Captain George Henderson.

I am indebted to James Whittaker, great-grandson of General James Willcocks, for sharing photographs and nuggets of information about the General.

I would like to thank Brigadier Vinod Raizada, Commandant, Garhwal Rifles Regimental Centre, Lansdowne, for his help with accessing the archives at the centre, and to Col Gautam Guha of Garhwal Rifles Regiment and his father, Lt Col Nitai Chandra Guha for background information.

I would also like to thank Wing Commander Rumy Chowdhury and Junior warrant officer, T.S Bisht from the Indian Air Force Museum, Delhi, for their help in allowing me to access the material at the Museum.

I am grateful to Dr Anthony Morton, Curator, Sandhurst Collection and to Angela Lucas, Collection Support Officer, for showing me around the historic Indian Army Memorial Room at Sandhurst.

I would like to thank Nelofar Bakhtyar of *Newsweek* Pakistan and Nabeel Anwar Dhakku of *The Dawn* for helping me trace the family of Khudadad Khan in Chakwal. I am grateful to my sister, Moushumi Basu, for helping me find the family of Gabar Singh Negi. My grateful thanks to my cousin, Pola Indrani Roy and her husband Klaas Van der Hoeven for driving me around Ypres in Belgium and helping me to locate the Indian memorials.

To Peter Bance, who generously showed me his collection of WWI memorabilia and allowed me to use postcards from his collection, I am very grateful.

The veteran librarian of *Ananda Bazar Patrika*, Saktidas Roy, can always be depended upon, and I am truly grateful to him for all the newspaper cuttings and articles he traced for me on Indra Lal Roy. I would also like to thank the staff and archivists at the British Library and the National Archives for all their help. Thanks to the National Portrait Gallery, London, British Library, London, The Royal Pavilion and Museums, Brighton & Hove and the Imperial War Museum for use of photographs from their collection. I would also like to thank K. Nandhakumar for his help with digitising some photographs.

I am very grateful to the Author's Foundation for giving me a generous grant which helped towards my travel and research.

For the journey from manuscript to book, I could ask for no better publishers. To Alexandra Pringle, Editor-in-Chief of Bloomsbury, who warmly welcomed me to the group and believed in my work, I am truly grateful.

I would have drowned in the vast mass of material had it not been for my wonderful editor at Bloomsbury, Diya Kar Hazra. It is her I have to thank for skilfully channelising my thoughts. Without her patience and gentle guidance, this book would not be possible. I am also grateful to the team at Bloomsbury: Nick Humphrey and Laura Brooke in London and the lovely Faiza Khan in Delhi who took the book to the final stage.

Thanks also to Himanjali Sankar, Arvind Booni and Rajiv Beri in the Delhi office.

Special thanks to my agent Anuj Bahri for all his help in publishing the book and for his enthusiasm at all times.

I would also like to thank Aveek Sarkar, my editor in chief at *Ananda Bazar Patrika*, for his constant support and encouragement with all my books.

For inputs and help in various ways, I would like to thank Kusoom Vadgama, Mike King, Tony McClenaghan, General Arjun Ray, Aruna Roy, Chetan Roy and Shanta Chatterji. I would also like to acknowledge the work of historians Gordon Corrigan, David Omissi, Santanu Das and David Olusoga, whose works on the subject have informed me.

My thanks to my friends and fellow Trustees of the Noor Inayat Khan Memorial Trust, who have always given me their warmth and moral support.

And finally I would like to thank my family: my parents, Chitta Ranjan and Gouri Basu, my sisters, Nupur and Moushumi and my brothers-in-law Sanjeev and Paramjeet, for always being there for me. To my daughters, Sanchita and Tanaya, who cast their critical eyes on my manuscript, act as my helpdesk for all technical problems and are my support troops in the trenches, I cannot be more grateful. To all of you, I owe this book.

Shrabani Basu
June 2015, London

Index

Afghan wars, xix, 13, 28–29
Afridis, 21, 51, 59
Ahmadiya Muslims, 156
Akhbar-i-Jang, 106, 109
Albert, Prince, 99
Alexandra, Queen, 9, 143, 145
Ali, Niyaz, 51
Ali, Sultan, 73
Alix of Hesse, 9
All India Muslim League, 43
Anderson, Lt General Sir Charles, 129
Andrews, C F, 20
Aryavarta Fund, 145
Asquith, H.H., 74
Atal, Major P, 68
Austria, 9, 189

Bagot-Chester, Captain W.G., 80
Baker, Herbert, xvi
Balfour, A.T., 170
Baluchis, 21, 29
Bande Mataram, 49
Banerjee, Surendranath, 13
Banerji, R.K., 101
Bareilly, 7–8, 35
Barker, Billy, 135–36
Barr, Sir David, 106
Barstow, Major, 106
Behn Meyer & Company, 74
Belgium, 10, 46–47, 61, 190
Bell, Dr Johannes, 187–88
Benson, Rex, 64, 70, 83
Bhakna, Sohan Singh, 50
Bhopal, Begum of, 43, 84, 156
Bhownagree, Sir Mancherjee, 14
Bikaner, 10
Boer War, 28, 32
Bombay, 22–23, 25, 75, 162, 189
Borden, Robert, 170, 173, 178
Bose, Bhupendranath, 13
Botha, Louis, 178
Brailey, Gertrude, 145
Brigade Report Centre, 111
Brighton and Hove Graphic, 144
Brighton Council, 141, 160
Brighton Gazette, 142
Brighton Palace, 140–41, 147
Britain, xxv, 10–14, 49, 176
  Common Imperial Policy, 173
  conscription, 171
  Dominions, 170, 172–73, 175, 178, 187

Hunter Committee enquiry, 184–85
Imperial Legislative Council, 180
Imperial War Cabinet, 168–72, 175, 177
Peace Conference, 177–79, 186
Royal Flying Corps (RFC), xxiv, 133–37
War Office, 50, 91, 101, 137, 141, 144, 149, 157, 160

British, the, 3–4, 72–75
British American Tobacco Company, 46
British Armed Forces, 134
British Infantry Division, 76
Northern Army, 28
British Empire, xxv, 5, 13–15, 19, 84, 89, 108, 117, 139, 162, 168, 170, 173, 176–78, 183
British Enfield Rifle, 27
British Expeditionary Force, 21, 24, 32, 76, 85, 166
British India Steam Navigation Company, 24
British Indian Army, 2, 4, 12, 28, 37
1/34th Sikh Pioneers, 23
1/39th Garhwal Rifles, 111, 113, 121
2/2nd Gurkhas, 76
2/3rd Gurkhas, 80, 129
2/39th Garhwal Rifles, 112
1st Punjab Infantry, 122
3rd Bengal Light Cavalry, 27
3rd Lahore Division, 24
3rd Queen Alexandra's Own Gurkhas, 25, 36, 130
5th Native Light Infantry, 107
6th Dragoon Guards, 27
6th Poona Division, 24
7th Meerut Division, 24–25, 36, 39, 81, 92
8th Gurkhas, 79
9th Bhopal Infantry, 61
9th Lancers, 64, 70
15th Sikhs, 23–24, 111, 114
34th Poona Horse, 75–76, 79
39th Garhwal Rifles, xxiii, 36, 38, 61, 68, 80, 130, 192
40th Pathans, 29–30, 51, 125–26
41st Dogras, 106
47th Sikhs, 23, 61, 63–64, 125–26, 130
57th Wilde's Rifles, xix, 23, 25, 35, 37–38, 47, 56–61, 67–68, 70, 88, 122, 124–26
58th Vaughan Rifles (Meerut Division), 24, 26, 76–77, 118, 152
59th Scindia Rifles, 24, 142
74th Punjabis, 51
129th Duke of Connaught's Own Baluchis, xix, xxiii, 24–25, 47, 56–61, 68, 88, 93, 124–25, 127, 152
Bareilly Brigade, 111
Dehradun Brigade, 113, 126
Ferozepur Division, 32
Ganga Risala, 168
Garhwal Brigade, 25, 111, 114
Honourable Artillery Company (HAC), 19
Jullunder Brigade, 20–21, 23, 32, 62, 113–14
Lahore Division, 21, 24, 26, 32–34, 37–39, 70, 81, 88, 92, 111, 115, 123–26
Ferozepur Brigade, 25, 46–47, 60, 124
Meerut Division, 36, 39, 81, 92, 114, 126

Secunderabad Cavalry Brigade, 24
Sirhind Brigade, 114
Broacha, Sir Shapurji, 152
Brunker, Gen. J.M.S., 88
Burns, John, 18

Cabrinovic, Nedel, 6
Calcutta, 18, 25
Cama, Bhikaji Rustom, 48–49
Campbell, J.S., 1
Campbell, Colonel Neil, 145
Carnegy, Gen. P.M., 88
Castalia, 31
caste, xxiv, 8, 87–88, 99, 155, 165
committees, 146
death rites, 164
markers, 163–64
Cawnpore, 8
Chamba, 2
Chamberlain, Austen, 144, 147, 160, 170, 172
Champaran, 179
Charles, Prince, 193
Charles, Sir Richard Havelock, 40
Chattopadhyay, Bankim Chandra, 49
Chelmsford, Lord, 169, 191
Chichester, Countess of, 145
Chindwara, 177
cholera, 2
Clemenceau, George, 176, 178, 186–88
Coldstream, William, 104–05
Commonwealth War Graves Commission, xix, 194
Crewe, Lord, 15, 73, 78, 118
Cubrilovic, Vaso, 6
Curzon, Lord, 11, 39–40, 95–96, 170

Dad, Sepoy Fazl, xix
Das Gupta, Lieutenant, 159
Dass, B., 43
Dast, Mir, xxiii, 24–25, 47, 56, 88, 118, 122, 124–25, 147–48, 189, 192
Dayal, Lala Har, 50
Delhi, 28
Dhingra, Madan Lal, 17, 49
Dill, Captain, 58
Doegen, Wilhelm, 131
Dogras, 8, 21, 29, 31, 59
Donnan, Lt Col W, 53
Duff, General Sir Beauchamp, 75
Durand, Sir Mortimer, 40
Dyer, Brigadier General Reginald E, xxvii, 181–85

Easdon, Isabel Mary, 181
East India Company, 27–29
Enlistment Act of July 1856, 27
Edward VII, King, 145, 187
Edward VIII, Prince of Wales, 160
Elizabeth II, Queen, 193
English Heritage and Woking Council, 195
Ernsthausen & Company, 74

Ferdinand, Franz Archduke, 5–7, 9, 186
Ferdinand, Sophie, 6–7
First World War, xv, 10, 16, 49, 183
Allies, 56, 61, 71–72, 123, 178
and censorship, xxvi, 48–53, 91, 143, 151
and Indian sweets, 52–53, 146
Battle of Passchendaele, 135
Battle of the Somme, 132–33, 171
British troops, 47
Comfort Committee, 40–45, 47, 52, 65, 93–94, 144
economic consequences for India, 173, 179

fear of sedition, 73–74, 149
gas attack, 124–25, 129
Hill 60, 122–23
hospitals, 40–42, 44, 48–50, 53, 70–71, 75, 79, 96–97, 99–106, 140–55, 157, 159–63, 166
Indian royalty, 12
Indian solidarity, 13–16, 19
Indian troops, xix, xxi–xxii, 13, 19, 22–27, 31–38, 41–48, 53, 61, 89–91
and British people, 146–47
and English nurses, 151–52
battle frontline, 59, 63–64, 70–72
casualties, xvi, xx, 75–78, 123–26, 130, 133, 162, 171–72
death rites, 98, 156–60, 164–65
desertion, 106–07, 118–20
despondency, 53–54, 62, 81, 118–20, 153–55
loyalty to the Raj, 143–44, 190
mutiny, 107
'*pinnis*', 52
Praise for, 116–17
war conditions, 58–63, 71, 81, 131
war convalescents, 96–100, 104, 140–55
restrictions, 149–51
war returnees, 140
trenches, 55–57, 61, 66–67, 70–72, 76–79, 83, 93, 104, 109
Christmas truce, 80–81
Victoria Cross, xx–xxi, xxiii, 4, 24–26, 29–30, 58, 60, 67, 69, 92–93, 110, 112, 125, 130, 135, 147–48, 189, 191–92
Flight, 139
Foch, Marshall, xvi
France, xxv, 10, 22, 26–27, 46–47, 49, 54, 71, 162, 171, 173, 178–79, 190
Frankfurter Zeitung, 63
French, Sir John, 60, 85, 91, 110, 116, 123, 128
Frontier Forces, 21, 28

Gandhi, Kasturba, 15
Gandhi, Mohandas Karamchand, xxiv, 15–16, 180, 185
Satyagraha, 180–81
Gangapur, 7
Garhwal Rifles Regiment, 1–3, 26
Garhwalis, 3–4, 8, 21, 66–68
Gazette Extraordinary, 74
George, David Lloyd, 169–70, 173, 175–78, 187–88
George IV, King, 141
George V, King, xxii–xxiii, xxv, 3, 8–11, 13–14, 19, 33, 39, 42, 58, 66, 68–69, 81, 84, 93, 96, 125, 141, 143–45, 147–49, 171, 187–88, 191
Coronation Darbar, 3
Germany, xxv, 4–5, 9, 12–14, 33, 68–74, 176, 178–79, 188–89
Ghadar, 49
Ghadar movement, 108
Ghadar Party, 50, 107
Goorkha, 101
Gorakhnath, Guru, 4
Gough, Major General Hubert de la Poer, 56
Grimshaw, Captain 'Roly', 75–77, 79
Guildford Castle, 101
Gurkhas, 3–4, 8, 21, 29–30, 37, 79, 88
Guru, Raj, 190
Guru Granth Sahib, 43–44

HMS Hampshire, 128

Haig, Lieutenant General Douglas, 110, 114–15, 117, 128, 132–33
Hamilton, Lord, 40
Hamper-Vincent, Captain, 57
Hardinge, Lord, xxv, 11, 37, 64, 70, 83, 169
Harrach, Lt Col Count Franz von, 6
Henderson, George, xxiv, 21, 23, 25, 62, 114–15, 134, 159, 189, 193, 195
Henderson, Ian, 115, 193, 195
Henderson, Robert, 115, 193
Henriques, E.C., 160
Hewett, Sir John, 39–41, 53
Hill, August Major Harry, 20, 32, 35
Hindus, 3–4, 13, 27
  funeral of soldiers, 159
Hitler, Adolf, 10
Holderness, Sir Thomas, 15
Hong Kong, 107
Honorary Artillery Company, 172
Horsell Common Preservation Society, 195
Howell, Second Lieutenant E.B., 50–51, 53
Hughes, Billy, 178
Humphreys, Major, 58
Hungary, 189
Hyderabad, Nizam of, 84

Imperial German Navy, 4–5
Imperial Indian Relief Fund, 40
India,
  Defense of India Act, 180
  dominion status, 168–69, 173
  effects of the war, 179, 190
  electricity, 2
  famine conditions, 108
  Government of India Act (1919),
  indigo, 179–80
  Jallianwala Bagh massacre, xxvii, 182–86, 190
  Mutiny of 1857, 8, 27–29, 40, 50
  nationalism, 190
  Rowlatt Act, 180–82
  telegraph, 2
India Council, 106
India Office Whitehall, 48, 53, 97, 101, 108, 116, 160
India Tea Association, 46
Indian Cavalry War Depot, 79
Indian Civil Service, 193
Indian Gift House, 145–46
Indian Medical Service, 159
Indian memorial Committee of Brighton, 159
Indian National Congress, 13, 169, 183
Indian Sappers and Miners, 62, 131, 133, 144
Indian Soldier's Club, 104
Indian Soldiers' Fund, xxvi, 39–41, 145
Indian Volunteer Corps, 100
Indians,
  discriminated against, 30
Indore, Holkar of, 84
Innes, C.A., 73
International Socialist Conference, 48
Irwin, Lord, 194

Jaan, Gauhar, 145
Jacob, Sir Swinton, 160
Jalandhar, 20
Jinnah, Mohammad Ali, 14, 156
Johal, Jaimal Singh, 115, 193, 195
John Jackson & Company, 40
Johnson, Gen. C.E., 88
Josef, Franz, 9

Kamaluddin, Khwaja, 156

Kandahar, 13
Karachi, 20, 22–23, 25–27, 31, 189
Karim, Abdul, 156
Kashmir, 95
Keary, Gen. H.D.V., 125
Kefarteer, 2, 21, 67–68, 191
Khan, Ashraf, 76
Khan, Azam, 118
Khan, Havildar Karim Ullah, 152
Khan, Hazrat Inayat, 145
Khan, His Highness the Aga, 40, 73–74, 101
Khan, Jemadar Muhammad, xix
Khan, Khudadad, xix, xxiii, 24–25, 30, 37–38, 47, 55–59, 67, 69, 88, 92–93, 125, 189, 192
Khan, Mir Osman Ali, 74
Khan, Muhammad Yakub, 153
Khan, Naik Ayub, 127–28
Khan, Sepoy Mehr, xix
Khan, Subedar Arsla, 59
Khan, Usman, 56–57
Khan, Wahab, 68
Khan, Zaman, 35–36, 47, 68
Khusro, Amir, 142
Kiel Canal, 4–5
King George V, 5
Kipling, Rudyard, xvi, xxiii, 96, 185
Kitchener, Earl, xxiii, xxv, 2, 12–13, 29, 32, 66, 96–98, 101–03, 128–29, 144, 151, 154, 158
Kitchener Hospital, 147, 149, 150–54
Kitchlu, Dr Saifuddin, 181
Kotdwar, 2, 26
Krishnavarma, Shyamji, 50

Lady Hardinge Hospital, 40, 99, 102, 140, 145, 152, 160–61, 164, 166
Lahore, 23
Lansdowne, xxiii, 1–2, 21, 26, 68, 112–13
Lansdowne, Lord, xxiii, 4
Law, Bonar, 170
Lawrence, Henry, 96
Lawrence, Lilian, 95–96, 194
Lawrence, Walter, 91, 93, 95–104, 106, 140–41, 144, 149, 151–52, 154–55, 158, 160, 194
Laymen's Society, 104
Le Temps, 60
League of Nations, 188–89
Lee Enfield Rifles Mark II, 37
Lee Enfield Rifles Mark III, 37
Leitner, Dr Gottlieb Wilhelm, 156
Lojka, Leopold, 7
London Gazette, 118, 125
Loyalty, 84
Lucknow, 8
Lukis, Sir Charles Pardey, 43
Lutyens, Sir Edward, xix

Macbean, Gen. F. 88
MacMunn, Sir George Fletcher, 164–65
Mahal, Begum Hazrat, 8
Maharaja of,
  Benares, 84
  Bikaner, xxiv, xxvi, 65, 70, 83–85, 87, 168–72, 177, 187–89, 194
  Darbhanga, 84
  Dholpur, 84
  Gwalior, 12, 46, 84
  Jaipur, 84
  Jodhpur, 84–85
  Kapurthala, xvi, 84
  Kashmir, 84
  Kishengarh, 11, 85, 87
  Mysore, 11
  Nepal, 11
  Patiala, xxiv, 11, 170, 172

Ratlam, 11
Rewa, 46, 84
Maharani of,
Bharatpur, 40
Bhownagar, 44
Mahinder, Sir Bhupinder Singh, 172
Malik, Hardit Singh, xxiv, 16–17, 19, 133–36, 184, 193
Malik, Prakash, 184
Manchester Regiment, 23
Manjood, 2, 21, 109, 113
Marseilles, 27, 33–39, 41, 49, 91, 97, 102, 190
Mary, Princess, 148
Mary, Queen, xxiii, xxv–xxvi, 113, 143–45, 148–49, 171
Massey, William Ferguson, 170, 178
Mast, Jemadar Mir, 118–20, 122, 127, 148, 189
McCall Anderson, Edith, 161
McLeod, Col J, 144
McLeod, Mr C. C., 40
Meerut, 8, 27
Meerut Stationary Hospital, 43
Mehmedbašić, Muhamed, 6
Mehta, Jivraj N, 15
Merewether, Lt Col, 31, 33, 126, 129
Meteor V, 4–5
Minh, Ho Chi, 179
Molony, Lieutenant, 59
Montagu, Lord Edwin Samuel, 172–73, 177, 187–88
Morning Post, 185
Mueller, Hermann, 187–88
Müller, Karl Friedrich Max von, xvi–xvii
Muhammad, Khan, 51
Munich, 10
Murdoch, Keith, 178
Murdoch, Rupert, 178
Murray, Lt Gen A.J., 48
Murree, 26
Muslims, 13, 27, 31–33, 107
burial of soldiers, 156–59
Mussoorie, 1

Naidu, Sarojini, 15
Naoroji, Dadabhai, 14
National Reserve, 102
Negi, Badri Singh, 2
Negi, Darwan Singh, xxiii, 2–4, 21, 25–26, 31, 36, 38, 66–69, 110, 189, 191
Negi, Gabar Singh, xxiii, 1–2, 4, 21, 25–26, 31, 36, 38, 66, 78, 109–13, 172, 191–92
Negi, Kamal Singh, 192
Nehru, Jawaharlal, 193
Nepal, 4
Nepalese War,
First, 4
Neuve Chapelle, xv, xx–xxi, xxiii–xxiv, 38, 61–64, 68, 70, 75, 78, 92, 109–23, 126–27, 130, 159, 190, 192, 195
Nicholas II, Tsar, 9
Nixon, General John, 74

O'Connor, Lt Col, 41
O'Dwyer, Michael, 185–86
Otter, John, 140, 159–60
Order of St John of Jerusalem, 46
Orlando, Vittoria, 176, 178
Orpen, Sir William, 188
Oudh, 27
Owen, Susan, xviii, 173–74
Owen, Tom, 173–74
Owen, Wilfred, xviii, xxvii, 174

Pacific Coast Hindustan Association, 49

Palmer, Edward, 52
Pakistan, 156
Pankhurst, Christabel, 48
Paris, 49
Paris Indian Society, 48–49
Parsees, 13
Pasha, Djemel, 168
Pathans, 8, 29, 33–34, 37, 107
Peshawar, 189
Pile, Seymour, 144
Pilgrim Camp, 23
Plumber, Sir Herbert, 125
Pollock, Major General, 28
Potiorek, Gen Oskar, 6–7
Prince of Wales, 8, 17, 68, 83, 85, 96, 141, 160, 187
Princip, Gavrilo, 6–7

Quran, 43–44, 157

RMS Takada, 24
RIMS Northbrook, 24
Rahim, Abdur, 14–15
Rai, Jasbahadur, 132
Rai, Lala Lajpat, 14
Rai, Surgeon Hakim, 68
Rajputs, 29–30, 107
Rana, Karan Bahadur, 25–26
Rana, Sardar Singh Rewabhai, 48–49
Ranjitsinhji, Maharaja of Nawanagar, 84
Reuters news agency, 32
Richthofen, Manfred von (aka Red Baron), 135, 139
Roberts, General Lord, xxiii, 4, 12, 29–30, 40, 65–66
Roos-Keppel, Sir George, 108
Rothenstein, William, 82
Rothschild, Lady, 161
Rothschild, Mrs Leopold de, 45
Roy, Indra Lal 'Laddie', xxiv, 18–19, 136–39, 172, 193
Roy, Lolit, 18
Roy, Lolita, 17–19, 136–38, 172
Roy, Piera Lal, 17–18
Roy, Poresh Lal, 18–19, 136, 172, 193–94
Royal Air Force (RAF), 139, 172, 184
Royal India Marine, 31
Royal Navy, 31
Royal Prussian Phonographic Commission (RPPC), 131
Rumbold, Sir Horace, 5
Russia, 10

SMS Emden, xvi–xvii, 25–26, 33, 74, 107
SS Akbar, 23, 25
SS Angora, 25
SS Arancola, 25
SS Coconada, 26
SS Edavana, 31
SS Taiyebeh, 33
Sadr-ud-din, Maulavi Qazi, 101, 156–58, 164
Sarajevo, 6–7, 9
Sassoon, Siegfried, xviii, 174
Satoori, 1, 21, 78, 109, 112–13, 191–92
Satyapal, Dr, 181
Savarkar, Veer, 17
Second World War, 115, 193–94
Secunderabad Indian General Hospital, 43, 52
Serbia, 9
Seton, Col. Bruce, 151, 154
Shah, Akbar, 68
Shah, Jalal, 101
Shah, Nawab Wajid Ali, 27

Shah Jehan Mosque, 156
Shapurji, Sorabji, 15
Sherwood, Marcella, 181, 184
Sikhs, 8, 16, 21, 29, 34, 42–44, 62, 88, 101–02
funeral of soldiers, 159
Simla, 1, 83
Singapore, 107
Singh, Assa Johal, 21, 115, 172, 193
Singh, Bhagat, 190
Singh, Bhawan, 132
Singh, Guru Gobind, 29
Singh, Havildar Gagna, 24, 56, 59–60, 88, 147
Singh, Jemadar Kapur, 59, 88
Singh, Jemadar Ram, 59
Singh, Jiwan, 53
Singh, Khem, 20
Singh, Maharaja Duleep, 100, 145
Singh, Maharaja Ganga, 10–11, 85–86, 168–71, 187–89, 194
Singh, Mall, 131–32
Singh, Naik Nika, 53
Singh, Princess Sophia Duleep, 145
Singh, Sir Pratap, 11, 31–32, 65, 83, 85, 87
Singh, Subedar Manta, xxiii, 20, 23, 25, 62, 64, 111, 114–15, 159, 172, 189, 193, 195
Singh, Sumer, 11, 32
Singh, Udham, 185–86, 190
Singhji, Ranjit, 12
Sinha, Sir Satyendra Prasanno, xxvi, 169–70, 172–73, 177, 187, 194
Sinhji, K.S. Sawai, 84
Smith, Sir Frederick, 31, 126, 129
Smuts, Lt Gen J.C., 170–71, 178
Smyth, Col Edward Carmichael, 27
South Africa, 178, 180
St John Ambulance Association, 45
Steel, Major R.A., 71
Stevenson, Frances, 177
Suez Canal, 31–32
Sukha, xxv, 7–8, 35, 160–66, 194
Sukhdev, 190
Swanston, Lt. Col. C.O., 76

Tagore, Rabindranath, xxvii, 19–20, 60, 82, 174–75, 183
Gitanjali, xviii
songs, 18
Talvar, 49
Tata, Sir Ratan, 14, 40
Teesta, 24
Thapa, Amar Singh, 4
Thapa, Kulbir, 25, 130
Thaper, D.R., 158
The Asiatic Home, 99–100
The Bengalee, 13
The Ceylon and Eastern Agency, 46
The Daily Mirror, 93
The Indian Sociologist, 49–50
The Times, 96, 159
The Times of India, 11, 13–14
Thomson, G.M., 181
Treaty of Versailles, xxvi, 187–89
Turkey, 72–74, 107, 127, 173

Undivided Servicemen's Association, 193
United States of America (USA), 189
Urquhart,Sligger, 134

Veeraswamy & Company, 52
Venn, Henry, 99
Victoria, Princess Royal, 9

Victoria, Queen, 4, 8–9, 11, 19, 141, 156
Violence,
  in Delhi, 28

Wallinger, W.H., 53
Watkis, Gen., H.B., 88
Wedderburn, Sir William, 169
Weller, Paul, 195
Whittaker, James, 195
Wilhelm I, Kaiser, 9
Wilhelm II, Kaiser, 4–5, 8–10, 83, 119
Willcocks, Captain William, 28
Willcocks, Lieutenant General Sir James, 26–28, 37–38, 41, 44, 48, 57, 61–65, 78, 85, 87–90, 98, 106–07, 109, 115–17, 120–21, 126–29, 152, 194–95
Willingdon, Lord, 14, 72–75
Wilson, Woodrow, 176, 178–79, 187–89
Woking Muslim Mission, 156–58, 164, 195
Wyllie, Sir Curzon, 17, 49

YMCAs, 101
Ypres, xix–xxiii, 47, 55, 57, 60–61, 67, 75, 88, 93, 100, 109, 122–27, 147, 190

Zetland, Lord, 186